Albania

Albanian Alps &
Northern Albania
p108

TIRANA
p46 ⊙

Tirana &
Central Albania
p43

Southeastern
Albania
p132

The Albanian
Riviera
p72

Joel Balsam

Mesi Bridge (p119)

CONTENTS

Plan Your Trip

The Journey Begins Here	4
Albania Map	6
Our Picks	8
Regions & Cities	18
Itineraries	20
When to Go	28
Get Prepared	30
The Food Scene	32
The Outdoors	36
Action Areas	38

The Guide

Tirana & Central Albania ... 43
- Find Your Way ... 44
- Plan Your Time ... 45
- Tirana ... 46
- Beyond Tirana ... 55
- Krujë ... 60
- Durrës ... 62
- Beyond Durrës ... 67
- Divjakë-Karavastë National Park ... 68
- Places We Love to Stay ... 71

The Albanian Riviera ... 72
- Find Your Way ... 74
- Plan Your Time ... 76
- Help Me Pick: Albanian Riviera Beaches ... 78
- Sarandë ... 80
- Beyond Sarandë ... 84

Speca me gjizë (stuffed peppers and aubergines)

- Ksamil ... 86
- Butrint ... 88
- Himarë ... 92
- Beyond Himarë ... 95
- Dhërmi ... 97
- Vlorë ... 101
- Beyond Vlorë ... 105
- Places We Love to Stay ... 107

Albanian Alps & Northern Albania ... 109
- Find Your Way ... 110
- Plan Your Time ... 111
- Shkodër ... 112
- Beyond Shkodër ... 119
- Theth ... 128
- Places We Love to Stay ... 131

Southeastern Albania ... 132
- Find Your Way ... 134
- Plan Your Days ... 136
- Berat ... 138
- Beyond Berat ... 143
- Gjirokastër ... 147
- Beyond Gjirokastër ... 153
- Përmet ... 156
- Korçë ... 159
- Beyond Korçë ... 163
- Places We Love to Stay ... 169

Toolkit

Arriving	172
Getting Around	173
Money	174
Accommodation	175
Family Travel	176
Health & Safe Travel	177
Food, Drink & Nightlife	178
Responsible Travel	180
LGBTIQ+ Travellers	182
Accessible Travel	183
Driving in Albania	184
Nuts & Bolts	185
Language	186

Storybook

A History of Albania in 15 Places	190
Meet the Albanians	194
World Heritage	196
Skanderbeg's Sword	198
Tourism Boom or Burden?	200

Petrelë Castle (p57)

ALBANIA
THE JOURNEY BEGINS HERE

During my multi-week journey through the Western Balkans, I resisted the urge to skip Albania. I was warned that it's dangerous, with an EU border guard telling me that Albanians 'shoot first and ask questions later'. The *furgon* (shared minibus) that broke down in the middle of the night further aimed to deter me. But what I found here was unlike anywhere else I'd been in Europe, and certainly nothing like what the detractors had warned me about. Instead of violence, I found some of the warmest people I've met on my many travels, with a curiosity and a welcoming attitude towards visitors that was much more hospitable than other destinations in the region. These days, Albania is far from undiscovered, but it has managed to maintain its warmth, its vibrant traditions and its optimism. When we visit, it's our responsibility to match locals' kindness – and to tell the haters elsewhere how wrong they are.

Joel Balsam

@joelbalsam

Joel Balsam is a Canadian freelance journalist based in Rio de Janeiro. He is the author of more than a dozen Lonely Planet guidebooks.

MY FAVOURITE EXPERIENCE

My favourite experience involves wandering around the ancient Ottoman-era stone alleyways of UNESCO-listed Berat (p138), snapping photos as the light strikes its cherished windows.

Mangalem (p141), Berat

PLAN YOUR TRIP

Valbonë Pass
Most popular hike of the Albanian Alps (p121)

Lumi i Shales
Hidden river beach (p126)

Bunk'Art 1
Communist bunker tunnels inspired by North Korea (p55)

Albanian Night
Cultural performance and artisanal shopping (p52)

House of Leaves
Communist spy and torture headquarters (p51)

Blue Eye Kaprre
Electric-blue natural pool (p128)

Marubi National Photography Museum
Albanian history through photos (p112)

Mrizi i Zanave
Albanian agrotourism and farm-to-table pioneer (p119)

Krujë Castle
Rebel fortress of a national hero (p60)

Durrës Amphitheatre
Arena where Roman gladiators fought (p62)

NATURAL WONDERS

You've seen the reels, so now come to see the beaches, pools and lagoons for yourself. Albania has waters for all ages and interests. Inland, venture within the snow-capped Albanian Alps (aka the Accursed Mountains) to find giant canyons, gushing waterfalls and pristine blue natural pools you won't believe are real. And that's before we even get to the tantalisingly turquoise waters along the Albanian Riviera.

Between Two Seas

Albania is flanked by two seas, the Ionian and the Adriatic. The turquoise-tinged Ionian south of Vlorë (pictured) is prettier, while the deep blue Adriatic in the north is wilder.

Scenic Drives

Albanian public transport is, to put it nicely, uncomfortable. You'll have more freedom to roam the beaches with your own vehicle. Read more about **driving in Albania** on p184.

Beaches by Boat

In high season, the best way to experience Albanian beaches without the crowds is to see the hidden coves by boat from Sarandë, Ksamil, Himarë or Dhërmi.

Divjakë-Karavastë National Park (p68)

BEST NATURE EXPERIENCES

Take a small boat through the Albanian Alps to reach the hidden ❶ **Lumi i Shales** (p126), a turquoise river beach that looks as if it belongs in Thailand.

Hike for 20 minutes to reach the stunning ❷ **Gjipe Beach** (p98), arguably the most beautiful on the Albanian Riviera.

Hop on a motorboat and sail through a lagoon in ❸ **Divjakë-Karavastë National Park** (p68) to go bird-watching for rare pelicans.

Soak in the mineral-rich ❹ **Benjë Hot Springs** (p158) at the mouth of a canyon near the adventure hub of Përmet.

Trek from the mountain village of Theth and plunge into the bright, natural spring of the ❺ **Blue Eye Kaprre** (p128).

House of Leaves (p51)

COMMUNIST SITES

Albania's communist dictatorship lasted from 1944 to 1992 and had a huge, painful impact on every aspect of the country, from its economy to the trauma felt by those who lived during it. Understanding its historical context and its dictator, Enver Hoxha, is not only fascinating but crucial for understanding Albania today.

Bunkers, Bunkers, Bunkers

Look out for the 175,000 concrete bunkers built during the dictatorship and scattered throughout Albania. There are some particularly cool bunker tunnels at the **Cape of Rodon** (p70).

Context Is Key

If locals are keen to talk about it, ask them about their perspective on the dictatorship and modern Albanian politics. They're bound to have stories and personal connections.

BEST COMMUNIST SITE EXPERIENCES

Wander the huge network of bunker tunnels inspired by North Korea at ❶ **Bunk'Art 1** (p55), just outside Tirana.

Visit the eerie ❷ **House of Leaves** (p51), a former spy and torture headquarters in Tirana that's now a museum.

Enter a prison cell that held political dissidents and learn about Shkodër's role in Albania's democratic revolution at the ❸ **Site of Witness & Memory Museum** (p115).

Tour the ❹ **Cold War Tunnel** (p152) in Enver Hoxha's hometown of Gjirokastër and learn about its chilling history.

Be sobered by the terrifying vibes at ❺ **Tepelenë Internment Camp** (p155), which had conditions akin to the Soviet gulags.

ALBANIAN FOOD

Albanian gastronomy is on the upswing, with chefs, cooks and grannies cooking up delicious dishes like *qofte* (meatballs), *fërgëse* (dip made with red peppers and ricotta cheese), and spit-roasted lamb with both gusto *and* fresh ingredients. A highlight is the countryside agrotourism restaurants/guesthouses that serve farm-to-table cuisine. And don't skip the drinks: producers of Albanian wine and *raki* (fruit brandy) are making names for themselves internationally.

Regional Specialties

Restaurants serve different food inland than they do on the coast. Beach areas lean towards Greek dishes, Italian pasta and seafood, while the heartland is more meat-heavy.

Sharing Is Caring

Dishes are served one at a time rather than as a mixed plate. Bring someone to share with, as it can be a lot.

Cooking Class

Learn to make traditional Albanian cuisine from a talented grandmother at **Për drekë tek Marjeta** (p152) in Gjirokastër.

BEST GASTRONOMIC EXPERIENCES

Feast on scrumptious farm-to-table multi-course feasts at ❶ **Mrizi i Zanave** (p119), the OG of Albanian agrotourism.

Try all the classics in a fun atmosphere at ❷ **Era** (p51), a tried, tested and true Tirana restaurant.

Enjoy tender service and home-style food with views of the beach at ❸ **Manxuranë** (p82) in Sarandë. Divine every time.

Taste award-winning Albanian wine and eat fresh food from the farm at ❹ **Alpeta Agrotourism** (p143) near Berat.

Sip *raki* at ❺ **Melesin Distillery** (p166); in an area known for its slow food, Melesin is turning *raki* into a luxury spirit.

ANCIENT RUINS

At the crossroads between Rome and Constantinople (now Istanbul), Albania has been attacked and occupied by various empires over the last 4000 years. Among them were the Illyrians (Albania's ethnic and linguistic ancestors), along with the Romans, Venetians, Greeks and Ottomans. These empires built fascinating cities – complete with theatres, basilicas, mosaics and tall ramparts, some of which have been excavated and preserved today. See these fascinating sites without the crowds of neighbouring countries.

Via Egnatia

Built in the 2nd century BCE by the Romans, the **Via Egnatia** (p65) linked Rome with Thessaloniki and Constantinople. Stops on the route included Durrës and **Apollonia** (pictured; p105).

Castle Views

While Albanian castles usually have little but their walls remaining, their placement on various hilltops make them terrific viewpoints, especially at sunset.

Read Up

There's usually very little historical information at Albanian archaeological sites. Read up in advance, and bring this book with you for some context.

Krujë Castle (p60)

BEST ANCIENT EXPERIENCES

Explore the UNESCO-listed ❶ **Butrint** (p88), which dates back 2800 years and is the pinnacle of Albania's archaeological sites.

Visit the town-sized ❷ **Berat Castle** (p138) to wander ruins of mosques and churches, as well as an excellent museum of Catholic art.

Wander between the white Italian villas and modern promenades of Durrës to find the ❸ **Durrës Amphitheatre** (p62), built by the Romans.

See the fortress where national hero Skanderbeg fought off the Ottomans at ❹ **Krujë Castle** (p60), and visit its two museums.

Learn about the villagers in Theth who protected family members caught up in Kanun blood feuds at the 400-year-old ❺ **Reconciliation Tower** (p129).

Venice Art Mask Factory (p117)

AMAZING ART

Despite thousands of years under occupation, Albanians have managed to maintain their vibrant artistic traditions in their garments, dances and jewellery. They're also proud to have riveting religious frescoes inside their prayer sites. Feast your eyes upon amazing Albanian art, and take some keepsakes home with you.

BEST ART EXPERIENCES

View thousands of gorgeous Orthodox paintings at Korçë's excellent ❶ **Medieval Art Museum** (p159).

Attend a traditional wedding at ❷ **Albanian Night** (p52) in Tirana, where the on-site shop has the best collection of artisanal art in the country.

See hundreds of intricate masks used at Venice Carnival and in Hollywood films at ❸ **Venice Art Mask Factory** (p117) in Shkodër.

Visit Shkodër's ❹ **Marubi National Photography Museum** (p112) to see the country's first photographs that are precious archives of its history.

Get a tattoo inside a concrete communist bunker at ❺ **Keq Marku Tattoo Art Studio** (p124) in the country's north; a bucket-list item.

Souvenirs

The best places to find souvenirs are at the **Bazaar** (p61) in Krujë and **Pazari i Ri** (p53) in Tirana, though most are, unfortunately, foreign-made.

Cover Up

Cover up bare skin as much as possible when visiting mosques and churches. It's worth it to see their flowing frescoes.

OTTOMAN BUILDINGS

The Ottoman Empire controlled Albania for 527 years, from 1385 to 1912. And while that period isn't remembered fondly, it did leave behind some intriguing architecture, especially in the UNESCO-listed 'museum cities' of Berat and Gjirokastër. You'll also see white villas dotted with charming wooden windows elsewhere, but you'll have to know where to look.

Museum Cities

Despite hostility towards religious and Ottoman architecture during the secular dictatorship, both Berat and Gjirokastër were graciously preserved as 'museum cities'.

Frescoes

Albania's churches and mosques aren't filled with drab, dark paintings as you might find elsewhere. Here, the art is bursting with vibrant blues, pinks and plenty of gold.

Ali Pasha

Look out for stone bridges, aqueducts and castles built and improved upon by Albanian despot Ali Pasha of Ioannina, who ruled under the Ottomans before the sultan had him killed.

BEST ARCHITECTURAL EXPERIENCES

Snap some pics in the neighbourhood of ❶ **Mangalem** (p141), a famous photo spot in Berat – the city of hundreds of windows.

Absorb the fascinating architecture of Gjirokastër, including hundreds of stone buildings and Ottoman residences such as ❷ **Zekate House** (p151).

Enter the ❸ **Et'hem Bey Mosque** (p47), bordering Tirana's Skanderbeg Sq, to gawp at its fabulous frescoes.

See Ali Pasha's daunting, triangular ❹ **Porto Palermo Castle** (p95) on the coast near Himarë.

Visit the little-known ❺ **Shkodër History Museum** (p115) in the north for an enchanting example of Ottoman architecture.

THRILLING ADVENTURES

Albania is rising as an adventure-sports destination, with a growing number of ways to spike your adrenaline scattered throughout the country. Get out on the country's many rivers, lakes and dazzling 400km coastline for rafting on not one, but two wild rivers. There's also kitesurfing, scuba diving, stand-up paddleboarding, treks across the Albanian Alps, horse riding, and roads perfect for cycling and scenic drives (ideally by motorcycle).

River Rafting

Take your pick between two wild rivers to go rafting. There's the **Vjosa River** (p156) and the **Osum Canyon** (pictured; p145), which cuts through steep cliffs near Berat.

Peaks of the Balkans

For the best of the Albanian Alps, trek the multi-national, multi-day **Peaks of the Balkans** (p123), or do a section, such as **Valbonë to Theth** (pictured; p120).

No Experience Necessary

You don't have to be a pro in order to adventure in Albania, as few activities require certification. The exception to this is diving, which requires a PADI licence or similar.

Rafters on Vjosa River (p156)

BEST ADVENTURE EXPERIENCES

Raft the wild ❶ **Vjosa River** (p156), Europe's first national river park, and soak in the nearby hot springs to warm up when you're finished.

Cross the Albanian Alps in the three-day ❷ **Valbonë to Theth** (p120) circuit that includes a three-hour ferry and a hike over the 1800m **Valbonë Pass** (p121).

Plunge beneath the crystal-clear Ionian Sea with ❸ **Saranda Diving** (p83) to find military and communist shipwrecks.

Soar along a stretch of windswept beach north of Vlorë, where you'll find the perfect conditions for kitesurfing. ❹ **Kitesurf Albania** (p106) can show you how.

Go stand-up paddleboarding on Lake Shkodër and look for rare bird species on a self-guided or guided trip with ❺ **Drini Times** (p118).

REGIONS & CITIES

Find the places that tick all your boxes.

Tirana & Central Albania

RISING CAPITAL & BATTLEWORN RUINS

Fly into the main international airport for a taste of Albania's communist history at some of the country's best museums and traditional restaurants. It's the best for nightlife, too. Outside the capital are ancient ruins from the Romans, Venetians and national hero Skanderbeg.

Tirana p46

Albanian Alps & Northern Albania

NATURE AT ITS PEAK

They might not be as tall as the Swiss Alps, but Albania's so-called Accursed Mountains certainly are enchanting, and far less touristy. Hike the mountains or cut through on a ferry, and see humble mountain villages seemingly stuck in time. Don't skip bike-friendly Shkodër, the north's main city that's also home to excellent museums.

Albanian Alps & Northern Albania p108

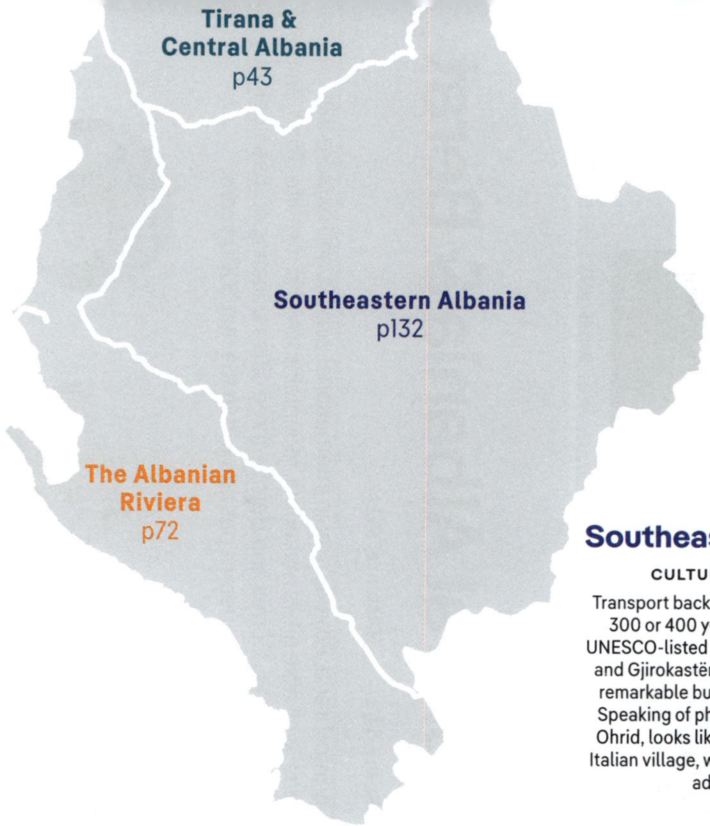

Southeastern Albania

CULTURAL CAPITALS

Transport back to the Ottoman period, 300 or 400 years ago, at Albania's UNESCO-listed 'museum cities' of Berat and Gjirokastër. You won't be short on remarkable buildings to photograph. Speaking of photos, Korçë, near Lake Ohrid, looks like a colourful French or Italian village, while Përmet is a hub for adventurers.

Tirana & Central Albania
p43

Southeastern Albania
p132

The Albanian Riviera
p72

The Albanian Riviera

TURQUOISE COAST

You've seen Albania's beaches on social media, now see them for yourself – they really are that turquoise and crystal-clear. Come for clubs and festivals, camping with backpackers or long sand stretches for relaxing with the family – there's a beach for everybody. The coast also has fascinating ancient ruins.

Durrës (p62)

ITINERARIES

Central Albania & Berat

Allow: 7 days   **Distance:** 172km

Fly into Tirana, Albania's main international airport, and explore this rising, walkable city's museums, mountaintops and nightlife. Then, time travel to Krujë, Durrës and Berat – three cities boasting archaeological sites from three different periods within the last 2000 years.

❶ TIRANA ⏱ 2 DAYS

In **Tirana** (p46), wander the many interesting buildings and museums around **Skanderbeg Square** (p46), especially the former spy headquarters of **House of Leaves** (p51). Then hit up the stylish **Blloku** (pictured; p52) neighbourhood for food and cocktails. The next day, bus or taxi to see the bunker museum of **Bunk'Art 1** (p55) and ride the **Dajti Ekspres** (p57) cable car up **Mt Tujani** (p57) for an enjoyable hike.

❷ KRUJË ⏱ 1 DAY

Hop in a *furgon* (shared minibus) to **Krujë** (p60) to see **Krujë Castle** (pictured; p60), where national hero Skanderbeg and his forces defied the Ottomans for a quarter of a century. The castle has two fascinating museums, plus B&Bs where you can stay the night. Stock up on souvenirs at the **Bazaar** (p61).

↪ *Detour:* Hike up the side of the mountain to see **Sari Salltik** (p61), a Bektashi teqe (shrine) carved into it.

❸ DURRËS ⏱ 1 DAY

Take a *furgon* from Krujë to Albania's second-largest city, **Durrës** (p62), where cute Italian villas stand next to ancient archaeological sites. See the Roman **Durrës Amphitheatre** (p62), the **Venetian Tower** (pictured; p62) and **King Zog Villa** (p65), once a summer home for Albania's 20th-century monarch. Catch sunset from the **Sfinksi** (p65) or a beach club.

④ BERAT ⏱ 3 DAYS

Take a *furgon* from the **Plepa Bus Station** (p62) in Durrës to **Berat** (p138), the UNESCO-listed city of windows. Soak up the fascinating architecture in **Berat Castle** (pictured; p138) and the stone neighbourhoods of **Mangalem** (p141) and **Goricë** (p141). The next day, take a tour to **Osum Canyon** (p145) to go rafting between canyon walls.

FROM LEFT: JOEL BALSAM/LONELY PLANET
JOEL BALSAM/LONELY PLANET

Amalia (p141), Berat

View from the Monastery of the 40 Saints (p83), Sarandë

ITINERARIES

Beach Hop the Riviera

Allow: 7 days   **Distance:** 140km

Fly into the Greek island of Corfu and take a 'Flying Dolphin' ferry over to Sarandë for an Albanian beach holiday. Explore the southeastern hub towns and the UNESCO World Heritage Site of Butrint, then beach hop up the coast to Himarë, Dhërmi and Vlorë, where there's a new international airport to take you home, or to your next destination.

❶ SARANDË ⏱ 2 DAYS

Sarandë (p80) has lost much of its charm, but it's a great base, with plenty of hotels, seafood restaurants and stylish bars. People-watch from its busy promenade, and hike or taxi up to **Lekursi Castle** (p82) for a spectacular sunset. The next day, do a short day trip to see the turquoise waters of the **Blue Eye** (pictured; p84).

❷ KSAMIL ⏱ 1 DAY

Ksamil (p86) is the undeniably sparkling hot spot of the Albanian Riviera. Lounge in a chair at fashionable beach clubs, and swim or pedal boat to remote islands. Experiences can plunge you below to see its shipwrecks with **Saranda Diving** (p83). Be warned: Ksamil teems with people in June, July and August. Don't dare skip the UNESCO **Butrint** (p88), Albania's most incredible archaeological site.

❸ HIMARË ⏱ 2 DAYS

Take a *furgon* (shared minibus) or bus up to **Himarë** (p92), which has a series of spectacular turquoise beaches and a budget-friendly vibe, with lots of fun backpacker campgrounds. Hike or taxi to two of the most beautiful beaches in Albania: **Aquarium** (pictured; p93) and **Gjipe** (p98), or take a boat tour.

🚗 *Detour:* See Ali Pasha's **Porto Palermo Castle** *(p95)*.

④ DHËRMI ⏱ 1 DAY

Dhërmi (p97) is a Greek-influenced beach town with a cute, church-filled **old town** (p99) up the hill and party vibes along the beachfront. It's also becoming a summer destination for electronic music festivals such as **Kala** (p99).

⑤ VLORË ⏱ 1 DAY

On your way to **Vlorë** (p101) zigzag up and over the **Llogora Pass** (p99) as Caesar's forces once did. Vlorë is a busy coastal city at the confluence of the Adriatic and Ionian seas. Take a boat tour to **Sazan Island** (pictured; p103), an uninhabited island soon to be developed into a resort by Donald Trump's son-in-law, and walk a winding wooden bridge to flamingo-frequented **Nartë Lagoon** (p103).

Nartë Lagoon (p103)

Shkodër (p112)

ITINERARIES

The North

Allow: 5 days **Distance:** 210km

Explore the Albanian Alps by starting from the main hub town of Shkodër, which has a youthful vibe and excellent museums. Then, embark on the Valbonë to Theth Circuit, the most straightforward and popular way to explore the Alps. This loop itinerary involves taking a three-hour ferry and a five- to seven-hour hike through the mountains.

❶ SHKODËR ⏱ 1 DAY

Shkodër (p112), the gateway to the Albanian Alps, is a quaint and colourful city with a few terrific museums and interesting monuments scattered around a charming historic core. Hop on a bike (cycling is really popular here) to see the **Rozafa Fortress** (pictured; p115) and **Lake Shkodër** (p118), where you can bird-watch while dining on tasty grilled carp.

❷ KOMAN ⏱ 1 DAY

Begin your three-day Valbonë to Theth circuit by taking a *furgon* (shared minibus) to **Koman**. From the **Koman Ferry Terminal** (p120), you'll board a ferry for a three-hour journey along the Drin River to Fierzë. Then, you'll board another *furgon* in Fierzë that heads to the mountain village of Valbonë. Accommodations can easily coordinate your transport.

❸ VALBONË ⏱ 1 DAY

Once you reach **Valbonë** (p121), spend the night in one of the guesthouses there and wake up the next morning to begin the region's most popular hike, which takes you over the 1795m **Valbonë Pass** (pictured; p121) from Valbonë to the village of Theth. The hike down to Theth is steep and should take between five and seven hours.

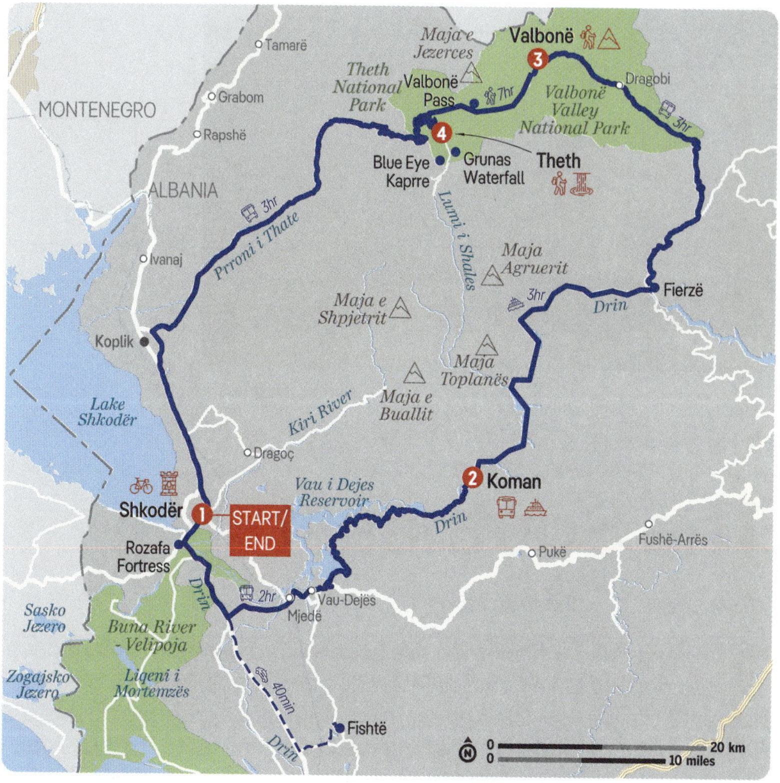

4
THETH ⏱ 2 DAYS

In **Theth** (p128), spend the night in one of the guesthouses lining the river and, if you have the energy, hike to the village's famous **Grunas Waterfall** (p128) and **Blue Eye Kaprre** (p128). Catch the afternoon *furgon* back to Shkodër the next day.

🢂 *Detour:* *If you have another day, after you travel back to Shkodër, spoil yourself with a meal at* **Mrizi i Zanave** *(p119) in* **Fishtë** *(p119). The simplest way to get there is by taxi.*

FROM LEFT: EVISDISHA/SHUTTERSTOCK
MEHMETO/SHUTTERSTOCK

Theth (p128)

Gjirokastër (p147)

ITINERARIES

The Southeast

Allow: 7 days **Distance:** 395km

From Tirana, road trip south to this under-explored region. You'll drive southeast along Lake Ohrid to Pogradec and Korçë, taking a quick detour to the church-filled ghost town of Voskopojë before driving a freshly paved mountain road along the Greek border to Përmet. After two days of adventure, head to the UNESCO stone city of Gjirokastër.

1 POGRADEC ⏱1 DAY

From Tirana, drive along **Lake Ohrid** (p165) and stop in the fishing town of Lin to see the 6th-century **Lin Mosaics** (pictured; p168). Continue down the lakefront to **Pogradec** (p165), a local favorite with a beach and promenade. Continue to Korçë, where you can spend the night.

🡒 *Detour: East along Lake Ohrid is* **Drilon National Park** *(p165), where dictator Enver Hoxha liked to vacation.*

2 KORÇË ⏱1 DAY

Colourful **Korçë** (p159) has a visibly French feel due to a short 20th-century occupation by France that greatly influenced its architecture. Wander around to see its **Bazaar** (p159) and the awe-inspiring Orthodox paintings at the **Medieval Art Museum** (p159). Cap off your day with an ice-cold (and very cheap) beer at the **Birra Korça** (pictured; p161) brewery.

3 VOSKOPOJË ⏱1 DAY

Voskopojë (p163) was once a thriving merchant city with two dozen churches, but it was ransacked by the Ottomans and became a ghost town. However, it's experiencing a second life as a tourist hub. Explore its crumbling churches and eat at restaurants serving Korçan *lakror* (baked spinach pie).

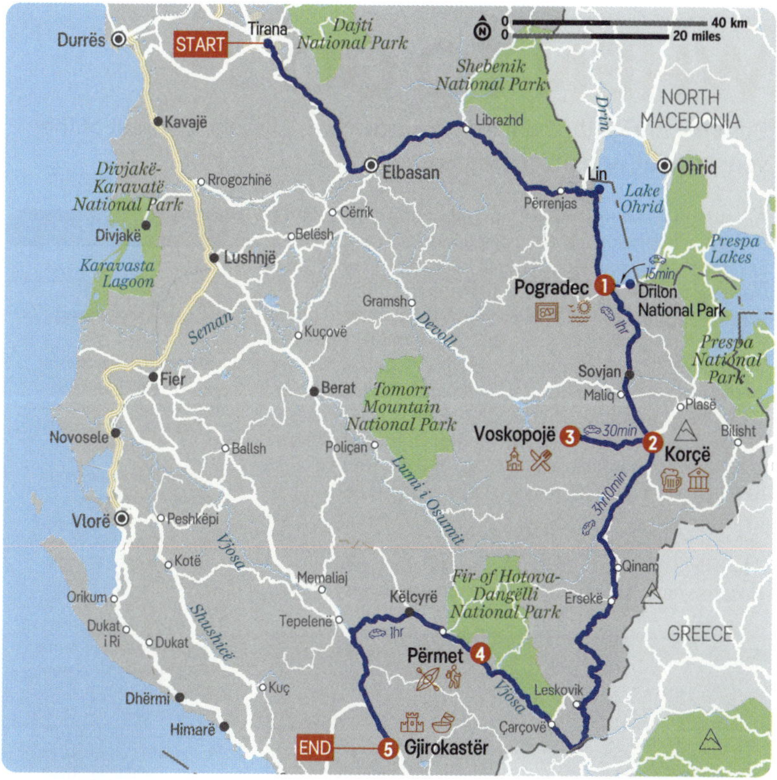

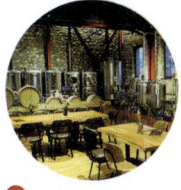

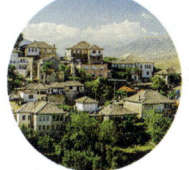

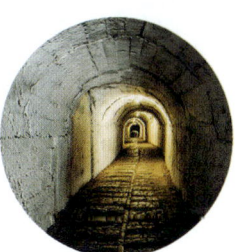

Cold War Tunnel (p152), Gjirokastër

4

PËRMET ⏱ 2 DAYS

Wake up early for a road trip along the Greek border on a crazy mountain road. Along the way, stop at **Melesin Distillery** (pictured; p137) to try its artisanal *raki* (fruit brandy), then spend the night in **Përmet** (p156). The next day, organise a rafting trip along Përmet's **Vjosa River** (p156) – Europe's first national river park – and warm up in the **Benjë Hot Springs** (p158) and/or hike the **Langarica Canyon** (p158).

5

GJIROKASTËR ⏱ 2 DAYS

The amazing stone city of **Gjirokastër** (p147) is filled with Ottoman-era buildings with slabs for roofs. There's plenty to see, including **Gjirokastër Castle** (p149), house museums and a **Cold War Tunnel** (p152). You can also do a cooking class with **Për drekë tek Marjeta** (p152).

FROM LEFT: JOEL BALSAM/LONELY PLANET, LEV LEVIN/SHUTTERSTOCK, INGRID PAKATS/SHUTTERSTOCK

WHEN TO GO

Summer brings the heat and the crowds to Albania. The rest of the year is quiet, and most places are closed.

Albania is a strange mix of up-and-coming destination that's much less touristy than neighbouring countries such as Greece, Italy and Croatia; and country on the brink of overtourism that gets chaotic in summer. June, July and August are crazy in Albania, especially in coastal beach towns such as Sarandë, Ksamil, Himarë and Dhërmi, and in the capital, Tirana. Expect high prices, queues and extreme heat (which subsequently means cranky people).

Travelling to Albania in the low season isn't so straightforward. Most of the main attractions outside of Tirana are shut from October through May, and the Riviera looks like a ghost town, with only a couple of hotels and restaurants open. It's also pretty lonely at this time of year without travellers around.

Ideally, travel to Albania in the shoulder season – as close as you can to summer – to avoid the biggest crowds.

⊕ I LIVE HERE

SPRING AWAKENING

Armando Muca, founder of **Albanian Night** (p52), celebrates Albanian culture in Tirana. *@albanian.night. official*

Springtime in Albania is my favourite because it's a feast for all the senses. I hiked through the Albanian Alps in spring as snow melted into rivers and wildflowers came out in all their glory; shepherds returned to the highlands, and villages slowly woke from winter's sleep. There's a rare magic in witnessing nature and tradition come together. Everywhere you look, details stand out: moss on stone, the sound of river water, flocks moving through valleys.

SHOULDER SEASON

For the fewest visitors and the most pleasant weather, travel to Albania in May or September. The seas should be warm enough for swimming, and most accommodation, sites and restaurants will be open.

Himarë Beach (p92)

Weather through the Year: Tirana

JANUARY	FEBRUARY	MARCH	APRIL	MAY	JUNE
Average daytime max: 11.6°C	Average daytime max: 12.9°C	Average daytime max: 15.6°C	Average daytime max: 19°C	Average daytime max: 23.8°C	Average daytime max: 27.7°C
Days of rainfall: 13	Days of rainfall: 13	Days of rainfall: 14	Days of rainfall: 13	Days of rainfall: 12	Days of rainfall: 7

COOL OFF IN SUMMER

The Albanian summer isn't just hot, it can be dangerous, with scorching sun roasting pedestrians when it bounces off the concrete. Pack your swimming gear, whether or not you're heading to the coast, as there are plenty of rivers and lakes to cool off in.

Music Festivals

On the coast, the **South Outdoor Festival** (p85) on Borsh Beach features concerts with DJs, as well as rock and traditional music. What's really special about this festival? It also encourages outdoor sports, including hiking, kayaking and beach volleyball. **May**

Dhërmi is becoming a fixture on the electronic music festival circuit. There's weeklong **Kala** (p99), which features a lineup of international DJs, as well as **Anjunadeep** (p99), a festival that combines music and wellness. **June**

For harvest month, head to the mountain village of Theth for its live concert series at **Zâ Fest** (p129). Expect rock and traditional folk music. **July**

Cultural Celebrations

Who needs Italy when you've got **Shkodër Carnival** (p118)? Locals parade through the streets in costumes, including masks made at the famous **Venice Art Mask Factory** (p117). Be warned: it's chilly. **February/March**

Albanians celebrate the return of warmer weather with two cultural festivals in the spring. The first is **Dita e Verës** (p54), which celebrates the arrival of the spring sun, followed by **Sultan Nevruz** (p54), the Persian New Year and Bektashi celebration. **March**

See Albanian folk dancing, choirs and orchestras in Durrës, Albania's second-largest city, at **Durrës Festival** (p54). **July**

The best place to see endangered Albanian art forms, including UNESCO-listed iso-polyphony singing and traditional *xhubleta* clothing, is the **National Folk Festival** (p150) in Gjirokastër. Unfortunately, it only comes around every five years, with the next one occurring in 2028. **June**

WINTER TIRES

Driving in Albania in the wintertime or shoulder seasons can be very dangerous, as the roads typically become slick with ice and snow. In such a mountainous country, the roads in winter are risky everywhere, but be especially careful in the Albanian Alps.

⊕ I LIVE HERE

AUTUMN IN ALBANIA

Eni Koço, guide and co-founder of **Albania My Way** (p51), is passionate about sharing Albania's diverse beauty. *@albaniamyway*

In small Albania, we are proud to have almost all natural landscapes: sandy and rocky beaches, mountains with green forests, rivers and lakes. With each season comes a different charm. In autumn, the country slows down, and you can enjoy the full panorama of smells and colours. I love guiding in autumn. In a single day, you can handpick fruit, walk through a thousand colourful leaves in the forest, taste pomegranate and dates, and watch the sunset in the Adriatic.

Bridge near Valbonë Pass (p120)

JULY	**AUGUST**	**SEPTEMBER**	**OCTOBER**	**NOVEMBER**	**DECEMBER**
Average daytime max: 30.7°C	Average daytime max: 30.7°C	Average daytime max: 27.3°C	Average daytime max: 21.8°C	Average daytime max: 17.1°C	Average daytime max: 13°C
Days of rainfall: **5**	Days of rainfall: **4**	Days of rainfall: **6**	Days of rainfall: **9**	Days of rainfall: **16**	Days of rainfall: **16**

Krujë (p60)

GET PREPARED FOR ALBANIA

Useful things to load in your bag, your ears and your brain.

Clothes

Cover up Albania might be secular, with few women wearing hijabs, but you're still expected to cover up in cities, on public transport and at prayer sites: they usually have shawls you can borrow in exchange for a small tip. Wearing a bikini on the beach is fine.

Footwear You'll want good hiking shoes or boots if hiking the Albanian Alps, where the terrain is steep and slippery. You also might want to have closed-toed shoes for walking the cobblestone streets of Berat and Gjirokastër.

Layers Even if it's hot in the day, it can get very cold at night, so bring layers. You'll also want a jacket for cooler destinations, including the Albanian Alps and Mt Dajti near Tirana.

Manners

Invitations for dinner or a drink are common – Albanians are warm and curious people.

Thorny topics in Albania are numerous. Among them are the dictatorship, the Kosovo–Serbian war and the mafia. Albanians who speak English usually have no trouble talking about them, but tread carefully.

Nodding your head traditionally means 'no' and shaking your head can mean 'yes', though this is less common nowadays.

📖 READ

 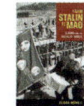  

Free (Lea Ypi; 2021) Bestselling memoir by a London School of Economics professor about growing up in Durrës under the communist dictatorship.

From Stalin to Mao: Albania and the Socialist World (Elidor Mëhilli; 2017) Understand Albania's dictatorship and its place within international geopolitics with this scholarly work.

The General of the Dead Army (Ismail Kadare; 1963) This book, about an Italian soldier who returns to Albania after WWII, catapulted Albania's finest writer to international fame.

The Highland Lute (Gjergj Fishta; 1937) Fishta's epic poem covers freedom and war and is considered one of Albania's best.

Words

Përshëndetje (per-shen-*deh*-tyeh): 'Hello'
Mirupafshim (meer-oo-*pahf*-sheem): 'Goodbye'
Ç'kemi (ch-*keh*-mee): 'Hi' or 'What's up?'
Mirëmëngjes (meer-muhn-*jess*) 'Good morning'
Mirëdita (meer-*dee*-tah): 'Good afternoon'
Mirëmbrëma (meer-*mbruh*-mah): 'Good evening'
Natën e mirë (*nah*-ten eh meer): 'Goodnight'
Si jeni/je? (see *yeh*-nee/yeh): 'How are you?' (f./inf.)
Ju/Të lutem (yoo/tuh *loo*-tem): 'Please' (f./inf.)
Faleminderit (fah-leh-meen-*deh*-reet): 'Thank you'
S'ka përse (ska per-*seh*): 'You're welcome'
Më falni/fal (muh *fahl*-nee/*fahl*): 'Excuse me' or 'I'm sorry' (f./inf.)
Po/Jo (poh/yo): 'Yes/No'
Gëzuar! (guh-*zoo*-ar): 'Cheers!'
Ju bëftë mirë! (yoo *buhf*-tuh meer): 'Bon appetit!'
Tualeti (too-ah-*leh*-tee): 'Toilet'
Ujë (*oo*-yeh): 'Water'
Ndihmë! (n-*dee*-muh): 'Help!'
A mund të më ndihmoni? (ah moond tuh muh n-dee-*hmoh*-nee): 'Can you help me?'
Unë jam i humbur (oon yuhm ee *hoom*-boor): 'I am lost'
A flisni anglisht? (ah *flees*-nee ahn-*gleesht*): 'Do you speak English?'
Ku është...? (koo *uh*-shtuh): 'Where is...?'
Ku është stacioni i autobusit? (koo *uh*-shtuh stah-*tsyoh*-nee ee ow-too-*boo*-seet): 'Where is the bus station?'
Çfarë është kjo? (ch-*fah*-reh *uh*-sht kyoh): 'What is this?'
Sa kushton? (sah *koosh*-ton): 'How much does it cost?'
A mund të paguaj me kartë? (ah moond tuh pah-*goo-aye* meh kahrt): 'Can I pay by card?'
A ka wi-fi këtu? (ah kah wee-*fee* kuh-*too*): 'Is there wi-fi here?'
Sa është ora? (sah *uh*-sht uh-rah): 'What time is it?'

🎬 WATCH

Waterdrop (Robert Budina; 2024) Albania's entry for the Best International Feature Film at the Academy Awards is about a woman living in Lake Ohrid whose son is accused of rape.

The Forgiveness of Blood (Joshua Marston; 2011; pictured) Drama about Kanun blood feuds that's set and filmed in northern Albania.

Alexander (Ardit Sadiku; 2023) True story about an Albanian mechanic who hijacked a warship in 1990 to escape the dictatorship.

Time of the Comet (Fatmir Koçi; 2008) Historical romance based on *Black Year*, a novel by Ismail Kadare.

Dear Albania (Nate Dushku; 2015) Travel documentary where American Albanian actress Eliza Dushku travels to Albania to learn more about its culture.

🎧 LISTEN

Zjerm (Shkodra Elektronike; 2025) Meaning 'fire' in the Gheg dialect, this was Albania's best showing at the 2025 Eurovision Song Contest.

Albanian Iso Polyphony: Southern Albania (Labëria) (Lab Polyphonic Group; 2010) Hear the UNESCO-listed iso-polyphony singing.

Inside Albania Podcast with Alice Taylor (EuroNews; Ongoing) Weekly podcast in English on Albanian culture, news and politics.

Rrjedh në këngë dhe ligjërime (Vaçe Zela; 1973) Classic Albanian song by Vaçe Zela, a beloved, award-winning singer/songwriter.

Qifqi (p35) and other traditional Albanian food

THE FOOD SCENE

Whet your appetite with this guide to Albania's diverse and delicious cuisine.

Like their formerly Ottoman-occupied neighbours, Albanians salivate for savoury grilled meats, flaky pastries, yoghurt and *raki* (fruit brandy). They spend hours sipping coffee (usually an espresso, though sometimes Turkish style), smoking cigarettes and feasting for Sunday lunches, weddings, birthdays, festivities – any excuse to eat, really. Dishes are served individually, and in heaping portions – *kokë* (lamb) cooked for hours on a spit; *qofte* (meatballs) dunked in *salsë kosi* (yoghurt dip akin to tzatziki); piles of grilled veggies; fresh village salads with hunks of fresh tomato, cucumber, olives and sheep's cheese – all edge-to-edge crowding a tablecloth like a game of Tetris. For dessert, think honey-soaked pastries like *bakllava* (layered filo dough with honey and nuts), cookies and cakes, along with, of course, more coffee.

Just when you think you've figured out Albanian cuisine, another dish you haven't seen before arrives to surprise you. Taste it, because it's probably made with heart, and certainly plenty of soul.

Ottoman Influences

More than half a century of Ottoman control has, understandably, had a major impact on Albanian cuisine. In Tirana, *furrë bukë* (bakeries) pump out *byrek* (flaky pastries filled with spinach, cheese or meat) as bakeries would in Istanbul. *Zgaras* (barbeque restaurants) dish out grilled meats like *qofte* and *sujukh* (sausage). You'll also find

Best Albanian Dishes

TAVË KOSI
Lamb baked in a cast-iron pan with yoghurt and rice.

LAKROR
Doughy Korçan pie usually stuffed with spinach and maybe cheese, leeks or meat.

SPECË/ PATËLLXHAN TË MBUSHUR
Baked peppers or aubergines stuffed with rice.

FËRGESË
Dip made with red peppers and ricotta cheese.

dishes like *japrak/dollma* (stuffed grape leaves) and *kafe turke* (Turkish coffee), served in small cups with a thick layer of grounds at the bottom.

Coastal Cuisine

Albanian cuisine shifts when you get to the beach, where dishes are more influenced by Greece, Italy and international trends. Virtually every restaurant serves *peshk në furrë* (grilled fish) – commonly sea bass or sea bream – along with seafood such as squid, shrimp and mussels brought fresh from Lake Butrint. *Pasta me fruta deti* (seafood pasta) is rarely a bad choice, with tasty ingredients and prices – at 700–800L, it's much cheaper than the same dish across the sea in Italy. You'll also see plenty of moussaka (layered potatoes, aubergines and meat), Greek salads and olive oil, especially in Hellenist-influenced cities like Himarë and Dhërmi.

Albanian Dairy Products

Albania is one of several European countries to be registered on UNESCO's Intangible Cultural Heritage List for transhumance – the seasonal migration of sheep, goats or cows, and their shepherds, to areas of grazing. You'll find proof of this ancient practice wherever you drive in the country. A major reason for transhumance? The production of milk, yoghurt and cheese – all of which Albanians adore.

Dairy is found in many dishes and most meals. A morning *byrek* is washed down with *dhallë* (salted yoghurt drink), and *tarator* is a delicious cold yoghurt and cucumber soup. Cheese is served in salads, mixed with meat in a *tavë* (cast-iron casserole pot) or on its own. Popular Albanian cheeses include *djathë i bardhë* (white cheese similar to feta), *gjizë* (ricotta-style curds) and *kaçkavall* (a hard cheese often served grilled).

Korça Beer Fest

FESTIVALS TO FEAST AT

Lakror Festival (*August*; p162) Eat Korçan *lakror* fresh from the *sač* (large metal pan) and baked in open fires in villages around the region of Korça, where it was born.

Korça Beer Fest (*August*; p162) Albania's largest beer festival also takes place in Korça and features more than 40 breweries, numerous live concerts and 100,000 attendees.

Wine & Stories (*October/November*; p162) Cheers with locals in Berat, Albania's top wine-producing region. The festival features tastings and live concerts.

Cheese, Fishtë (p119)

JAPRAK/DOLLMA	FLIA	KOKË	PESHK NË FURRË
Stuffed grape leaves.	Layered crepes that can be sweet or sour; from Kosovo and the northern regions.	Lamb, baked on a spit and served on its own or in a soup.	Grilled fish. Look for *karpe* (carp) or *koman* (trout) by the lakes.

Raki

Vegan & Vegetarian

Albanian cuisine is meat-heavy, but there are some dishes to look out for if you're on a plant-based diet. Many restaurants serve *perime në zagarë* (grilled vegetables) and *fasulë* (white bean soup), which works as a tasty protein. Village salads, usually with cheese and bread, are very filling, and you're never far from a pasta. Specialities like *fërgesë me perime* (red peppers in cottage cheese) and *speca të mbushur* (baked peppers stuffed with rice, tomatoes and fresh herbs) are delicious options for vegetarians, though they're sometimes made with *mish* (meat), so make sure to ask if they've added any. Restaurants that specifically cater to vegans and vegetarians are most common in Tirana and Sarandë.

Booze

Many Albanians really do kick off their day with a shot of *raki,* and you're bound to be offered one if you're in a family-run B&B. *Raki,* usually made with grape or plum (though increasingly with intriguing flavors such as saffron, fig or blackberry), is also a remedy for when you're sick (both medically and from wounds of the heart).

Albanian wine is increasing in both popularity and taste, with small producers in Berat, Tirana, Vlorë and the northern regions producing some enticing wines in their vineyards. Albanian indigenous grape varieties include kallmet (red grape often compared to pinot noir), shesh i zi (black grape often barrel-aged), shesh i bardhë (full-bodied white grape), pulëz (white grape from Roshnik near Berat), vlosh (rare red grape from the Vlorë region) and serina (red or white grape from southeastern Albania).

Beer-wise, Albanians love their local lagers, with Birra Korça and Birra Tirana the most popular choices, along with Birra Peja from Kosovo. Craft beer is slowly becoming more common, though you'll likely only find it in Tirana.

TOP LEFT: AGROFRUTI/SHUTTERSTOCK
TOP RIGHT: JOEL BALSAM/LONELY PLANET

AGROTOURISM & SLOW FOOD

The biggest trend in Albanian cuisine is unquestionably agrotourism. Part guesthouse, part farm-to-table B&B, agrotourism establishments were inspired by the fine work at Mrizi i Zanave in the north and are now found in rural areas throughout the country. Agrotourism restaurants are some of the best dining experiences in the country. Stop in for a Sunday feast, or spend the night in tranquil, filling bliss.

A parallel trend is the slow-food movement around the southern town of Përmet. Founded as a branch of the Italian Slow Food Foundation for Biodiversity *(fondazioneslowfood.com),* restaurants, guesthouses and small producers (like a cheesemaker in a bunker) adhere to ecofriendly principles, including cooking with local ingredients, avoiding chemical additives and using traditional recipes passed down through generations. Dishes don't necessarily arrive slowly (in case you're in a rush), but they are made with care.

Specialities

Cheap Eats & Snacks

Byrek Parcels of flaky pastry usually stuffed with meat, cheese or spinach.
Pispili Cornbread mixed with leeks and feta.
Qofte Round or log-shaped meatballs.
Paçe kokë Soup with a sheep's head and/or other parts.
Qifqi Rice-and-egg balls fried in a 105-year-old special pan; orginates from the city of Gjirokastër.

Non-alcoholic Drinks

Caj Mali Mountain herbal tea.
Boza Fermented cornmeal beverage.
Dhallë Refreshing salted yoghurt drink.

Sweet Treats

Petulla Fried doughnut balls often served with honey, sugar or jam.
Gliko Fruit or vegetable preserve in a sugar syrup.
Bakllava Layered filo dough and nuts bathed in honey.
Treleçe (aka Tri Leche) 'Three milk' sponge cake.
Ballokume Butter and cornflower cookies from the city of Elbasan.
Shendetlie Honey and walnut cake.
Sultiash Albanian rice pudding.
Asullde Simple caramel pudding.

Qifqi

MEALS OF A LIFETIME

Mrizi i Zanave Multi-course feasts, wine and/or *raki*, all produced on their compound south of Shkodër.

Rapsodia Chef Alfred Marku serves small plates with local and foraged Albanian ingredients from this restaurant near Lezhë.

Era Go-to restaurant for traditional Albanian cuisine in the trendy Blloku neighbourhood of Tirana.

Manxuranë The coast's best dining experience, with home-style cooking and attentive service.

Fustanella Farm Organic farm-to-table restaurant and vineyard near Tirana. Try their *berxolle vici* (T-bone steak).

Lili The kindest service you'll ever have, in a small dining room in Berat's Mangalem neighbourhood.

Alpeta Agrotourism Delicious, award-winning wine and fresh ingredients from the farm in Roshnik.

THE YEAR IN FOOD

SPRING

March to May is the time for farmed and foraged herbs such as leeks, spring onions and wild garlic, along with lamb for Easter. See if you can find *lakror* stuffed with wild nettles (pictured).

SUMMER

From June through August, vendors alongside the highways sell piles of strawberries, cherries, watermelons and tomatoes. Pick up some snacks for a road trip. This is the season for fresh village salad.

AUTUMN

The harvest, from September to November, brings pumpkin, squash and aubergines, along with a fresh crop of grapes for wine (pictured) and *raki*. Look out for *byrek* filled with courgettes.

WINTER

December to February is comfort-food season. Eat baked casseroles, pickled vegetables, slow-cooked lamb and soups like *pacë kokë*.

Ksamil (p86)

THE OUTDOORS

Psych yourself up for the many adventures this thrilling country offers, from hiking the Albanian Alps and rafting through canyons to plunging beneath turquoise water to military shipwrecks.

Albania has a wide range of landscapes. There's the remote Albanian Alps for hiking (just be careful not to get lost – after all, they *are* also known as the Accursed Mountains). There's also 450km of coastline to be explored, both under and above the water, with scuba and kitesurfing equipment. Inland, wild rivers, steep canyons and calm lakes are perfect for exploring on a raft or stand-up paddleboard. That said, Albania has room to grow as an adventure destination, as there isn't much competition among outfitters.

Walking & Hiking

The Albanian Alps are perfect hiking territory. In summer, climb mountain peaks for stunning views, stopping at humble cafes for mountain tea and to fill up your water bottle. You don't need to be a mountaineer to do it, though unfortunately, many trails are unmarked, so you will require a guide. The big exception is the hike from Valbonë to Theth (p120), which is popular from spring through autumn. It's a safe and well-trodden hike but shouldn't be attempted in spring or winter, as the weather can be snowy, cold and dangerous (an Australian man went missing on the hike in November 2024). The Valbonë to Theth hike is part of the Peaks of the Balkans Trail (p123), a multiday trek that crosses Albania, Kosovo and Montenegro.

Outdoor Pursuits

PARAGLIDING
Fly off Mt Dajti and float down to the ground on a paragliding trip with Tirana's **SkySports Paragliding** (p57).

JET-SKIING
Show off on a jet-ski at Durrës Beach with **Shark Water Sports** (p65).

SCUBA DIVING
Plunge to see WWII shipwrecks, reefs and fishies in the turquoise water off **Sarandë** (p80).

FAMILY ADVENTURES

Strap in for some high-altitude fun at **Dajti Adventure Park** (p57) just outside Tirana.

Head south of Durrës to see pelicans and other rare birds on a motorboat trip through **Divjakë-Karavastë National Park** (p68).

Soar through the mountains along the 1110m **Theth Zipline** (p129).

Take your toddler castle crawling around **Berat Castle** (p138).

Saddle up and go horse riding through Gjirokastër's hillsides with **Visit Gjirokastra** (p153).

House of Horses (p163) is another excellent horse-riding experience that offers multi-day trots just outside of Korçë.

Rent a pedal boat from **Bora Bora** (p86) and sail through turquoise water to islands just off Ksamil Beach.

Other amazing mountains to climb include Mt Tujani (1513m; p57) and Mt Vajushë (2057m; p125), which involves hiking from Lëpushë into Montenegro. Mt Tomorr (2416m; p144), located near Berat, is another great option, while Mt Tarabosh (593m; p118) is a less demanding hike near the town of Shkodër. You can also climb Albania's tallest mountain, Mt Korab (2764m; p122), on the border with North Macedonia.

Langarica Canyon (p158) is also a great hiking spot, as you can hike through the shallow water or above the 100m-deep canyon and then finish with a soak in Benjë Hot Springs (p158) when you're finished.

Hike between Valbonë and Theth (p120)

Biking & Motorcycling

There are few cities in eastern Europe more bike-friendly than Shkodër (p112) in Albania, so rent a bike and cycle to Lake Shkodër (p116) for some grilled carp. Cycling is also popular in Tirana, though to a much lesser extent. There, cycling around the artificial lake in Tirana Park (p54) is a must.

Road touring is also increasingly popular in Albania – just be prepared for mountain climbs wherever you go. The coastal road is a scenic cruise, as is the up-and-down road from Shkodër to Vermosh (p124).

Watersports

The Albanian coast is perfect for more than just sunbathing. Plunge into the crystal-clear water off the coast of Ksamil (p86) and organise a scuba-diving trip from Sarandë with Saranda Diving (p83). Or swim through the calm water to the Tre Ishujt islands (p86), just offshore from Ksamil.

Albania has not one, but two wild rivers for white-water rafting. There's the Vjosa River (p156), declared Europe's first national river park in 2023. You can organise your Vjosa rafting trip from the adventure hub of Përmet (p156). And then there's Osum Canyon (p145), located near Berat (p138).

Spring is best for the wildest rapids – by late July, they're slowly fading.

BIRD-WATCHING
Head to the lagoon and coastland of **Kune-Vain-Tale Reserve** (p126) to see Dalmatian pelicans, pygmy cormorants and greater flamingos.

KITESURFING
Learn to kitesurf or hone your skills at the windswept **Seman Beach** (p106) north of Vlorë.

STAND-UP PADDLEBOARDING
Rent a board or go on a guided trip to see rare birds and lily pads on **Lake Shkodër** (p118).

SKIING
Hit the slopes at **Ski Pista Begell** (p164), the only ski resort in Albania, located just south of Korçë.

ACTION AREAS

Where to find Albania's best outdoor activities.

Walking/Hiking
1. Mt Tujani (p57)
2. Mt Tarabosh (p118)
3. Valbonë to Theth (p120)
4. Mt Tomorr (p144)
5. Langarica Canyon (p158)
6. Theth National Park (p128)

Vineyards/Wineries
1. Mrizi i Zanave (p119)
2. Cobo Winery (p143)
3. Alpeta Agrotourism (p143)
4. Melesin Distillery (p137)

National Parks
1. Mt Dajti National Park (p57)
2. Divjakë-Karavasta National Park (p68)
3. Kune-Vain-Tale Reserve (p126)
4. Nartë Lagoon (p103)
5. Llogorë Pass National Park (p99)
6. Theth National Park (p128)
7. Vjosa River (p156)

Extreme Adventures

1. SkySports Paragliding (p57)
2. Saranda Diving (p83)
3. Kitesurf Albania (p136)
4. Drini Times (p118)
5. Theth Zipline (p129)
6. Albania Rafting Group (p145)
7. Vjosa Rafting Albania (p157)

Beaches

1. Durrës Beach (p65)
2. Shengjin Beach (p123)
3. Ksamil Beach (p86)
4. Aquarium Beach (p93)
5. Gjipe Beach (p98)
6. Drymades Beach (p98)

PLAN YOUR TRIP THE OUTDOORS

ALBANIA

THE GUIDE

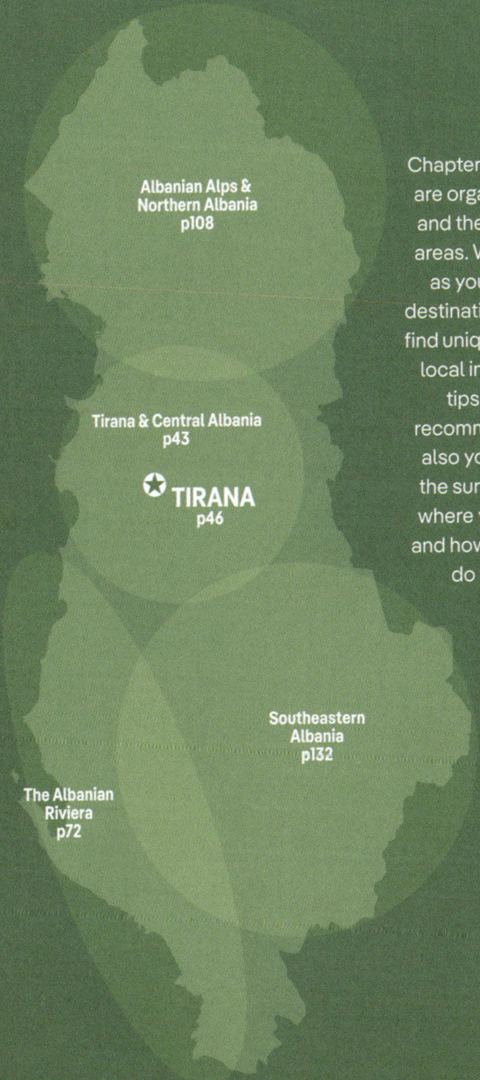

Albanian Alps & Northern Albania
p108

Tirana & Central Albania
p43

★ **TIRANA**
p46

Chapters in this section are organised by hubs and their surrounding areas. We see the hub as your base in the destination, where you'll find unique experiences, local insights, insider tips and expert recommendations. It's also your gateway to the surrounding area, where you'll see what and how much you can do from there.

Southeastern Albania
p132

The Albanian Riviera
p72

Berat (p138)

THE GUIDE

TIRANA & CENTRAL ALBANIA

For places to stay in Tirana and Central Albania, see p71

Left: beach near Durrës (p62); Above: Krujë Castle (p6

Tirana & Central Albania

RISING CAPITAL & BATTLEWORN RUINS

Land in Albania's compact and walkable capital, then day trip to ancient ruins and a national park known for bird-watching.

Many travellers will find themselves spending at least a day in the country's centre, which is home to Albania's main international airport and, since 1920, its capital. Don't leave too soon, as there's plenty to see here that doesn't involve beaches or mountains – though there are those, too.

Tirana is an everyone-knows-everyone type of place, petite for a European capital, but that makes it delightful to explore on foot. See a hodgepodge of architectural styles that ex plain Albania's many foreign takeovers, including Ottoman houses, Italian neo-Renaissance buildings constructed during the 1939–43 Fascist takeover, and Soviet-style concrete apartments freshly painted with colourful facades and murals. But a coat of paint and stylish modern skyscrapers (of which Tirana has many) aren't enough to cover the memory of Albania's brutal dictatorship under Enver Hoxha that lasted nearly half a century, from 1944 to 1992. Learn about the country's painful isolation with visits to concrete bunker museums, spy headquarters and the former private neighbourhood of the Communist Party leadership that's now a party zone.

Outside Tirana, climb up to Krujë, where national hero Skanderbeg defied the Ottomans for decades, and chill in the stylish beach city of Durrës, where Roman and Venetian ruins are nestled up against white Italian villas and breezy promenades. There are outdoor adventures, too, including hikes to caves and mountain peaks, and Albania's best bird-watching.

ANDREW ANGELOV/SHUTTERSTOCK

THE MAIN AREAS

TIRANA
Dictatorship history and cool nightlife. **p46**

KRUJË
National hero's hilltop war fortress. **p60**

DURRËS
Sun-kissed beach city and ruins. **p62**

THE GUIDE

TIRANA & CENTRAL ALBANIA

Find Your Way

Smack in the centre of the country, Tirana is Albania's best-connected city, with the country's main international airport and public transport to all major cities and neighbouring countries. Hire a car to see more, especially if you're on a tight schedule.

FURGON

There are plenty of *furgon* (shared minibus) connections between Tirana and Krujë or Durrës, though don't expect them to leave at fixed times or be of any comfort. Still, *furgons* are the most affordable way to get around.

CAR

Your own vehicle will give you the most freedom to explore, and it's required to visit natural sites like the **Cape of Rodon** (p70) and **Bovilla Lake** (p59). There are plenty of car-hire companies in Tirana, though few international brands that accept credit card.

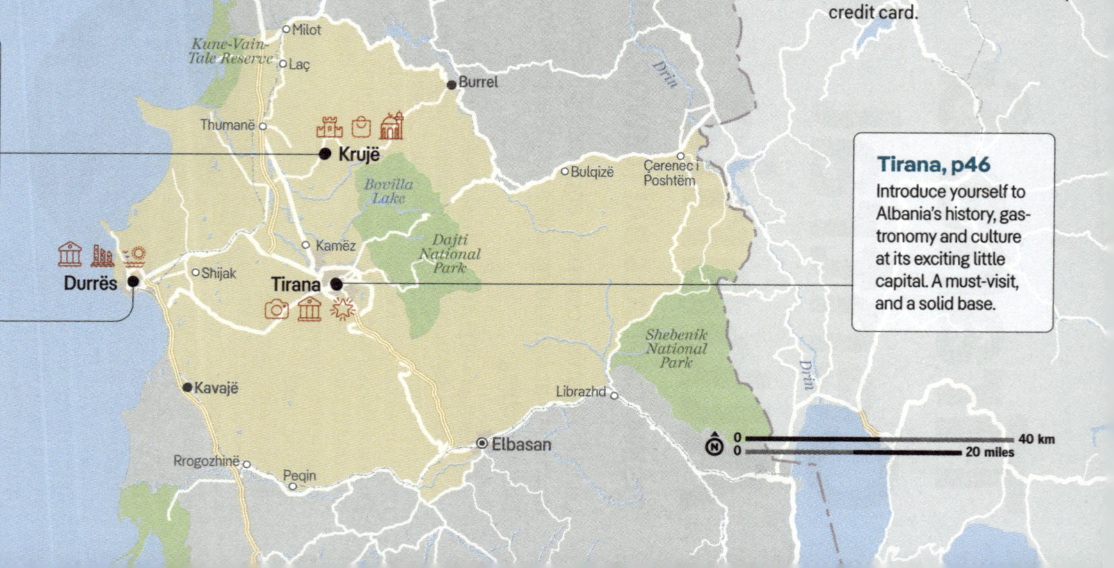

Tirana, p46

Introduce yourself to Albania's history, gastronomy and culture at its exciting little capital. A must-visit, and a solid base.

Krujë, p60

Day trip to Krujë to climb to a Bektashi shrine and learn about Skanderbeg, Albania's national hero, from within his hilltop fortress.

Durrës, p62

Escape to the coast for some sun soaking and to see ancient ruins next to Italian villas before enjoying a beach club sunset.

Skanderbeg Square (p46)

Plan Your Time

Reserve at least a day or two for walking around Tirana, but leave time for day trips to the cities and natural sites nearby.

Weekend in the Capital

- Start in Tirana's **Skanderbeg Square** (p46) and admire the odd mixture of architectural styles. Close is the **House of Leaves** (p51), once the dictatorship's spy and torture headquarters.

- Bus or taxi to **Bunk'Art 1** (p55), a museum in a communist bunker tunnel, then ride the **Dajti Ekspres** (p57) cable car up the mountain. Back in Tirana, dance and feast at staged wedding performance **Albanian Night** (p52).

A Week around Tirana

- Drive or taxi south to see **Petrelë Castle** (p57) and hike to the **Black Cave** (p58) in Pëllumbas, then feast at **Fustanella Farm** (p57). Head up to **Krujë** (p60), where Skanderbeg became legend, and to the **Cape of Rodon** (p70) to hike to bunker tunnels carved into a hillside. Visit **Durrës** (p62) for Roman and Venetian ruins and **Divjakë-Karavastë National Park** (p68) on a boat tour to spot flamingoes and pelicans.

SEASONAL HIGHLIGHTS

SPRING
Albania celebrates Dita e Verës (Summer Day; p54) on 14 March with *ballokume* (cookies) and flowers. Elbasan hosts the biggest celebrations.

SUMMER
See migrating birds in Divjakë-Karavastë National Park (p68) and avoid the Tirana crowds with an adventure to the Cape of Rodon (p70).

AUTUMN
Fewer crowds and cooler temperatures. Catch Albanian and international cinema at the Tirana International Film Festival (p54).

WINTER
Celebrate Dita e Pavarësisë (p54) on 28 November. Many tourist sites and beaches are closed; warm up in a Tirana bar with a *raki*.

Tirana

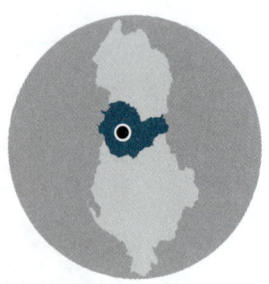

HISTORY | CUISINE | NIGHTLIFE

✅ TOP TIP
Albanians are firmly committed to cash payments, and few businesses accept credit cards. Both lekë and euros are accepted (buses only take lekë), so there's no need to exchange. Bank ATMs dispense lekë – Credins and Tirana Bank usually have the lowest withdrawal fees.

GETTING AROUND
An airport bus runs every hour on Rr Luigj Gurakuqi, near Skanderbeg Sq. The trip takes 30 minutes. Tirana also has more than 20 municipal bus lines – these are traditional buses, not *furgons* (shared minibuses).

Without Uber or Bolt, Tirana's taxis are pricey, and drivers rarely speak English. The city's electric taxi companies – try **Lux Taxi** *(069 844 4487)* – are cheaper than official cabs and can pick you up wherever you are; order via WhatsApp. Ask about rates to go beyond the city, and see if they can wait or pick you up when you're ready to go back.

Lively Tirana (Tiranë) has come a long way from its decades under a brutal dictatorship, which lasted from 1944 to 1992. The Albanian capital is bursting with colour, from parks and thoroughfares flourishing with foliage to Soviet-style apartment buildings painted with vibrant murals. Busy traffic rolls past captivating mosque minarets and church domes in this secular, though still faithful, city, while chic locals stroll through clean, safe streets to sprawling patios for an espresso, *raki* (fruit brandy) or fancy cocktail in the dapper Blloku neighbourhood. Look at the modern skyscrapers popping up everywhere, especially around Skanderbeg Sq, for more evidence that this aspiring European Union capital is on the rise.

Spend a day or two visiting Tirana's former spy headquarters and walking around its religious buildings before partying in Blloku or catching an amazing cultural performance at Albanian Night. If there's time, visit smaller museums and galleries, or stroll the city park.

The Heart of Tirana

A hero's welcome in Skanderbeg Sq
Start exploring the Albanian capital at its bustling epicentre of **Skanderbeg Square** *(Sheshi Skënderbej)*. Initially a roundabout with a fountain under Italian occupation (1939–43), the communists added the **Skanderbeg Statue**, an ode to Albania's national hero, in 1968. The square has been upgraded in the past decade, with stone slabs added from regions where many Albanians reside (including Kosovo and North Macedonia). It's now the tourist focal point of the city.

In the northwestern corner is the **National History Museum** *(Muzeu Historik Kombëtar; mhk.gov.al)*, which has a socialist-realist mosaic facade featuring Albanian soldiers across the centuries. Closed until 2028 for much-needed updates, the museum's collection includes artefacts dating back to the 6th century BCE, when Illyrian tribes ruled what is now Albania.

Et'hem Bey Mosque

To the northeast, see Tirana International Hotel (p71), the city's main hotel during the communist era, along with a skyscraper in the shape of Skanderbeg's face (yes, really). There's also the **Palace of Culture** *(Pallate Kulturës; tkob.gov.al)*, which features an active opera and ballet theatre, a strip of cafes and an excellent bookshop, Adrion (p53).

Southeast is the early-19th-century **Et'hem Bey Mosque** *(donations requested)*, one of Albania's most important prayer sites, with flowing foliage frescoes inside and out. Take off your shoes before entering and cover up – shawls are provided to women free of charge. Next to it is the 35m **Clock Tower** *(Kulla e Sahatit)*, built around the same time. Climb its 90 steps for views of the square and a close-up of the mosque's minarets.

Take a breather on the benches in the rectangular green space to the south of the square and look around at the administrative buildings constructed during the Italian occupation.

Grim Communist Past

Painful memories in museums and bunkers

Following Italian and German occupation, Albanians elected the Albanian Communist Party in 1943. Led by Enver Hoxha,

continues on p51

IS ALBANIA SAFE?

Many who've never been to Albania will warn you not to visit – ignore them. Albania is as safe as anywhere in Europe, if not safer, with a crime rate lower than Canada's. Pickpocketing isn't common, and local people appear friendly, curious and welcoming.

Stereotypes mainly stem from centuries-old ethnic conflicts between Slavs and Illyrians, and Christians and Muslims. They also derive from Albania's long, mysterious communist period, mafia crime elsewhere in Europe, and the 2008 film *Taken*, which featured a pissed-off Liam Neeson chasing down the Albanian mobsters who had kidnapped his daughter. As Albania develops, and cracks down on corruption in an effort to join the European Union, this discrimination will inevitably decline. In the meantime, it's the responsibility of travellers to share the truth.

 EATING IN TIRANA: BEST INTERNATIONAL

TëDuKtu: If you fancy a Western brunch, this place does artfully crafted plates in a space that's just as decorative. *9am-midnight* €

Pasta Da Pucci: A dizzyingly long list of pasta combinations served inside adorable dollhouse decor. Not your nonna's pasta, that's for sure. *11.30am-10.30pm* €€

Mugo: Feed your Instagram highlights along with your tummy with tasty tacos, sushi and cocktails at this stylish Blloku spot. *8am-midnight* €€

Fishop: Pick your fish caught from Albania's two seas and have it cooked however you like. *noon-11pm, to 6pm Sun* €€

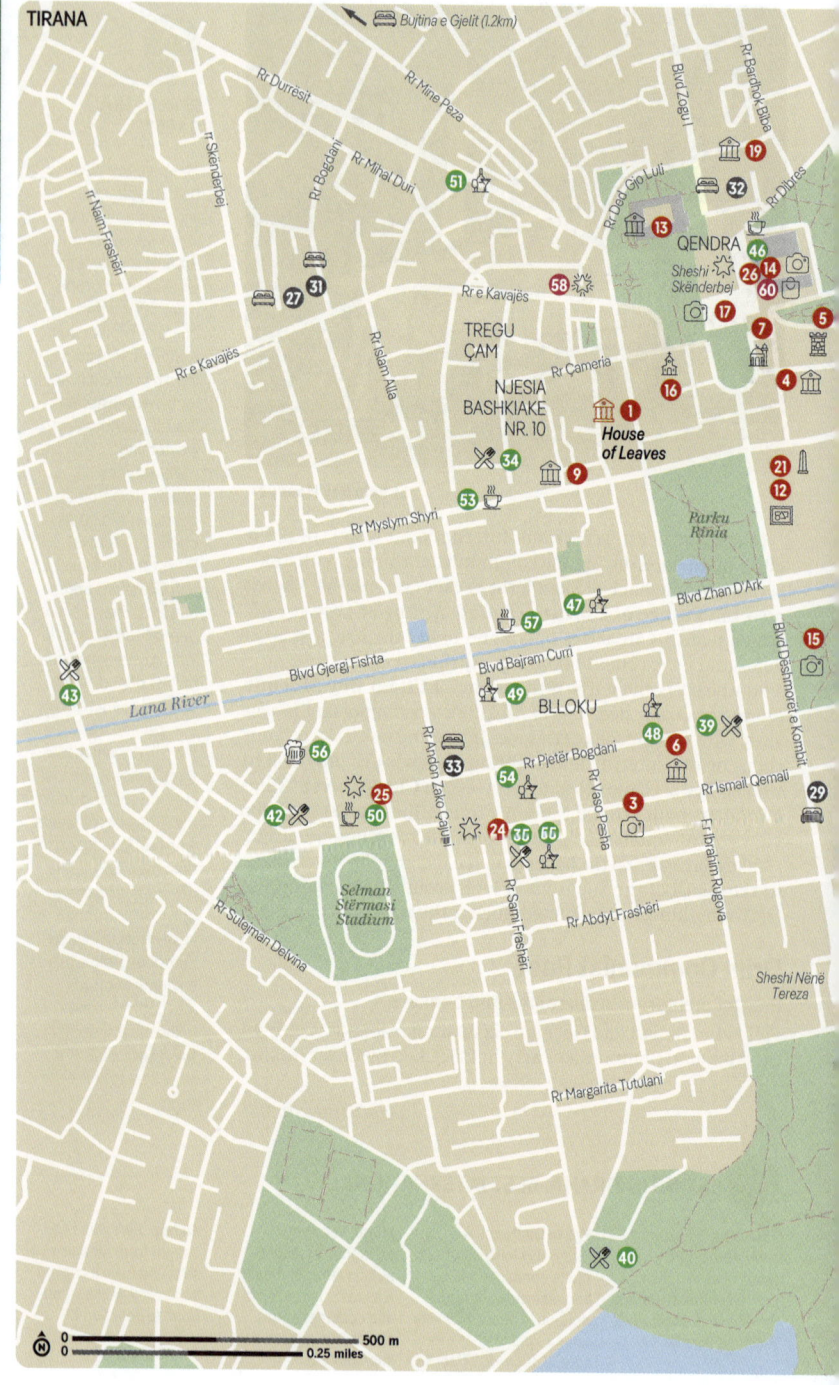

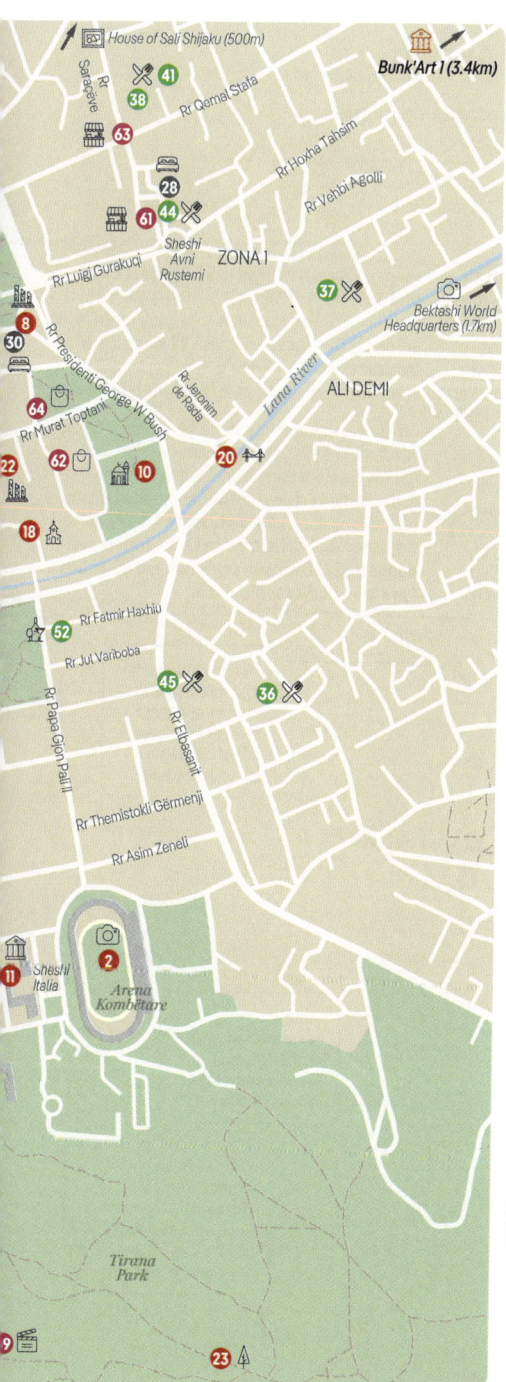

★ HIGHLIGHTS
1 House of Leaves

● SIGHTS
2 Arena Kombëtare
3 Blloku
4 Bunk'Art 2
5 Clock Tower
6 Enver Hoxha's Former Residence
7 Et'hem Bey Mosque
8 Kaplan Pasha's Tomb
9 MiG
10 Namazgah Mosque
11 National Archaeological Museum
12 National Gallery of Arts
13 National History Museum
14 Palace of Culture
15 Pyramid
16 Resurrection of Christ Orthodox Cathedral
17 Skanderbeg Square
see 17 Skanderbeg Statue
18 St Paul's Cathedral
19 Studio Kadare & Agolli House
20 Tanners' Bridge
21 The Cloud
22 Tirana Castle
23 Tirana Park

● ACTIVITIES
24 Albania Holidays
25 Outdoor Albania
26 Tirana Free Tour

● SLEEPING
27 Art Hotel
28 Hotel Boka
29 Rogner
30 The Plaza
31 Tirana Backpacker Hostel
32 Tirana International Hotel
33 Vanilla Sky Boutique Hostel

● EATING
34 Byrektore Albani
35 Era
36 Fishop
37 Gjelltore Sauku
38 Lakror TeEla
39 Mugo
40 Mullixhiu
41 Oda
42 Pasta Da Pucci
43 Taverna Amazona
44 Te Met Kodra
45 TëDuKtu

● DRINKING & NIGHTLIFE
46 Botanica
47 BUFE
48 Charl's
49 Duff
50 Hana
51 Hemingway
52 Komiteti
53 Mulliri i Vjetër
54 Nouvelle Vague
55 Radio
56 The Taproom
57 The Tea Room

● ENTERTAINMENT
58 Albanian Night
59 Open Air

● SHOPPING
60 Adrion
see 58 Albanian Night
61 Pazari i Ri
62 Seferi
63 Street Market
64 Tirana Castle

TIRANA CURIOSITIES ON FOOT

See lesser-known sights on this walk around Tirana.

START	END	LENGTH
Resurrection of Christ Orthodox Cathedral	Tirana Park	4.8km; 1½ hours

Start at ❶ **Resurrection of Christ Orthodox Cathedral** (Katedralja Ortodokse Ngjallja e Krishtit), a cathedral built in 2012 that looks a lot like a mosque (how Albanian!). Don't miss the cathedral's concrete candles that noodle their way up the clock tower. Try to spot concrete communist-era bunkers in Rinia Park before stepping inside ❷ **The Cloud** (Reja), a 2017 art installation by Japan's Sou Fujimoto. Walk past Italian-style government buildings on Blvd Dëshmorët e Kombit to a 19th-century monument with eight white columns: ❸ **Kaplan Pasha's Tomb** (Tyrbja e Kapllan Pashës).

Continue south through ❹ **Tirana Castle** (p53), a Byzantine-era fortress now filled with high-end shops and bars. Turn right to ❺ **St Paul's Cathedral** (Katedralja e Shën Palit), which is graced by a statue of Albanian Macedonian philanthropist Mother Teresa. Turn back east to visit ❻ **Namazgah Mosque** (Xhamia e Namazgjasë) – the largest mosque in the Balkans, paid for mostly by Türkiye.

Cross over 18th-century stone ❼ **Tanners' Bridge**, which looks tiny compared to the city that surrounds it, before turning back along the Lana River to the formerly closed-off neighbourhood **Blloku** (p52). Climb the ❽ **Pyramid** (p52), a memorial to the late Enver Hoxha, and see his ❾ **former residence** (p52). Finish with a stroll around ❿ **Tirana Park** (p54) and its artificial lake.

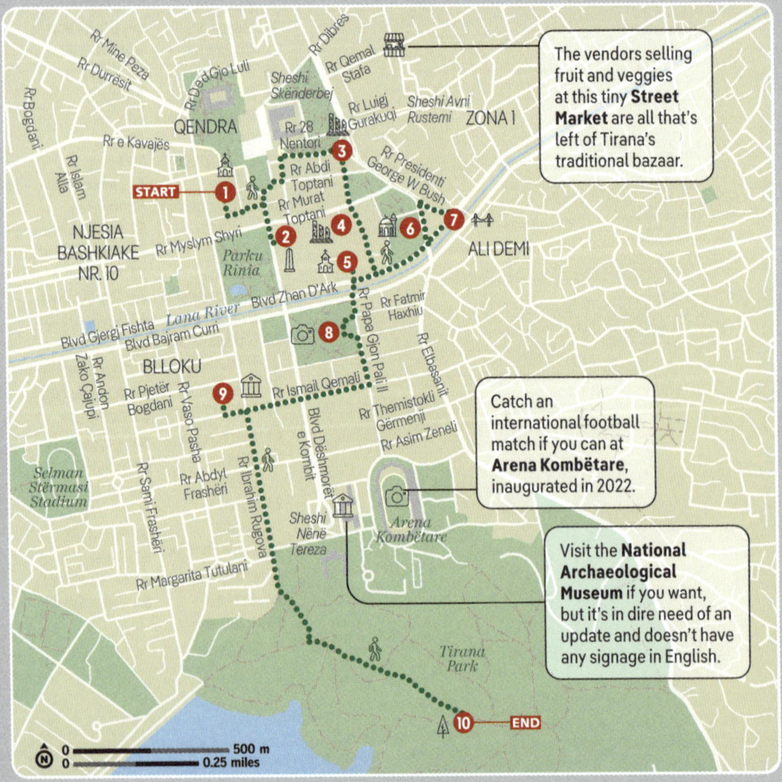

> The vendors selling fruit and veggies at this tiny **Street Market** are all that's left of Tirana's traditional bazaar.

> Catch an international football match if you can at **Arena Kombëtare**, inaugurated in 2022.

> Visit the **National Archaeological Museum** if you want, but it's in dire need of an update and doesn't have any signage in English.

continued from p47

the party went on to rule the country for roughly half a century under a dictatorship considered to be one of modern history's most repressive. Repercussions of Albania's experiment with communism, which ended in 1991, are many, and still felt today through Albania's stunted economic growth, the PTSD experienced by those who lived through those difficult years and its lust for everything foreign – popular music like The Beatles, and food and drinks like bananas and Coca-Cola, were all banned during communism.

One of the most brutal forms of repression under Hoxha was the vast network of spies largely coordinated out of a redbrick building in Tirana that was a former obstetrics hospital. Now known as the **House of Leaves** (*muzeugjethi.gov.al; 700L*), it's named after the dense trees that obscure it from the busy street, as well as the whispers of informants reminiscent of rustling leaves. The museum is Tirana's finest. Inside, multimedia exhibits with fittingly eerie vibes highlight the extensive spying that fuelled Hoxha's paranoia. Watch video propaganda from the period, read shocking statistics, and see the brooms, jackets and radios implanted with tiny mechanical 'bugs' and used as spy devices. Watch what you say – the bugs are on and listening.

The grim communist education continues in **Bunk'Art 2** (*bunkart.al; 500L*), one of approximately 175,000 bunkers built across Albania as protection should the isolated country be attacked. The dark and dingy museum tells the story of the restrictive communist policies in place during the dictatorship, such as closed borders. Visitors can also see soldier garb throughout the bunker's rooms and tunnels. Unfortunately, the lengthy

HOXHA'S HOMETOWN

In the southeastern stone city of Gjirokastër is the house where Enver Hoxha grew up. It is now the excellent **Ethnographic Museum** (p151) and is dedicated to vibrant Albanian traditions such as northern clothing and singing.

TIRANA-BASED TOURS

Tirana Free Tour (@tiranafreetour) The highlights of the city are covered in two hours and offered five times a day. Available in English, Spanish, Italian and German.

Albanian Food Tours (@albanianfoodtours) Local guides take you to try their favourite spots and stir in some history along the way.

Albania My Way (*albaniamyway.com*) Weeklong tours around the country, run by well-informed local guides. Also offers trips to other Balkan countries.

Outdoor Albania (*outdooralbania.com*) Running active and cultural tours around Albania since the fall of communism. Great for winter trips, too.

Albania Holidays (*albania-holidays.com*) Offering multi-city tours around Albania and the Balkans since 2004.

EATING IN TIRANA: BEST TRADITIONAL

Lakror TeEla: Taste Korça specialty *lakror* (baked spinach pie) washed down with *dhallë* (salted yoghurt drink). *5am-3pm, to 2pm Sat & Sun* €	**Byrektore Albani**: Arguably the best *byrek* (flaky pastry filled with spinach, cheese or meat) in Tirana. Come early before they run out. *8am-2pm* €	**Te Met Kodra**: There's just one thing to order here: freshly grilled *qofte* (meatballs) made with meat straight from the farm. *8am-10pm, to 4.30pm Sun* €	**Gjelltore Sauku**: Backstreet spot run by two ladies who speak little English but serve superb traditional food like *paçe koke* (sheep's head soup). *7am-9pm Mon-Sat* €
Taverna Amazona: The decor is nothing special, but the meat is perfectly juicy and served in generous portions. *7am-11pm* €	**Era**: Widely considered Tirana's best restaurant for traditional dishes, with excellent service and reasonable prices. *11am-midnight* €€	**Oda**: Top-quality Albanian food since 2005, served in a historic home and its pretty garden. Traditional music most nights. *noon-11pm* €€	**Mullixhiu**: Fine dining and bakery in the park. Chef-owner Bledar Kola (an ex-footballer) is a slow-food pioneer. *noon-4pm & 6-10pm* €€

MUST-TRY TIRANA EATS

Guide **Linda Alia** of **Albanian Food Tours** (@albanianfoodtours) shares her favorite local bites.

Flia: Layered crepe dough traditionally made in a *saç* (large metal pan). It takes six to eight hours to make, which explains the name: *flia* means 'sacrifice'.

Fërgesë: A light summer dip made with pan-fried peppers and ricotta cheese.

Tavë kosi: Baked lamb with yoghurt and a little bit of rice. The yoghurt combined with the richness of the lamb makes it really unique.

Boza: Fermented corn-meal drink. Here we have it with a scoop of ice cream.

Speca të mbushur: Baked peppers stuffed with rice, tomatoes and fresh herbs.

---

texts are incomprehensible in English, and contrary to the name, Bunk'Art 2 barely has any art. Go there to cool down on a hot day or if you only have limited time and can't make it to the much better Bunk'Art 1 (p55), 6km east. If you plan to visit both within 72 hours, a combo ticket will save you 200L.

Party with the Cool Kids
In Bloku, former home of Hoxha

The stylish **Blloku** neighbourhood, located south of the Lana River, is the place to see and be seen in Tirana. Streets are lined with trendy plant-filled patio bars frequented by well-heeled locals, and the upscale restaurants serve sushi and seafood with Instagrammable decor reminiscent of Bali or Tulum. Blloku also has some dance clubs – single guys aren't usually let in unless they buy a bottle or come with some ladies.

Blocked off for nearly half a century as a heavily guarded home to Communist Party officials, Blloku's gates were thrown open in 1991 and it quickly started filling up with modern bars and restaurants. Look out for **Enver Hoxha's Former Residence** (closed to visitors) and the brutalist **Pyramid**, erected after his death by his daughter, Pranvera Hoxha, to lionise the dictator, as if he were an Egyptian pharaoh. Nowadays, Hoxha's residence is vacant, though maintained, while the pyramid is a mixed-use space popular for sunset snaps.

Experience an Albanian Wedding
Dress up and dance

Many of Tirana's top sights involve learning about its communist dictatorship – but there's so much more to Albanian culture. That's where **Albanian Night** (*albaniannight.com; 3800L*) comes in. Created in January 2024 by world-travelling local Armando Muça, Albanian Night invites guests to a traditional Albanian wedding, complete with dancing by trained performers – and you, the guest. There's singing, traditional clothing (you'll be dressed up in vibrant clothing collected and made by Albanian artisans), and like any good wedding,

---

 DRINKING IN TIRANA: BEST BARS

Komiteti: Try 35 flavours of *raki* – including quince, saffron, cinnamon and coffee – amid funky vintage Albanian decor. *8am-midnight*	**Radio**: Creative cocktails with an Albanian twist, r.g. a Brazilian caipirinha with *raki*. Vintage audio devices and the hippest of locals. *9am-1am Mon-Sat, from 5pm Sun*	**Charl's**: Join Albanians in coordinated line-dancing to popular songs at this much-loved bar on Blloku's main drag. *7am-1am*	**Hemingway**: Sip cocktails (they don't serve much beer) and munch bar snacks beneath vibey lighting in honour of the famous author. *6pm-1am*
Duff: Surprisingly cool decor for a sports bar, and a massive outdoor screen to watch the big game. Great place to meet expats. *7am-1am*	**Nouvelle Vague**: In-vogue Blloku bar and terrace, with tables filled inside and out any night of the week. Serves local craft beers. *7pm-2am*	**The Taproom**: Taste funky craft beer and kombucha flavours along with pub grub in the beer garden. *8am-midnight*	**BUFE**: Millennial decor and an intriguing wine collection, including small-batch, natural and orange wines. *8.30am-12.30am*

plenty of gossip – the father of the bride is suspicious of the in-laws, etc.

The venue is an experience in itself, with finely carved wooden balconies to replicate an Ottoman-era courtyard and artwork by artist **Memento** (*@memento.artstudio*) that literally pops out of the frame. It's a real privilege as a foreigner to experience something as unique as an Albanian wedding, even if it *is* a staged performance – it's so cool to see local guests' eyes light up in pride when they sing their favourite songs. For an extra 2200L, you can eat a seven-course feast of traditional Albanian dishes, including *japrak/dollma* (stuffed grape leaves), *speca me qumësht 'të çartun'* (peppers with cultured milk) and *sultiash* (rice pudding).

The on-site gift shop has authentic art from 650 Albanian artists, including silver filigree, canvas paintings and earrings.

Shopping in Tirana
The best options

The 14th-century Byzantine-era Fortress of Justinian, also known as **Tirana Castle**, is transformed, somewhat sadly, into a strip mall selling Albanian wine and souvenirs. Its best shop, **Seferi**, has been making artisanal pottery of folk characters, some filled with 24 carat gold, since 1968.

Pazari i Ri, the former town bazaar, is now a covered market selling souvenirs including carpets, honey – and pistol-shaped lighters.

Adrion is a bookshop on Skanderbeg Sq with English titles.

Dive Deeper into Albanian Culture
Small, off-beat museums

If you've seen all of Albania's main sights and are looking for more, there are several small museums to visit that allow for a better understanding of this fascinating country and culture.

MiG (*womenmuseumalbania.com; 500L*) is a museum run *by* an Albanian woman *about* Albanian women. Said Albanian woman, Elsa Ballauri, oversees the museum from inside her apartment (find the door in the alley behind Rr Myslym Shyri 2). Inside, there's an interesting collection of traditional Albanian women's clothing, some of which are from Ballauri's family, along with jewellery and artefacts from both Butrint (p88) and communism – there's a chunk of the Enver Hoxha statue that used to be on Skanderbeg Sq.

ENVER HOXHA'S FIST

Born in Gjirokastër and a former teacher, 34-year-old Enver Hoxha was 'elected' leader of Albania in March 1943, in a contest with no challengers. To be fair, the country had been controlled by a slew of dictators following its independence in 1912, including Fascist Italy, Nazi Germany, western puppet Prince Wilhelm and self-anointed King Zog I.

Hoxha went on to rule Albania as dictator with his own form of brutal, paranoid communism that involved mass surveillance, closed borders and imprisonment of political dissidents in internment camps as terrifying as the Soviet gulags.

Hoxha died in 1985 of natural causes, and communism continued for six more years until student-led protests erupting from Shkodër and Tirana toppled the regime in favour of today's parliamentary democracy.

DRINKING IN TIRANA: BEST CAFES

| **Hana**: LGBTIQ-friendly cafe with excellent cakes and a cosy atmosphere. Laptop friendly. *10am-11pm* | **Mulliri i Vjetër**: Beloved local chain filled with locals day and night having an espresso and a pastry. Multiple locations. *6.30am-10pm* | **Botanica**: Plant-filled Skanderbeg Sq–facing cafe with a big terrace, good Wi-Fi and healthy food. *7am-midnight* | **The Tea Room**: Baby-pink teahouse with a range of black and green teas, dainty homemade cakes and delectable cheesecake. *9.30am-9.30pm* |

CENTRAL ALBANIAN FESTIVALS

Dita e Verës Meaning 'Summer Day', this national holiday on 14 March celebrates the arrival of the springtime sun. Festivities are largest in Elbasan.

Sultan Nevruz Bektashi Muslims celebrate the birthday of Ali ibn Abi Talib (599–661), along with the arrival of spring, on 22 March.

Durrës Festival A week of summer concerts and traditional dance performances take place in and around Durrës, including at its Roman amphitheatre.

Tirana International Film Festival (tiranafilmfest.com) A more than two-decades-old film festival held in September, with over 1000 annual submissions.

Dita e Pavarësisë Gaze at a sea of red and black flags on 28 November as the country celebrates its independence from the Ottomans in 1912.

Fans of Albania's greatest author, Ismail Kadare (1936–2024), and those with a love of mid-century architecture, will find **Studio Kadare & Agolli House** (@shtepite_studio_kadare_agolli; 500L) very interesting. Kadare lived in this Tirana pied-à-terre and studio from 1974 to 1990, and it was turned into a museum in 2019. Some of his books and his typewriter (which he didn't use much, as he preferred to write by hand) are on display. The most interesting aspect is the modernist design of the apartment, which ended up landing architect Maks Velo in prison during the dictatorship because it looked too foreign. Upstairs is another apartment designed by Velo that was home to Albanian poet and politician Dritëro Agolli.

The **House of Sali Shijaku** (350L) displays the artwork of the eccentric expressionist painter and sculptor Sali Shijaku (1933–2022) in his 300-year-old home. Shijaku's finger paintings are wild (especially the artist's hair in his self-portraits), vibrant and sultry (kids, be warned). It's a wonder that he wasn't sent to prison by Hoxha – in fact, the communist dictator liked his paintings and wanted one of his sculptures in Skanderbeg Sq. Stick around for a coffee in the verdant courtyard in front of the stunning house adjacent, recently built by Shijaku's kids.

Tirana's **National Gallery of Arts** (Galeria Kombëtare e Arteve) was undergoing renovations during research, but it usually has a sizable collection of socialist realist paintings.

Stretch Your Legs

Wander Tirana Park

Escape the concrete jungle by going for a walk in lovely **Tirana Park**, at the southern end of the city. Built in the 1950s under communism, the nearly 2-sq-km park has a botanical garden, 120 species of trees, and decorative shrubs and flowers alongside an artificial lake that's frequented by migrating birds. Go for a run or a bike ride, see a movie at the **Open Air** (openair.al) outdoor theatre or go for a xhiro (after-dinner stroll).

Proposed Vatican-like Microstate

Visit Bektashi World Headquarters

Soon, you might not have to leave Albania to add another country to your list. During research, the Albanian parliament was debating whether to add a microstate within Tirana's borders, just 3km from Skanderbeg Sq. The Sovereign State of the Bektashi Order, now the **Bektashi World Headquarters**, would be a Vatican-like city for practitioners of Bektashism, an Islamic Sufi sect that originated in Türkiye in the 13th century. Bektashis set up their official headquarters in Tirana after being kicked out of Türkiye in 1925 by secularist Mustafa Kemal Atatürk (who many believe was ethnically Albanian), and now they are estimated to account for 5% of Albania's population. Even before the state becomes official, travellers can visit the site for free to see its impressive green and white central mosque and wander the spacious grounds.

Beyond Tirana

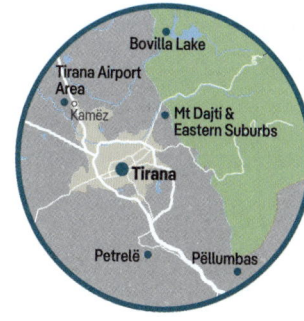

Add to your Tirana trip with visits to a communist bunker museum, a mountaintop (via cable car), castles, caves and serene bodies of water.

There are several worthwhile sites close to Tirana that are easily accessible by electric taxi or municipal bus. The bunker tunnel museum of Bunk'Art 1, located on the city outskirts, is not to be missed, and it's as eerie as expected. And the cable car up Mt Dajti for views and a hike is just around the corner from the museum.

Slightly farther away, there's Petrelë Castle, which was formerly occupied by rebel leader Skanderbeg's sister; as well as a hike to the Black Cave and the little-known blue eye spring of Cyclops Eye. Northbound, Bovilla Lake, the city's water reservoir, is a popular day tour, and there's Magic Blue Water, a kids' waterpark for cooling off from the summer heat. Wherever you go, make time for a delicious meal at a farm-to-table restaurant.

Places

Mt Dajti & Eastern Suburbs p55
Tirana Airport Area p57
Petrelë p57
Pëllumbas p58
Bovilla Lake p59

Mt Dajti & Eastern Suburbs

TIME FROM TIRANA: **20 MINS**

Creepy communist bunker

A short taxi or bus ride from Tirana city centre will take you into the paranoid logic of Enver Hoxha and his regime. **Bunk'Art 1** *(bunkart.al; 500L)* is a vast network of tunnels over five levels, with a surface area of 2685 sq metres. The tunnel, which was inspired by a state visit to North Korea in 1964 and opened in 1978, is one of some 175,000 bunkers built during the dictatorship as a backup in case enemies (pretty much everyone but North Korea) chose to attack Albania. While Hoxha didn't end up getting the 220,000 bunkers he wanted, the 175,000 that were built were still enough to shelter one in every 11 Albanians at the time.

With English explanations far better written and grammatically accurate than Bunk'Art 2 (p51) in Tirana, Bunk'Art 1 provides interesting facts on how the shelter was ventilated and built, and important historic context on the Italian and German occupation during WWII. It gives visitors an idea of what life was like during communism, though the exhibit on the children that went missing during the dictatorship is quite disturbing.

Walking through the underground halls is chillingly creepy, especially when entering the room that would have sheltered Hoxha.

The combo ticket (800L) gets you into Bunk'Art 1 and 2 within a 72-hour period.

GETTING AROUND

Most sites are accessible by a combination of city buses – just 40L per ride – and walking or electric car taxis, which are cheaper than city cabs, plus they can pick you up wherever you want. If driving, you'll be taking highways and paved roads most of the time, with the exception being the dirt road to Bovilla Lake, which has so many potholes it looks like it's recently been through a war.

CLIMB MT TUJANI

Get the best views over Tirana on this hike up Mt Tujani. Board the cable car from the Dajti Ekspres Lower Station and start your hike from the Upper Station.

START	END	LENGTH
Dajti Ekspres Upper Station	Dajti Ekspres Upper Station	7.2km round-trip; 2½ hours

Get out of the cable car at the ❶ **Dajti Ekspres Upper Station** and walk away from the view, past the horses, until you reach a ❷ **construction fence**. Turn right on the 4WD road until you see a ❸ **clearing** to your left. Make a U-turn through the clearing and head up the steep hill, where red and white trail markers will lead you the rest of the way. Follow the ridge, in line with the construction fence, until you see a ❹ **wooded area** with trail signs that will point you up the mountain. This forest of thin alpine trees is one of the prettiest segments of the trail. You'll cross a couple of 4WD roads along the way, but continue hiking up until you reach flat ground with a ❺ **T junction** with an option to turn left or right. Turn left and take the wide 4WD road, which zigzags up to a ❻ **view over Tirana** – but don't stop there. Another 10 minutes or so will take you to the top of ❼ **Mt Tujani**, at 1531m. Continue on the wide 4WD trail 10 minutes more for spectacular views over the national park and Bovilla Lake (p59). Return the way you came and board the cable car at the Dajti Ekspres Upper Station.

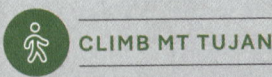

Dajti Adventure Park is accessed by following the 4WD road left from the construction fence.

Extend your hike with a climb up **Mt Dajti** by turning right at the fork.

SkySports Paragliding lead tandem trips off Mt Dajti. Book a 15- to 20-minute flight for 10,000L.

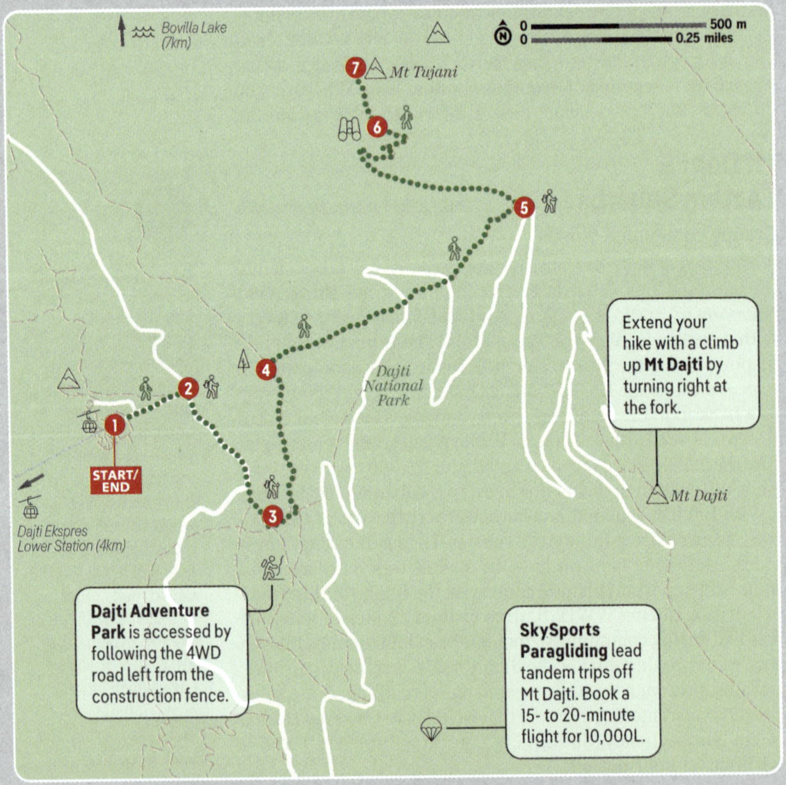

Cable car up Mt Dajti

A few blocks from Bunk'Art 1 is the **Dajti Ekspres** (*dajtiekspres. com; adults/children 5-12 round-trip 1400/800L*), a cable-car station with gondolas that zip passengers up to a balcony at the foot of Mt Dajti (1613m), located in **Mt Dajti National Park**. The Austrian-built cable car is the longest in the Balkans, and the 15-minute trip has stunning views over Tirana – well, as long as you're not in a car with scratched Plexiglass.

Once you get to the upper cable-car station, there are unobstructed views over Tirana and a grab-bag of touristy attractions, including a mini-putt course, buggies, a pellet-gun shooting range and horse rides through a patch of grass.

There's also **Dajti Adventure Park** (*@dajtiadventurepark; children 5-7/8+ 1200/1600L*), replete with ziplines and elevated courses, or you can fly over Tirana for 15 to 20 minutes with **SkySports Paragliding** (*skysports.al; 10,000L*). At the very least, the view out the windows of the **Dajti Balcony** restaurant is awesome, and the pizza is good.

If you have more time, it's a relatively easy and gratifying 7.2km climb up **Mt Tujani** (1513m).

Tirana Airport Area
TIME FROM TIRANA: **20 MINS**

Kids' Waterpark & Castle

Tirana gets scorching hot in the summertime, with average daily temperatures in July and August reaching 35°C or even 40°C. If you're travelling with kids (Albania in general is very child-friendly), escape the city cauldron by cooling off at **AquaPark Magic Blue Water** (*aquapark.com.al; families with kids aged 4-9/aged 10+ 1200/1500L*). The park is quite small, with just four pools, but it's worth the splash, and there's a solid restaurant inside.

To make a day of it, add a visit to the 14th- or 15th-century **Prezë Fortress**. The castle belonged to the Topias, who were local lords, and it has panoramic views.

Petrelë
TIME FROM TIRANA: **30 MINS**

Visit a hilltop castle

Dramatically set on a hilltop overlooking Tirana, **Petrelë Castle** (*Kalaja e Petrelës; free*) was initially built as early as the 4th century, but the current structure dates from the 15th century. For a time, it was under the command of Mamica Kastrioti – the sister of national hero Skanderbeg – after it was liberated from the Ottomans.

BUNKER BLITZ

When Albanian communism kicked off in 1944, it could rely on its comrades in the Soviet Union if anyone dared to invade. But when Joseph Stalin died, Albanian leader Enver Hoxha broke ties with the Soviet Union and turned east to Mao Zedong's communist China, getting yuan, grain, weapons, workers (for infrastructure projects) and soldier training out of the relationship. But Hoxha broke ties with China after Mao shook hands with President Richard Nixon, and Albania was left all alone. Paranoid Hoxha went on to launch a bunker blitz: one mushroom-shaped concrete shelter or tunnel for every adult male in Albania. Around 170,000 were built across Albania, and many are still visible, even visitable, today, with some being repurposed as tattoo shops or cheese factories.

SLOW FOOD AROUND TIRANA: BEST SPOTS

Fustanella Farm	Ceren Ismet Shehu	Uka Farm	Huqi Agrotourism
Fustanella Farm: One of Albania's best dining experiences has views over the fields and vineyards where the food on your table was grown. *10am-11pm* €€	**Ceren Ismet Shehu**: A growing powerhouse in Albanian dining, with a restaurant in the countryside and inside Tirana Castle. *noon-10.30pm* €€	**Uka Farm**: Organic farm restaurant and winemaker founded in 1996 by former agriculture minister Rexhep Uka. *noon-10pm Tue-Sun* €€	**Huqi Agrotourism**: Lamb is hung from hooks and then cooked in a pit the traditional Turkish way. Summer only. *noon-10pm* €€

VAIDOTAS GRYBAUSKAS/SHUTTERSTOCK

ILLYRIAN ORIGINS

Albanians trace their roots and language (a European linguistic oddity) to the Illyrian tribes and kingdoms that occupied the Western Balkans for as many as 2000 years. Illyrians occupied modern Albanian cities including Krujë and Berat, and built fortified cities such as Apollonia (p105) and Byllis (p146). They mastered silver and copper mining and were adept at sailing the Mediterranean, as boldly proven by 'pirate' Queen Teuta. The Illyrians frequently battled with Greeks, Slavs and Romans – with the Romans responsible for naming the country after the Albanoi Illyrian tribe that was living in central Albania at the time. Rome finally defeated the Illyrians in 229 BCE, slotting the region into its eastern Byzantine Empire in 395 CE.

Walk up to the castle on the short trail and enter – it's free to visit. Up and inside is a traditional cafe with panoramic views of the city – there are also tables inside the watchtower, which has a fireplace and garlic to keep the evil spirits away.

Petrelë Castle is especially worth a trip if you're not planning on visiting the better-known castles in Krujë and Berat.

Zipline over the Erzan River

Cry like Skanderbeg did while fighting the Ottomans when you're flying along one of the longest ziplines in the Balkans. **Zipline Albania** (*@ziplinealbania; 2000L*) extends for 1km some 200m over the Erzan River at maximum speeds of up to 90km/h. The minimum age is 10 years old, and they can take a drone video of you for an extra 10,000L.

Pëllumbas

TIME FROM TIRANA: **35 MINS**

Cave tour

South of Tirana, about 30 minutes downhill from the town of Pëllumbas, is the 360m-long **Black Cave** *(Shpelle e Pëllumbasit)*. Tours are coordinated by **Bardhyl Duqi** *(068 555 1305)*, also the owner of the town's **Pasha** restaurant, and they last about 1½ hours.

On your visit, you'll hike down to the cave and walk for about 20 minutes through the stalactite- and stalagmite-filed caverns. A guide costs 2000L per group, and you'll need to rent a flashlight (400L) and helmet (200L).

Alternatively, you can take a day tour of the cave with Tirana Backpacker Hostel (p71) *(tiranahostel.com/day-tours; 2500L)*.

MORE ALBANIAN CASTLES

Haven't had your fill of Albanian castles yet? Then head to **Krujë** (p60) and **Berat** (p138).

Bovilla Lake

Hike to a canyon & blue eye

Hilltop Pëllumbas is also a good starting point for a hike down to the **Erzen Canyon** *(Kanioni i Erzenit)*. A four-hour, 6.2km hike takes you past the Black Cave (don't visit without a helmet), down to the Erzen River to reach Erzen Canyon before looping back uphill to town.

Another nearby hike, best started from the town of **Krrabë** (the next mountain town south of Pëllumbas), leads to the turquoise **Cyclops Eye** *(Syri i Cikllopit)*, a natural blue-eye pool and waterfall. The hike is 4.2km and lasts two hours or so. Find hiking maps for both on the **Wikiloc app** *(wikiloc.com/outdoor-navigation-app)*.

Bovilla Lake

TIME FROM TIRANA: **1 HR 10 MINS**

Lakeview from the cliff

Fourteen kilometres northeast of Tirana is the artificial **Bovilla Lake**, the city's most important reservoir for drinking water. The 4.6-sq-km lake has striking electric water and is surrounded by hills, making for pretty pictures. Despite the fact that you can't swim in the lake, it's a popular day trip, especially for Tirana package tours. Note that if you plan to drive instead of taking a tour, the road to the lake is riddled with deep potholes.

Visits to the artificial lake usually centre around **Bovilla Restaurant**, which serves traditional Albanian food and can be found up a zigzagging road. From there, it's an easy 30- or 45-minute climb up **Mt Gamti** (845m) along a well-trodden path and a metal staircase bolted to the cliffside. The path leads up to a viewpoint for more pics of the lake. You'll be charged 100L to access the staircase.

DUA LIPA

Keep your eyes peeled in Albania for one very special tourist: Albanian-English pop singer Dua Lipa. According to the paparazzi, the Grammy Award-winner, known for songs like 'Levitating' and 'Cold Heart' (featuring Elton John), vacations on the Albanian Riviera and is building a multi-million-dollar mansion in Ksamil. Born in England to ethnic Albanian parents, Lipa lived four years of her childhood in Kosovo, an experience she said 'really helped me become who I am'. Lipa's family immigrated to the United Kingdom in 1992 as tensions were mounting in Kosovo due to the fall of Yugoslavia. In 2022, Lipa was granted Albanian citizenship, with President Bajram Begaj saying she had made the country 'proud with her global career and engagement in important social causes'.

Krujë

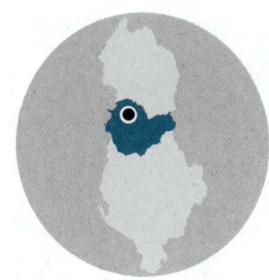

REBEL RUINS | SOUVENIRS | MOUNTAIN VIEWS

☑ **TOP TIP**

Consider spending the night within the walls of Krujë Castle. A couple of restaurant-hotel combos have been doing it for decades, and you'll get to wake up to stunning views that reach the Adriatic Sea.

After wandering around Tirana's Skanderbeg Sq and seeing his statue, you can learn about the warrior who gives it its name (and who appears on the country's currency) by visiting the citadel where Albania's hero and his forces held off the Ottomans from 1444 until 1478, 10 years after his death. High in the mountains and 30km northeast of the capital, Krujë (Kruja) has an impressive number of ruins for an Illyrian Albanoi stronghold that was settled as early as the 4th century. The main reason to visit is to wander the fortress from where Gjergj Kastrioti, aka Skanderbeg, impressively fended off the Ottomans. The castle has a couple of worthwhile museums, a clock tower and restaurants that also have beds to stay the night.

Outside the castle walls, wander Krujë's photogenic bazaar, which has some of the best souvenir shopping in Albania at rock-bottom prices, and hike up to a Bektashi shrine carved into the mountain.

GETTING AROUND

Krujë's main visitor area is a short walk between the bazaar and the castle. If you take a *furgon* (shared minibus) here, note that some stop at Fushë Krujë, a different town that's 30 minutes' drive southwest, so make sure you're going up to the Krujë on the hilltop.

If you have a vehicle, park in one of the lots in the old town (per day 500L). A car is also useful if you don't want to hike up to the Bektashi shrine.

Skanderbeg Stronghold

Rebel castle and museums

Visit **Krujë Castle** (Kalaja e Krujës), first built by the Byzantines in the 5th or 6th century, to see the existing ramparts and to visit a 12th-century stone watchtower turned **Clock Tower** *(Kulla e Kalasë së Krujës)*, now held together with straps after an earthquake in 2019 nearly destroyed it. The castle also contains the white-stone **Skanderbeg Museum** *(muzeumet-kruje. com; 500L)*, which was designed by Enver Hoxha's daughter and son-in-law and opened in 1982. Inside are bold sculptures of Skanderbeg, and socialist realism art and murals, including the chaotic *Endurance*, which depicts scenes from Ottoman-led sieges on Krujë. The castle grounds are also home to the **Ethnographic Museum** *(600L)*, an Ottoman home built in 1764 that reopened in July 2024 following years of renovations. This fascinating museum shares details about Ottoman-era trades such as woodworking and olive-oil distilling, along with examples of period dress, including a UNESCO-listed *xhubleta* (long woollen dresses often adorned with metals that chime with movement).

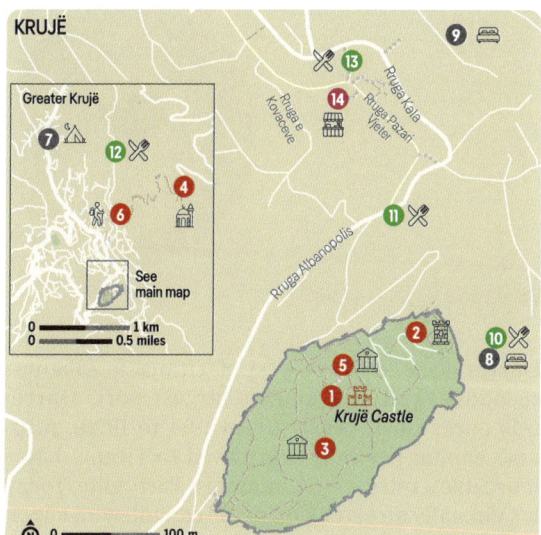

- ★ **HIGHLIGHTS**
- 1 Krujë Castle
- ● **SIGHTS**
- 2 Clock Tower
- 3 Ethnographic Museum
- 4 Sari Salltik
- 5 Skanderbeg Museum
- ● **ACTIVITIES**
- 6 Trailhead
- ● **SLEEPING**
- 7 Krujë Camping
- 8 Merlika
- 9 Panorama Hotel
- ● **EATING**
- 10 Emiliano
- 11 Fabiani
- 12 Horizont
- 13 Panorama
- ● **SHOPPING**
- 14 Bazaar

Shop for Albanian Souvenirs
Krujë's beautiful bazaar

Outside the castle, Krujë's 15th-century **Bazaar** is deservedly one of Albania's most photographed sites, with a curving cobblestone street lined with dingy stalls that recall centuries of commerce. Sift through carpets, wooden spoons, delicately painted plates, silver filigree jewellery and antiquities – much of what you'll find is mass-produced foreign-made souvenirs, but some are made by local artisans. As with any good bazaar, be sure to haggle.

Shrine in a Cave
Where spirituality is palpable

High above the castle on the hillside is **Sari Salltik**, a Bektashi prayer site with stunning views. Reach it by hiking 1.9km up the mountain – the **trailhead** is on Rr e Malit. The high-elevation shrine is in honour of Sari Salltik, the man credited with bringing Bektashism, an Islamic Sufi sect, to the Balkans in the 13th century. Walk down steep steps into the cliff face, where believers light candles and wash in the spring water. Yes, the hooks outside are used for exactly what they look and smell like – animal sacrifices.

SKANDERBEG

United under a red and black flag with two eagles (Albanians call this territory Shqipëria, or 'Land of the Eagles'), and with funding from neighbouring kingdoms, Skanderbeg and his rebels shocked the Ottomans by resisting for 34 years. His forces lost in 1478, a decade after he died, leading to 439 more years of Ottoman rule. Skanderbeg and his flag remain strong national symbols for Albanians today. Read more in our essay, **Skanderbeg's Sword** (p198).

 EATING IN KRUJË: OUR PICKS

Emiliano: Castle restaurant and hotel with a *byrek* (flaky pastry filled with spinach, cheese or meat) and cheese platter for 7000L. *7.30am-11pm* €

Fabiani: Can't beat the location of this *piceri* (pizzeria) between the castle and the bazaar. *8am-midnight* €

Panorama: The most recommended eatery in town is worth the hype, with excellent Albanian cuisine, including a range of baked dishes. *7am-11pm* €€

Horizont: Superb panoramic views and traditional Albanian mezze plates, served high above Krujë. *9am-11pm* €€

Durrës

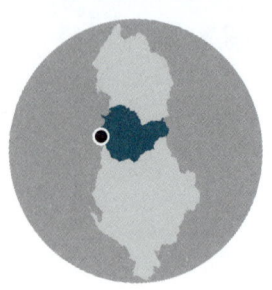

BEACHES | RUINS | CLUBS

GETTING AROUND

The city's main sites are within walking distance of each other, and there are plenty of metered taxis around. City buses don't come on a strict schedule. Note that Durrës has two main *furgon* (shared minibus) terminals – **Durrës Bus Terminal** by the port, with connections to Tirana, and the **Plepa Bus Terminal** near Durrës Beach (p65), with southbound transport. Keep an eye out for the train line between Durrës and Tirana, planned for 2026.

Durrës, located 30km west of Tirana, is Albania's second-largest city and its largest port. Durrës was once, albeit briefly (from 1914 to 1920), Albania's capital before it was moved to Tirana. Later, it became a retreat for Communist Party elite. Today, it's virtually an extension of the capital, with superstores and fuel stations lining the highway all the way to Tirana.

Chic Italian-style hotels and apartments give Durrës a fresh, airy vibe, though there isn't much to do beyond a day or two. The main reason for coming to Durrës isn't for the beaches (for those, you're better off going south to the Albanian Riviera), but for the interesting Roman amphitheatre and ancient ruins of the city's many conquerors, including the Venetians, Greeks and Illyrians. Otherwise, stroll on the expansive new boardwalk and have a drink at one of the many beach clubs on the waterfront.

Ancient Ruins in a Modern City
Remnants of empires

Imagine you're Spartacus battling a lion in front of thousands of screaming spectators by walking around the **Durrës Amphitheatre** *(300L)*. Built on the hillside inside the city walls in the early 2nd century CE, it had the capacity to seat nearly 20,000 in its prime. These days, it's little more than tunnels and ruins with few signposted explanations, though the mosaics inside are some of the finest in Albania. A visit won't take longer than 30 minutes.

BUTRINT
Albania's most impressive ruins are in the former city of **Butrint** (p88) in the southern coast. The scenic coastal park has plenty of ancient structures dating back 2800 years.

Another quick, though necessary, visit is to the **Venetian Tower** *(600L)* beside Durrës' main roundabout. It's one of the few structures that remain from the city's Byzantine era (490–540) under emperors Anastasius I and Justinian. It's

DURRËS

HIGHLIGHTS
1 Durrës Amphitheatre

SIGHTS
2 Aleksandër Moisiu Theatre
3 Archaeological Museum
4 Byzantine Forum
5 Durrës Beach
6 Freedom Plaza
7 Great Mosque
8 Kallmi and Currila
9 King Zog Villa
10 Sfinksi
11 Shëtitorja Vollga
12 Venetian Tower
13 Watchtower

ACTIVITIES
14 Shark Water Sports

SLEEPING
15 Adriatik Hotel
16 Giulia Albèrgo
17 Hostel Durres
18 Hotel Epidamn
19 Hotel Nais Beach

EATING
20 Artur
21 Meison Bistro
22 Neps
23 Te Nona N'Durrës

DRINKING & NIGHTLIFE
24 Cinco Cavalli
25 Sunset Bar
26 Traiano
27 Vinum

TRANSPORT
28 Adria Ferries
29 Durrës Bus Terminal
30 Plepa Bus Terminal

believed that Anastasius built three lines of ramparts in the city (then called Dyrrhachium), with a perimeter of 4.4km and a height of 12m. Towers like this one were placed every 60m to 65m. After an earthquake in 1273, most of the ramparts were destroyed, but the Angevins and Venetians added large round towers in their place, as with this one. Renovations in 2023 added multimedia exhibits, including VR and dome projections.

Nearby and just back from the seafront, Albania's largest **Archaeological Museum** (*Muzeu Arkeologjik*) has been undergoing major renovations since 2010 and was slated to reopen in late 2025. It usually has a huge collection of historical

☑ TOP TIPS

Ever dreamed of crossing the Adriatic by boat? **Adria Ferries** (adriaferries.com) travels to Italy from Durrës, with frequent departures to **Ancona** *(from €35, 16 hours)* and **Bari** *(from €25, eight hours)*. Cabins are available on board if you plan to take the ferry overnight.

DURRËS ARCHAEOLOGY WALK

Pass pretty Italian apartments as you hop from ruin to ruin on this tour of Durrës' main sites.

START	END	LENGTH
Freedom Plaza	Sfinksi	3km; 1 hour

Start from ① **Freedom Plaza** (*Sheshi Liria*), Durrës' white stone and palm tree-filled central square. The square was renovated in 2005 and is now a popular local hangout. Inside the plaza, see the ② **Great Mosque** (*Xhamia e Madhe*), the city's main mosque with its large yellow dome. It was first built in 1930, closed and partially destroyed in 1967 under communism, then restored in 1993. Only the faithful are allowed in. The square also contains the ③ **Aleksandër Moisiu Theatre** (*Qendra Kulturore Aleksandër Moisiu*), a cultural centre and theatre named after the Albanian-Austrian actor.

Detour north to see the remains of a 6th-century ④ **Byzantine Forum**. The site, which has some intact colonnades, was also used as thermal baths by the Romans in the 1st century. Back through the plaza, see Durrës' most interesting attraction, the 2nd-century CE ⑤ **Durrës Amphitheatre** (p62). You can walk around the Roman ruins, or pay to enter and see the tunnels. Walk down pretty Blvd Epidamn, lined with Italian-style buildings, until you reach the ⑥ **Venetian Tower** (p62). It's one of the few remains of the Byzantine ramparts that once stretched 4.4km around the city. Stroll along the freshly renovated boardwalk to ⑦ **Sfinksi**. Contrary to the name, it isn't a noseless Egyptian artefact but a series of white stone steps that cascade into the Adriatic.

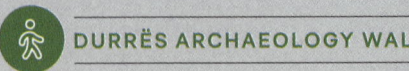

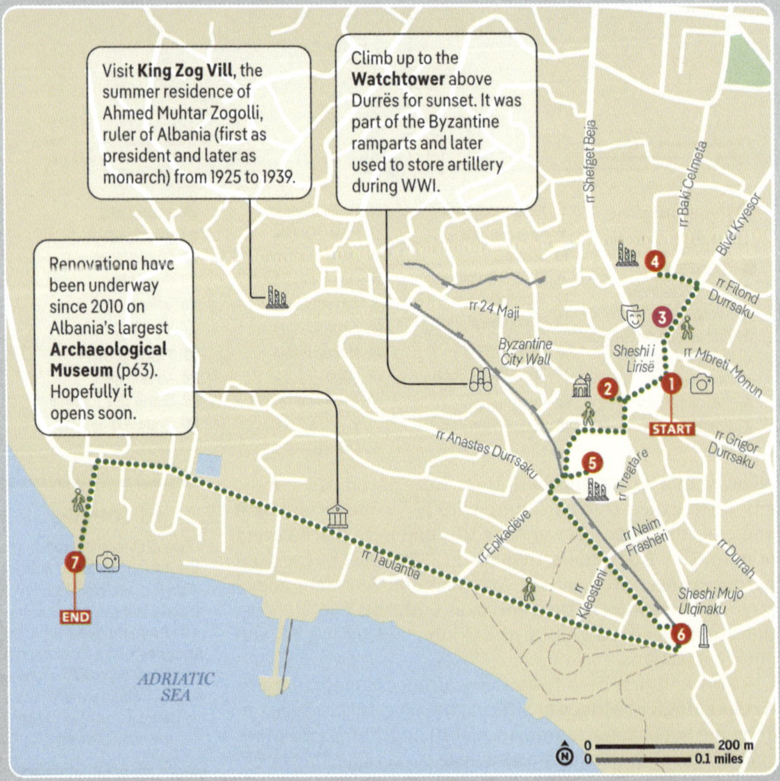

Visit **King Zog Vill**, the summer residence of Ahmed Muhtar Zogolli, ruler of Albania (first as president and later as monarch) from 1925 to 1939.

Climb up to the **Watchtower** above Durrës for sunset. It was part of the Byzantine ramparts and later used to store artillery during WWI.

Renovations have been underway since 2010 on Albania's largest **Archaeological Museum** (p63). Hopefully it opens soon.

artefacts, including amphoras recovered from the seafloor, delicate gold jewellery and preserved vases. The museum was already more modern than most in Albania, so it's reopening is exciting.

Stroll the Seafront
Breezy beaches and boardwalks

Durrës is a popular retreat for Tirana urbanites, especially during the scorching summer months. But measure your expectations – the beaches here aren't nearly as fine as those south of Vlorë (p104) on the Albanian Riviera.

Southeast of the historic centre is **Durrës Beach**, a long strip of sand with sunbathing chairs and umbrellas, volleyball competitions and an attractive blue track for runners and cyclists. Rent jet-skis or go parasailing with **Shark Water Sports** (@sharkwatersports). Don't spend much time in the water though, as it's notoriously polluted. While in the area, step into the lobby of the **Adriatik Hotel** – one of the few hotels opened during the Hoxha dictatorship – to see an excellent collection of photos of both traditional clothing and beachgoers in 1900. Some of the pictures were taken by Albania's treasured Marubi photography family.

Quieter, less polluted strips of sand are found just north of the city at **Kallmi** and **Currila**.

Durrës' seafront promenade and the **Shëtitorja Vollga** park have recently finished renovations and make for a lovely stroll. See the white steps of **Sfinksi** (*Sphinx*) and enjoy a coffee or meal facing the sea.

The seafront northwest of the promenade can't be traversed along the water – you'll have to walk on Rr Currila to get there. If you do, you'll find a row of trendy Tulum-style bars with three- or four-letter names; perfect for sunset sips.

Abandoned King's Villa
King Zog's summer villa

On a hilltop overlooking Durrës is a pink and white mansion, once the summer residence of King Zog I during his reign as self-proclaimed monarch of Albania from 1928 to 1939. The **King Zog Villa** (*300L*) is open for visits and occasional parties, though don't expect much remaining opulence. Despite hosting international leaders during the socialist era, including Soviet leader Nikita Khrushchev and US President Jimmy Carter, the building's interior is a shambles. Peeling

---

VIA EGNATIA

In the 2nd century BCE, the Romans sought to connect their capital with Constantinople (now Istanbul) through Thessaloniki (in modern-day Greece). Forty years later, Rome had the Via Egnatia, an 800km trading route that began in Durrës (Dyrrachium). Throughout its millennia of activity, the Via Egnatia was used by missionaries to spread Christianity in the Balkans, by Crusaders who plundered Constantinople in the 13th century, and by Ottoman traders and tax collectors.

Little of the Via Egnatia remains, but you can still visit pivotal stops on its route, including Petrelë Castle (p57), Apollonia (p105), the Bashtovë Fortress (p67) and the working-class city of Elbasan. The **Via Egnatia Foundation** (*viaegnatiafoundation.eu*), a Dutch organisation, sells a hiking guidebook to the route and occasionally organises treks.

 EATING IN DURRËS: OUR PICKS

Te Nona N'Durrës: Cosy locals' lunch spot just outside the touristy zone with a changing menu of home-style dishes. *11am-5pm* €

Neps: Appetizing pizzas, salads and *piadini* (sandwiches) from across the sea, served in a youthful atmosphere. *7.30am-11.30pm Tue-Sun* €€

Meison Bistro: Tasty market-fresh seafood served in a chic ambience; close to the promenade. *noon-11pm* €€

Artur: Upstairs views of the sea and Sfinksi are accompanied by risotto and seafood dishes. *9am-11.30pm* €€

King Zog Villa (p65)

KING ZOG I

In 1922, two years after Albania joined the League of Nations, Ahmed Muhtar Zogolli was elected prime minister at just 27 years old. A few years later, Zogolli became president and, with Benito Mussolini's Fascist Italy backing him, declared himself King Zog I in 1928.

Late in history for a new European monarch, and looked down upon by the continent's royal families for not coming from blood lineage, Zog aimed to modernise and secularise Albania – even marrying a Catholic Hungarian countess in 1939 (quite rare for a Muslim in those days). A day after his wedding, Mussolini turned on Zog and Italy took over Albania, sending the 'king' into exile in France, where he died in 1961.

paint, ripped-up floors and a gutted fireplace are all that remain of this former palace – it was ransacked during the chaos of the 1997 pyramid scheme crisis (p83), leaving little but the marble flooring. But it's fun to wander through the abandoned building, and there's a view of the city behind. Why an entrance fee is charged when virtually nothing is being done to preserve the building is anyone's guess.

 DRINKING IN DURRËS: OUR PICKS

Sunset Bar: Great spot for sunset sips and not as pretentious as the rest on Durrës' bar-lined western coast. *7am-midnight*

Vinum: Taste Albanian sheshi wine from the nearby Duka region with a plate of charcuterie. *4-11pm Mon-Thu, to 1am Fri & Sat*

Traiano: This cafe and bar on tree-lined Blvd Epidamn is busy day and night with espresso and Aperol-spritz drinkers. *8am-midnight*

Cinco Cavalli: If you're looking for some dancing, this club over Kallmi Beach is the place to be. Summer only. *11pm-late*

Beyond Durrës

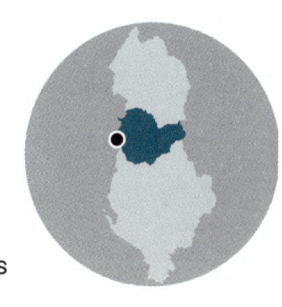

Don't expect many international visitors – this is local territory. But if you like going off the beaten track, there are surprises in store.

South of Durrës, find Divjakë-Karavastë National Park, Albania's best national park for bird-watching, where a boat tour through the country's largest lagoon is a thrill. And don't leave without trying some local seafood. You'll also find a couple of beaches and a fortress on UNESCO's tentative protections list.

Northbound, an adventure to the historic Cape of Rodon is for the wild at heart. There, you'll find trails leading to castle ruins, peculiar bunker tunnels and a lovely little church (and also, we hate to say it, trash-filled beaches).

Places
Spille p67
Cape of Rodon p70

Spille

TIME FROM DURRËS: **40 MINS**

Lounge at the beach

Down the Adriatic Coast, **Spille Beach** (*Plazhi i Spilles*) is a popular getaway for city dwellers. Stretching 3km, the beach is lined by restaurants with lounge chairs beneath umbrellas, and the surrounding town has all your amenities for a beach day, including eateries and hotels.

Or for a more isolated beach, drive along shoddy roads to **General Beach** (*Plazhi i Gjeneralit*), a 400m cove named after an Italian general who would visit on his yacht. Be careful not to step on the sea turtle eggs, as the beach is a nesting spot.

Visit Bashtovë Fortress

Less than 10km from Spille, find the sort of castle you think of when you close your eyes: the 15th-century Venetian-built **Bashtovë Fortress** (*Kalaja e Bashtovës*). With circular towers and walls that climb to nearly 12m high, the castle was built

continues on p70

GETTING AROUND

You'll need a car to get the best out of the areas surrounding Durrës. A 4WD vehicle is ideal, especially if you plan to drive in Divjakë-Karavastë National Park (p68) or to the Cape of Rodon (p70). If you have a large camper, you'll have to pay a higher fee to enter the Cape of Rodon – in that case, it might be best to just park outside and walk in.

 EATING BEYOND DURRËS: OUR PICKS

Ali Kali: Just one (delicious) option: all-you-can-eat fish or shrimp, plus salad, yoghurt and potatoes for 1700L. *10am-6pm* €€

Pelikan: Buck-a-crack blue crabs, fresh seafood and salads just outside the busy strip in Divjakë-Karavatë National Park. *noon-9pm* €€

Agroturizëm Gjepali: Lovely restaurant and guesthouse surrounded by verdant fields. A fixed three-course menu of farm-fresh food costs 2200L. *noon-11pm* €€

Rodon Fish: Just you, splashing waves and huge plates of the freshest fish. Does candle-lit dinners in the evening. *8am-11pm* €€

Karavastë Lagoon

TOP EXPERIENCE

Divjakë-Karavastë National Park

Encompassing a vast 222 sq km, including the huge Karavastë Lagoon, **Divjakë-Karavastë National Park** is the most organised of Albania's reserves, and the best place in the country for birdwatching. The park is home to four lagoons, sand dunes, deciduous and umbrella pine forests, and an enticing lineup of seafood restaurants. It's also free to enter, but don't expect environmental preservation to be up to western European standards.

DON'T MISS
- Rare birds
- Lagoon boat tour
- Tower views
- Fresh seafood and blue crab
- Hiking trails

Park Orientation

About an hour's drive south of Durrës, Divjakë-Karavastë National Park is the best place in Albania for spotting rare birds – huge populations of Dalmatian pelicans and greater flamingos rest and breed here. There's also a small network of hiking trails and tranquil boat tours through Albania's largest lagoon.

PRACTICALITIES
Scan this QR code to download an English trail map of the park.

Get started at the ivy-covered **Divjakë Visitor Centre**, which has a small museum with facts about the park's flora and fauna. Next to the visitor centre, climb up (and up and up) the 36m cylindrical **tower** for views of the Adriatic, the park's forests and some birds, if you're lucky.

A few minutes' drive south of the visitor centre is a lineup of seafood restaurants that fill to the brim every summer (400,000 visitors come to the park every year, though just 10% of those are international).

The road doesn't continue for much longer after that – your best bet is to park your car at the visitor centre and continue on foot. If you head towards the coast, you'll find a long beach. Inland, you'll meet the lagoon and possibly some towers, but we wouldn't trust climbing them – many are crumbling and long past due for repairs.

Wildlife

Bird-watchers come from far and wide to see **rare birds**. Some of the world's largest populations of Dalmatian pelicans and greater flamingoes are here (1% of their global populations nest and breed in the park). The park is also home to 2% of the planet's pygmy cormorants, Eurasian wigeons and collared pratincoles.

Aside from birds, Divjakë-Karavastë National Park is home to squirrels, frogs, otters, golden jackals, lynxes, seahorses and nesting sea turtles. You can also see four endemic orchid species.

Hiking

There are seven marked **hiking trails** in the park, ranging from 30-minute strolls of a few kilometres to four-hour forest hikes that stretch for more than 22km. The terrain is mostly flat, with barely any elevation. While there are some towers throughout the park for bird-watching, many are unfortunately in disrepair and dangerous to climb.

Lagoon Tour

A must-do when visiting the park is the 30-minute **lagoon boat tour**. The trip is tranquil yet fused with anticipation, as you're pretty much guaranteed to see pelicans and flamingoes in spring or summer. Reserve ahead by contacting Kristi *(069 816 1355)*. The trip costs 2500L for the full boat and can fit up to five passengers.

Seafood

Come hungry for the **fresh seafood** sourced from the park's bodies of water. Just off the main road, under the cover of trees, is Ali Kali (p67). This is possibly the most popular spot with just one option on the menu: a seafood extravaganza of all-you-can-eat fried fish or shrimp, plus salad, yoghurt and potatoes for 1700L. Or if you're not that hungry and/or prefer à la carte, Pelikan (p67), just off the restaurant strip, is a solid and affordable option. Try their local **blue crab** – just 600L buys you six crabs. It also has plenty more seafood options and a playground for kids.

PARK AT RISK

Despite the protections afforded it as a national park, the Albanian government and Prime Minister Edi Rama have floated the idea of opening up the area for tourist development. A large beach resort, among other plans, could be in store, putting the sensitive habitat and wetlands at risk. Nothing was confirmed as of writing, but if something does happen, rest assured that international environmental groups won't be happy.

TOP TIPS

● The only way to get to the national park is with your own vehicle or on an organised tour.

● The park is open year-round, and entrance is free.

● Visit in spring and summer for the best weather and the best chances of seeing wildlife. This is also the busiest time for local tourists, so go during the week if possible.

● Bug spray is a must, especially in late spring, when the mosquitoes come out in swarms.

● The visitor's centre is open from 9am to 5pm.

● Don't worry about climbing on those hikes – the terrain is mostly flat.

2019 EARTHQUAKE

Earthquakes aren't unheard of in Albania. After all, a 17th-century earthquake damaged the watchtower in Krujë Castle (p60), prompting it to be transformed into a Clock Tower (p60). But no one can ever be fully prepared for a quake, and one came at 4am on 26 November 2019. The earthquake struck about 30km northwest of Tirana at a magnitude of 6.4, killing 51 people, injuring 3000 and causing serious damage to 53 monuments across the country. Durrës and Krujë suffered some of the most damage, including to the Clock Tower in Krujë – straps were holding the tower together on our latest visit. Tragedy just goes to show that these precious historic monuments won't last forever.

Tower (p69), Divjakë-Karavastë National Park

continued from p67

in a pivotal position at the mouth of Shkumbin River, close to the old Via Egnatia road (p65) to Constantinople. The fortress, which is in line for UNESCO recognition, was closed during our visit due to the addition of a fancy looking visitor centre.

Cape of Rodon

TIME FROM DURRËS: **1 HR 10 MINS**

Bunker and beach peninsula

Little known to international visitors, the **Cape of Rodon** *(Kepi i Rodonit; 300L)*, named after the Illyrian sea god, is a peninsula jutting into the Adriatic with unique historic sites, stunning sea views and short trails. Getting to the cape is an adventure in itself. A narrow road winds and dips along a string of coastal hills – stop to inhale on a viewpoint of the windy coastline, or grab a meal at one of the many fresh seafood restaurants, such as **Peshk i Freskët Deti Nori**.

Near the tip of the cape, pay to enter and pay 100L for parking. Visible from the parking lot is **St Anthony Church** *(Kisha e Mumlves)*, an adorable little church founded by Skanderbeg's sister in the 15th century. The Franciscan church was damaged in the 2019 earthquake but restored in 2022 with funding from the European Union.

The beach next to the church is a popular summer spot for locals but is sadly filled with trash. Similarly, the communist bunker tunnels that pierce the hillside would be cool if not for the mini-mountains of empty beer bottles.

Left of the parking lot, follow trails to stunning views of the waves crashing into tiny **White Beach** *(Plazhi i të Bardhë)*. North on the well-trodden trail are cool bunker tunnels with murals and graffiti inside. Also on this trail are the remains of **Rodon Castle** *(Kalaja e Rodonit)*, built between 1450 and 1452 by Skanderbeg before being destroyed by the Ottomans 15 years later.

Places We Love to Stay

€ Budget €€ Midrange €€€ Top End

Tirana p48

Tirana Backpacker Hostel € Albania's oldest hostel is still going strong, with a funky, vibrant decor reminiscent of the glory days of backpacking. Serves an all-vegetarian communal breakfast.

Vanilla Sky Boutique Hostel € If you prefer to stay in Blloku (Tirana's nightlife zone), this stylish hostel is a good choice. It has cool decor and furniture cut from a magazine, as well as air-con in the dorms.

Hotel Boka €€ Cute pastel-pink hotel in a prime location steps from Pazari i Ri, the new bazaar. The rooms are spacious and elegant – a steal for the price.

Art Hotel €€ Tucked behind the main road in a historic-looking white building, this midrange hotel is owned by an art collector and comes filled with Albanian paintings.

Tirana International Hotel €€ History buffs will love this hotel, connected to Tirana's socialist era and overlooking Skanderbeg Sq. Its views of the mountains, unfortunately, are now blocked by the huge yellow Intercontinental hotel behind it.

Bujtina e Gjelit €€€ Tirana's most charming hotel has Ottoman-era vibes with brick archways centred around a pool courtyard. The drawback? It's far from the centre.

The Plaza €€€ The first of many stylish skyscrapers to open near Skanderbeg Sq was finished in 2016. Modernist designed, it's a great option for those accustomed to business hotels.

Rogner €€€ Luxurious Blloku hotel that feels like a private club, with an enclosed tropical garden and lobby bar.

Krujë p61

Krujë Camping € Pitch your tent or park your camper here, with exquisite views of the Adriatic and nearby mountains. Also has a couple of double rooms.

Merlika € Stay the night within Skanderbeg's Krujë Castle walls at this B&B. Despite being a rustic, century-old building, the rooms were renovated in 2010.

Emiliano € Another B&B within the castle walls with stunning views and a play area for kids. Find it at the top of the castle, in line with the Watch Tower.

Panorama Hotel €€ Steps from Pazari i Ri, this hotel is Krujë's most comfortable option. If only it was designed to look more historic.

Durrës p63

Hostel Durrës € Backpacker's hostel in a 1930s' Italian villa in an unbeatable location steps from the main plaza. Particularly great for meeting fellow travellers.

Giulia Albèrgo €€ The mid-century Italian vibes are strong at this picturesque hotel, located down a quiet side street. The buffet breakfast is great, too.

Hotel Epidamn €€ Roman-style pillars, palm trees, claw-footed tubs and funky wallpaper...photos of this five-star hotel on Blvd Epidamn will light up your Instagram feed.

Adriatik Hotel €€ One of the few remaining hotels from the communist era (1957), this beach-facing hotel was renovated in 2003 and is now run under the Best Western chain. The historic photos in the lobby are a highlight.

Hotel Nais Beach €€ This hotel is aging and the rooms are plain, but it's your best, most affordable option for sea views close to the historic centre.

The Albanian Riviera

TURQUOISE COAST

Yep, Albania has gorgeous beaches at a fraction of the price of neighbouring countries – but the secret's out, so come before it's too late.

The Albanian Riviera was a revelation roughly two decades ago, when backpackers discovered the last virgin stretch of coast in Europe and proceeded to flock here in droves, setting up ad-hoc campsites and exploring scores of little-known beaches fronting the out-of-this-world turquoise Ionian Sea. Since then, things have become significantly less pristine, especially around Sarandë, where development has blighted once-charming beachside villages (see: Ksamil).

But worry not: the water is still a dream to swim in, and if you drive north you'll find plenty of space to throw down a towel and while away the day under a beaming sun, or hire a boat to take you to remote beaches. And all the better if you're looking for fun vibes, as electronic music festivals and beach clubs keep the party popping throughout the summer. Outside of summer, much of the Albanian Riviera is abandoned, so if you like sea views and don't need to swim, that's your chance.

Aside from the beach, the Albanian Riviera has some worthwhile archaeological sights built by various empires, including Hellenistic tribes, as well as the Romans, Venetians and the Albanian-Ottoman despot Ali Pasha. The most obligatory of these sights is Butrint, an ancient city inhabited for thousands of years and home to an array of excavated ruins. The coast is also perfect for bird-watching, shipwreck diving, kitesurfing and spinning your fork into some fresh seafood pasta.

THE MAIN AREAS

SARANDË
Riviera hub and ferries to Greece.
p80

KSAMIL
The Riviera's most famous turquoise beaches. **p86**

HIMARË
Budget-friendly beachside base.
p92

DHËRMI
The electronic music festival circuit. **p97**

VLORË
Seaside city on the rise. **p101**

For places to stay in the Albanian Riviera, see p107

THE GUIDE

THE ALBANIAN RIVIERA

Left: Vlorë (p101); Above: Bora Bora (p86), Ksamil

THE ALBANIAN RIVIERA   THE GUIDE

Find Your Way

The Albanian Riviera stretches from the confluence of the Adriatic and Ionian seas in Vlorë, down the turquoise-tinted coastline to the Greek border. The Riviera's major cities have ferry connections to Greece and Italy.

FURGON
Albania's infamous *furgon* (shared minibuses) drive up and down the coast, stopping to pick up passengers at vaguely identified stops and without fixed timetables. A good option if you're on a budget and have time to spare.

RIVIERABUS
RivieraBus (*rivierabus.com/albania*; €50), a seven-person air-conditioned minivan, drives from Tirana to Sarandë and back three days a week in summer. It stops at all major beach towns, and the price is the same wherever you stop. It also does Vlorë to Sarandë (€30) on weekdays from 2 July.

CAR
You'll have the most freedom – and a lot of fun – if you rent a car and road trip the coast. The highway is well paved with beautiful vistas throughout, especially from the zigzagging **Llogorë Pass** (p99).

Vlorë, p101
Albania's third-largest port city is transforming into a summer tourist hot spot with a new airport and controversial resort developments linked to the White House.

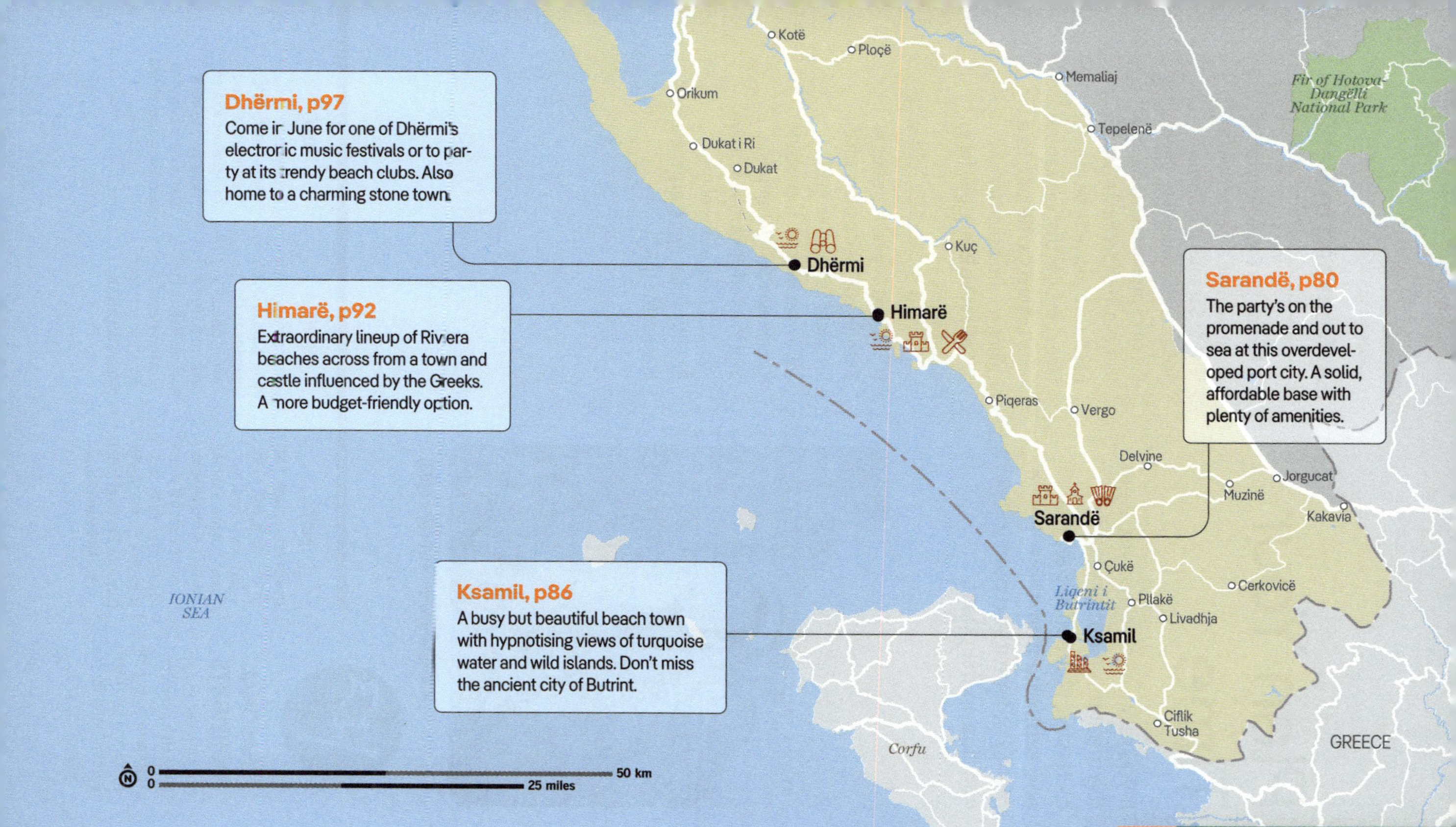

Dhërmi, p97
Come in June for one of Dhërmi's electronic music festivals or to party at its trendy beach clubs. Also home to a charming stone town.
Himarë, p92
Extraordinary lineup of Riviera beaches across from a town and castle influenced by the Greeks. A more budget-friendly option.
Sarandë, p80
The party's on the promenade and out to sea at this overdeveloped port city. A solid, affordable base with plenty of amenities.
Ksamil, p86
A busy but beautiful beach town with hypnotising views of turquoise water and wild islands. Don't miss the ancient city of Butrint.
Kotë
Ploçë
Memaliaj
Orikum
Tepelenë
Fir of Hotova-Dangëlli National Park
Dukat i Ri
Dukat
Kuç
Dhërmi
Himarë
Piqeras
Vergo
Delvine
Jorgucat
Muzinë
Kakavia
Sarandë
Çukë
Cerkovicë
Liqeni i Butrintit
Pllakë
Livadhja
Ksamil
Ciflik
Tusha
GREECE
Corfu
IONIAN SEA
0
0
50 km
25 miles

Plan Your Time

If you're short on days, you'll get the most bang out of your trip by basing yourself in Sarandë and exploring from there. Leave plenty of time if you plan to take a minibus up the coast.

Monastery of the 40 Saints (p83)

A Weekend to Relax

● Fly into the Greek island of Corfu and take a 'Flying Dolphin' ferry to **Sarandë** (p80), where you'll stay for two nights. Stroll the city's **promenade** (p80) and tuck into fresh seafood at **Haxhi** (p82). Give yourself a bit of a time cushion so that you can taxi up to **Lekursi Castle** (p82) for a stunning sunset, then taxi over to **Collective Room** (p81) for a nightcap.

● The next day, take the bus to **Butrint** (p88) and picture what life might've been like in this 2600-year-old city. Then bus to **Ksamil Beach** (p86) and swim over to its offshore islands. Have your last meal at one of the Riviera's finest dining experiences: **Manxurane** (p82).

SEASONAL HIGHLIGHTS

The Albanian Riviera becomes a tourism madhouse from June to August and then is abandoned for the rest of the year.

MAY
Beach season won't be in full swing, and some businesses will be closed, but there should be days warm enough for the beach if you don't mind chilly dips. Also time for the **South Outdoor Festival** (p85) on **Borsh Beach** (p85).

JUNE
Grab your tickets for either **Kala** (p99) or **Anjunadeep** (p99) – two of Dhërmi's electronic music festivals held in the first two weeks of June. Expect top international DJs.

JULY
Peak season on the Albanian Riviera, especially around Sarandë and Ksamil. Make sure to book accommodation (and everything else) ahead of time.

Five Days to Travel Beyond

● Add another beach day by taking a boat trip from **Sarandë** (p80) to more secluded beaches like **Kakomë** (p85), or go plunging to shipwrecks with **Saranda Diving** (p83).

● Taxi to the striking natural phenomenon that is **Blue Eye** (p84), a hypnotic pool of blue water, and return for another special Sarandë sunset at the **Monastery of the 40 Saints** (p83). Have a festive dinner of grilled meat or seafood at **Taverna Labëria** (p82).

● On your last day, taxi to the former ghost town of **Upper Qeparo** (p96), and have lunch at **Te Rrapi në Qeparo** (p96), which serves plenty of Albanian specialities. Finally, taxi down to **Porto Palermo Castle** (p95) to see the imposing fortress of the 19th-century ruler Ali Pasha.

Riviera Road Trip

● Rent a car in **Sarandë** (p80) and beach hop up the coast. Stop for a dip at the spacious **Borsh Beach** (p85), and visit **Upper Qeparo** (p96) and **Porto Palermo** (p95) on your way to **Himarë** (p92). Spend a day walking to the secluded **Aquarium Beach** (p93) and snap memorable photos atop **Himarë Castle** (p94). Continue to **Dhërmi** (p97) to see its old **stone town** (p99) and meander its long beaches. Follow in Julius Caesar's footsteps up the **Llogorë Pass** (p99) to **Vlorë** (p101), where you'll take a **boat tour** (p103) to the Karaburun Peninsula and Sazan Island. Don't miss the medieval **St Mary Monastery** (p103) on the **Nartë Lagoon** (p103), and be on the lookout for flamingos and pelicans.

THE GUIDE

THE ALBANIAN RIVIERA

AUGUST
Albania's hottest month, with temperatures eclipsing 31°C in parts of the Riviera. Beach hop to find a quieter beach – it ain't easy, but you'll be rewarded with beautiful turquoise water wherever you go.

SEPTEMBER
The best time to visit the Albanian Riviera, with temperatures consistently hitting highs of 28°C. You'll find fewer tourists, and the water will still be warm enough to swim.

OCTOBER
With the Albanian Riviera winding down for the year, this is a good time for hiking in **Llogorë Pass National Park** (p99) and enjoying Himarë's **beaches** (p92) without having to worry about getting overheated.

NOVEMBER TO MARCH
The Albanian Riviera becomes a ghost town in winter, save for some spots in Sarandë and Vlorë. If sea views with no one around appeal to you, you'll find rock-bottom prices.

HELP ME PICK:

Albanian Riviera Beaches

Albania's beaches are the main reason many travel to the country, and they're well worth the hype, with shimmering water tinted a tantalising turquoise or azure blue, and fine sand or small pebbles so smooth you'll want to pick one to rub for good luck. The thing is, the secret's out, and some get shoulder-to-shoulder packed every summer. But with a little planning, you can find your Albanian beach bliss.

Where to go if you love...

Turquoise Water

Gjipe Beach (p98) You'll have to hike 20 minutes to get here, but this is arguably Albania's most stunning secluded beach.

Aquarium Beach (p93) Hike or 4WD drive down to this tiny, hidden beach, where crystal-clear turquoise water splashes under the rocks.

Ksamil Beach (p86) Yes, this public beach is jam-packed every summer, but the water is a hypnotising blue, plus you can paddle to nearby islands.

Pulëbardha Beach (p87) Climb down from the road to this amazing beach at the foot of steep cliffs. It's slightly less busy than the main Ksamil beaches.

Blue Eye (p84) While it's not a beach and you can't swim here, the natural phenomenon that creates electric-blue water is a must-see.

Beachside Adventures

Seman Beach (p106) Learn to kitesurf or improve your skills at this long, windswept beach north of Vlorë.

Sazan Island (p103) Bounce along the confluence of the Ionian and Adriatic seas on a tour to a ghost island and pirate's cove.

Kakomë Beach (p85) Go stand-up paddleboarding in front of this private beach, or take a boat trip here from Sarandë.

Porto Palermo Castle (pictured left; p95) See the triangular fortress built by tyrant Ali Pasha, then go for a dip at the beach next to the impressive structure.

To Party

Bora Bora (p86) It's not quiet, but this Ksamil beach is a party every summer day, with chill house music from the bar and party boats.

Dhërmi Beach (p97) Back-to-back electronic music festivals in early June attract those who like to shake it to have a good time, and there's wellness mixed in, too.

Borsh Beach (p85) Home to a unique festival with live music as well as adventures such as kayaking and windsurfing.

Luxury

Arameras Beach Resort (p107) Stay at this resort with its own private beach southwest of Ksamil village for a more exclusive experience.

Jalë Beach (p93) While it's a shame that this formerly pristine beach has been developed, what's done is done, and it's now home to several luxury resorts.

Radhimë Beach (p104) Fly to Vlorë's new international airport (scheduled to open during research) and head for this strip of beach resorts fronting turquoise water.

Kitesurfing school, Seman Beach (p106)

HOW TO

When to go June, July and August see the best beach weather, but they're also the busiest months. Come in May or September to avoid the crowds.

Budget Prices skyrocket in summer. Save by pitching a tent or sleeping in a caravan. Many campgrounds provide tents if you don't have one.

Meals In summer, most beaches are served by bars and seafood restaurants. Bring food in low season and when heading to remote beaches like Aquarium.

Be warned Some beaches, such as Ksamil, get so busy in summer that there's little space to put down a towel. If you do, a server might hassle you to rent a chair.

Avoiding the Crowds

Many people see reels on Instagram of beautiful Albanian beaches and book a trip to the Albanian Riviera at the peak of summer, only to arrive shocked when they find the beaches crowded. Don't be one of those people. The Riviera, especially Sarandë and Ksamil, *will* be packed in June, July and August (everyone else saw those same reels). But there are ways to steer clear of the loudest areas.

In most beach towns, agencies along the waterfront offer boat trips that take you to secluded beaches inaccessible by car, then either leave you there for a few hours or tour you around.

You could also rent a car and make a road trip out of finding your favourite beach. Beaches that involve hiking, such as Gjipe (p98) and Aquarium (p93), tend to be less busy (but don't count on it). Long beaches, such as Borsh (p85) and Drymades (p98), don't feel as busy since there's so much space.

Also consider moving your trip to spring or autumn – it's remarkable how empty the beach towns get out of season.

And the last piece of advice might sound a bit woo-woo, but *embrace it*. Other people are enjoying their beach holidays, so why not just join the party?

Sarandë

SEAFRONT | CASTLE SUNSETS | SEAFOOD

☑ TOP TIP

If beaches are your target, fly to the Greek island of Corfu and take a ferry to Sarandë. **Finikas Lines** *(finikas-lines.com)* and **Ionian Seaways** *(ionianseaways.com)* run several daily trips between the two by 'Flying Dolphin' high-speed hydrofoil (per person €30, 30 minutes) or car ferry (per person €20, 1¼ hours).

Two decades ago, Sarandë (Saranda) was a sleepy beach port located next to a vast stretch of pristine beaches lapping cobalt-coloured water. While few outside of Albania knew these beaches existed, the cat is now out of the proverbial bag, and Sarandë is a full-on city with rows of hotels and a boardwalk where music blasts both ears. Still, the unofficial capital of the Albanian Riviera is an unavoidable and worthwhile base for sunseekers, while the seafood restaurants here are some of the best in the country, remarkably costing just a fraction of what they would across the sea in Greece or Italy. The hilltop castle and monastery are the best show in town every evening at sunset, and you can dive to military shipwrecks offshore. Just make sure you leave time to explore the area's surrounding beaches, which are much more enjoyable than the city's main beach.

Sarandë's Seafront

It's party time

Sarandë's busy boardwalk might be touristy, but it's still good fun for a drink. On the water are party ships that blast music and entice passengers to join for a booze cruise – *yaaarr*! Lining the boardwalk are bars – many with rooftops – that are perfect for sipping a cold drink or tucking into a seafood pasta – a speciality in Sarandë, with Italy being so close by.

 GETTING AROUND

Furgon (shared minibuses) stop in front of the ferry port from 6.30am to 6.30pm on their way to Ksamil (150L). Payment is cash only. If you can manage to score a seat, the bus is much better than driving or taking a taxi, as the seaside road becomes a virtual car park in the summer.

A vehicle is necessary, however, if you'd like to visit the less crowded beaches, and Sarandë has plenty of local car-hire agencies and a few international brands, such as Enterprise and Sixt. You can also book a tour or embark on a boat trip for your beach-finding needs.

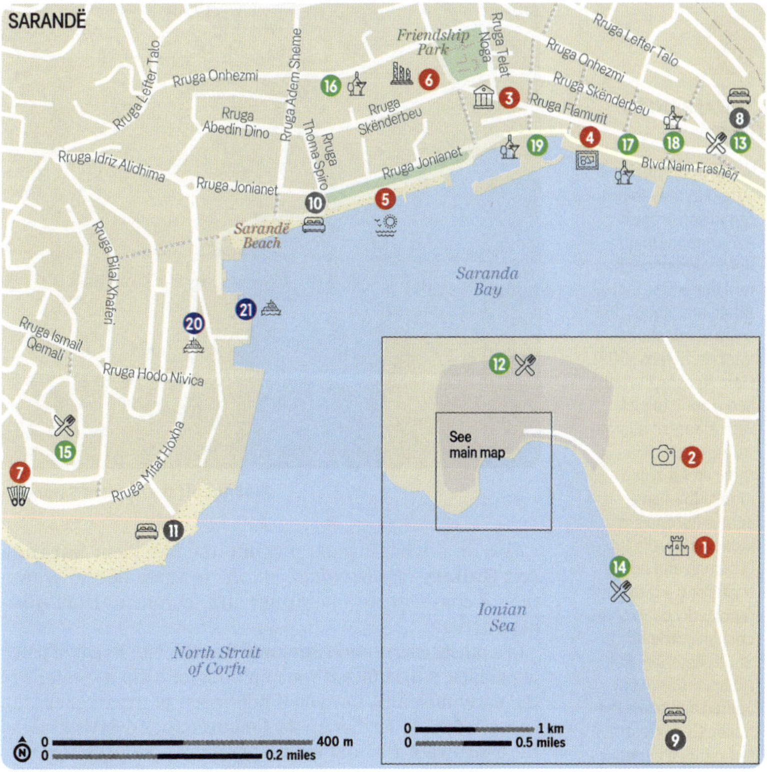

★ **HIGHLIGHTS**	6 Synagogue
1 Lekursi Castle	● **ACTIVITIES**
● **SIGHTS**	7 Saranda Diving
2 Monastery of the 40 Saints	■ **SLEEPING**
3 Museum of Archaeology	8 Central Boutique Hostel
4 Saranda Art Gallery	9 Harmony Hotel
5 Sarandë Beach	10 Titania Hotel
	11 Vila Kalcuni
● **EATING**	17 Hojza Lounge
12 Green Life Market	18 Jericho
13 Haxhi	19 Limani
14 Manxuranë	● **TRANSPORT**
15 Taverna Labëria	20 Finikas Lines
● **DRINKING & NIGHTLIFE**	21 Ionian Seaways
16 Collective Room	

Jericho (*@jericho.cocktail.bar*) is a local favourite, and **Hojza Lounge** (*@hojza.lounge*) usually has funky house music on its rooftop terrace. Or jutting out on a mini peninsula, have drinks at **Limani** (*@restorant_limani*) – a greedy piece of real estate if there ever was one, but as they say, don't hate the player, hate the game. The best watering hole in town, however, is **Collective Room** (*@collective_room_*), found in a back alley in the town. Here, the cocktails are good, the beats are great (the owner is also a DJ) and the vibes are as immaculate as the religious murals adorning the walls.

QUIETER COASTAL BEACHES

Your best shot at a peaceful and quiet beach is to take a boat tour or drive up the scenic coastal road for at least an hour to beaches near **Himarë** (p92) and **Dhërmi** (p97).

Probitas off the coast of Sarandë

THE ALBANIAN MAFIA

When many hear 'Albania', they think organised crime. A European Union border agent once told this writer that Albanians 'shoot first and ask questions later'. In *Taken* (2008), Liam Neeson certainly had a bone to pick with Albanian human traffickers. But is there an Albanian mob? Albanians across Europe are indeed a deadly force in human and drug trafficking – they reportedly control the cocaine route from South America. But Albanians aren't a unified mafia like the Italian Cosa Nostra, but rather a network of crime cells. The reasons why many Albanians turn to illegal activity are complex, but they can be traced to the fall of communism, when the country's Sigurimi had spies with skills suited to crime, and the 1997 pyramid scheme crisis, which left thousands poor and desperate.

Also on the boardwalk, pop into the basement **Saranda Art Gallery** *(@sarandaxhemajli)* to see a decent collection of contemporary paintings and sculptures from Albanian artists.

In a pinch, coarse-sand **Sarandë Beach**, with its small patch of pebbles, will suffice if you're pining for a dip, especially in the early morning, but you'll find much prettier beaches in Ksamil (p86) or farther up the Ionian coast. Advertised along the boardwalk are **boat tours** *(per person 2500L, prepare to negotiate)* that can take you to Ksamil or other remote beaches only accessible by boat.

Special Sunset Spots

Views from a castle and monastery

An hour's walk (or a taxi ride) from the boardwalk uphill, you'll reach Sarandë's must-see sunset spot: the ruins of **Lekursi Castle** *(Kalaja e Lekursit)*. Built by the Ottomans in 1537 to defend against the Venetians, only its ramparts remain. The setting makes a romantic backdrop for photos, and there's a classy restaurant to enjoy after your photos (the food is just OK, but the ambience is unparalleled, especially when there's

 EATING IN SARANDË: OUR PICKS

Taverna Labëria: This lovable family-run restaurant off the boardwalk serves terrific, generous portions of steak and seafood on its two busy terraces. *8am-midnight* €€

Green Life Market: Sarandë's only vegan restaurant serves creative, ever-changing homemade meals made by its friendly Canadian and Argentine owners. *5-10pm Wed-Sun* €€

Haxhi: Seafarer-themed upper-floor restaurant with creative lighting and quality seafood. All we have to say about the voluptuous glassware is: why? *noon-11pm* €€

Manxuranë: Inspired by his mother's cooking, local Fatmir's carefully prepared plates are a knockout – as are the views. One of Albania's best. *10am-11pm* €€€

live folk music). Go at least an hour before sunset (before the mountain obscures the light).

Sunset from the ruins of the 6th-century **Monastery of the 40 Saints** *(Manastiri i 40 Shenjtorëve)* is just as stunning. The 40-room Eastern Orthodox monastery was built to welcome pilgrims on their way to Sebaste, where 40 Romans were martyred for refusing to renounce their faith. The monastery was mostly destroyed in WWII by British artillery, but the church's legacy lives on in the name Sarandë, which means '40' in Greek.

Dive to Military Shipwrecks
Albania's best dive site

During WWII, when Albania was controlled by Italy and Germany, the Allies managed to sink an Italian cargo ship, the SS *Probitas*, 50m offshore. The ship, sunk in 1943, is still there, and in good condition – perfect for a dive if you have a PADI licence or equivalent certification.

Book at least a day ahead with **Saranda Diving** *(sarandadiving.com; per dive 7000L)*. Your day on the water begins by diving to a maximum depth of 18m to see the 100m-long *Probitas*. You'll also have a chance to visit the **Hunda e Mërtesë** dive site. It's 15m deep, and the water is typically a pleasant 17°C; moray eels and ray fish are frequently seen here. Ask about other dives, including to see intentionally sunken military ships, and about certification courses.

Millennia-old Mosaics
Ruins steps from the sea

In the middle of Sarandë, a foundation of ruins, including a 5th-century **Synagogue**, evidences the Jewish community that once lived here. The synagogue had a mosaic floor featuring a menorah (candlestick) and shofar (ram's horn). The synagogue was later covered by a basilica, with Byzantine-style mosaics added. Unfortunately, the mosaics are covered for protection, but you can snap a photo of the building's layout.

A visible mosaic from around the same period can be viewed inside Sarandë's one-room **Museum of Archaeology** *(100L)*. The almost 13m by 11m mosaic, which once covered the floor of a 6th-century basilica, was unearthed in the 1960s. The museum is often closed, but you should be able to see the mosaic through the window.

PYRAMID SCHEME CRISIS

When communism collapsed in 1991, Albanians were finally able to earn and spend money on products most of them had never seen before, including Coca-Cola and bananas. They could also invest, and private companies popped up with promises of high returns. By 1997, two-thirds of Albanians had invested in these companies. When the companies turned out to be pyramid schemes, tens of thousands of Albanians went bankrupt.

The country descended into chaos, with widespread protests, especially on the Albanian Riviera, where a hunger strike at the University of Vlorë turned bloody. Fighting then turned to Sarandë, where rebels ransacked government buildings and seized weapons until a multinational force, Operation Alba, arrived to return order. Despite avoiding a full-blown civil war, the crisis dealt a devastating blow to the young democracy.

Beyond Sarandë

Leave Albania's southwestern hub to see the electric Blue Eye and search for quieter beaches.

Places
Krongj p84
Lukovë p85
Borsh p85

Sarandë is a great base, but you should by no means stick around the busy city for your entire visit, as there's even more to do in the surrounding area. Witness the magical Blue Eye in the mountains, stopping on the way to see St Nicholas Monastery, which is adorned with carvings of mythical creatures. Northbound, you'll find several turquoise water beaches with few international visitors. The drive alone is worth the trip, as you'll get spectacular views along the way. Check and see if the South Outdoor Festival is on while you're here.

Krongj
TIME FROM SARANDË: **30 MINS**

Natural springs
The **Blue Eye** *(Syri i Kaltë; pedestrian/car 100/300L)* really is magical. The hypnotic pool of deep blue water, with electric-blue edges that resemble the iris of an eye, is one of Albania's top attractions – tour groups come from far and wide. Go early or outside of June, July and August to avoid the largest crowds.

The natural phenomenon starts over 50m underground (divers have never made it to the bottom), where water gushes out of karstic subsoil at a rate of 18,400 litres per second. The water rises to become the main source for the Bistricë River, which empties into the Ionian Sea. The pool is part of a natural park that's home to long-eared bats, wolves and golden jackals, as well as 600 plant species, including oaks, sycamores and pines.

It's 22km east of Sarandë on the road to Gjirokastër. After parking or getting dropped off by a taxi, walk for 20 minutes on the paved path that gets piping hot in summer until you reach the restaurant. Enjoy a drink over the stunning views of the water and mountains, but don't miss the bluest water by walking for another five minutes on a short bush trail. Even though you'll probably see many people jumping from the wooden platform into the refreshing water, which ranges between 10°C and 13°C, swimming is prohibited here in order to protect the sensitive biome.

Monasteries
On your way to the Blue Eye, stop in the village of Mesopotam to see the 13th-century Byzantine **St Nicholas Monastery** *(Manastiri i Shën Nikollës)*. It's not always open, but you can still enjoy the carvings of mythical animals on its facade.

GETTING AROUND

Unfortunately, buses are no longer available for the Blue Eye due to the construction of a new highway, but tours *are* offered by virtually anyone in Sarandë, and they may also include stops at Butrint. Or hire a taxi (return trip 4000L).

Minibuses go up the coast – tell the driver to stop wherever you'd like. Keep in mind that most beaches are a long walk from the highway, and there are no dedicated sidewalks. You'll have the most freedom if you hire a car in Sarandë.

St Nicholas Monastery

Lukovë

TIME FROM SARANDË: **30 MINS**

Serene and pebbly beaches

While the beaches near Ksamil are prettier, they also tend to be much busier, and pushier, than those north of Sarandë. In 30 minutes, you'll reach the town of Lukovë, which features the pebble **Shpellë Beach**, located 10 minutes downhill. This beach is small and has food and drink service, and from the shore, you can hire a boat captain (2500L) to take you to swim at the much prettier, paradisiacal **Kakomë Beach**. As Kakomë is private, you unfortunately won't be able to go ashore. Alternatively, explore Kakomë Bay by arranging a full-day kayak or stand-up paddleboard trip with **Albania Rafting Group** *(albrafting.org; €80)*.

Borsh

TIME FROM SARANDË: **1 HR**

Explore Ionian beaches

Farther north, **Buneci Beach** is easily accessed from the highway (which makes it less scenic) and has the type of aquamarine water many fly to Albania for. There's beach service, and it tends to be less busy. Or, continue for just under an hour to 6km-long **Borsh Beach**, the country's longest. The water is shallow (great for kids), and there are plenty of restaurants with playgrounds. Also, you won't be hassled if you don't pay for a beach chair or umbrella, unlike in Ksamil. While in Borsh, check out **Borsh Castle** *(Kuluja e Borshit)*, which has splendid views of the sea.

Adventure festival

In May, the five-day **South Outdoor Festival** *(southoutdoor.al)* on Borsh Beach has a bit of everything, including live concerts (house DJs to rappers to pop singers) and dozens of different activities: trike flying (gliding through the air on a bike propelled by a fan), sea kayaking, mountain biking and hiking up the coastal mountains. The event is fun for the whole family, with activities and games for young children as well.

DELTA AT RISK

Albania's Vjosë-Nartë Delta is rich in biodiversity, with nearly 250 bird species, loggerhead turtles and endangered monk seals. It's also the gateway to Vjosë Wild River National Park, Europe's first national river park, protected in 2023. The delta is one of Europe's few pristine ecosystems, but environmentalists are raising concerns for the delta's future, as it's slated for tourism development.

In 2021, the Albanian government approved plans to build an international airport within the Vjosë-Nartë Delta Protected Area. Recently, Donald Trump's son-in-law, Jared Kushner, and daughter, Ivanka Trump, sponsored a 6000-room luxury resort beside the lagoon, which was being considered by the government during research. This is in addition to the luxury resort community on Sazan Island, a protected national marine park, which was approved in December 2024.

Ksamil

BREATHTAKING BEACHES | ANCIENT CITY | LUXE CLUBS

☑ TOP TIP

Everything, from the beach chairs (which bars force you to purchase) to the hotels to the restaurants, is more expensive here than anywhere else in Albania. To save money, stay in Sarandë (p80) and make day trips to Ksamil and Butrint.

GETTING AROUND

If Ksamil is your primary target while in Albania, fly to the Greek island of Corfu and take a ferry to Sarandë, then bus over. Buses run from the port in Sarandë to Ksamil from 6.30am to 6.30pm and cost 150L. They also go to Butrint.

Having your own vehicle in Ksamil is a detriment rather than an advantage. Thankfully, taxis are plentiful.

If you've seen photos or videos on social media of tantalisingly turquoise water on the Albanian Riviera, they were probably taken in Ksamil. The coastal town is lined with breathtaking beaches backed by stark cliffs and stylish beach bars playing melodic deep house. Bliss out in a beach chair under an umbrella, ice-cold drink in hand, and then paddle out to the uninhabited islands just offshore. But be warned: you won't be the only one enjoying this beach paradise. Ksamil gets well and truly swarming with people every summer. Ksamil pretty much shuts down from November to May.

While here, don't dare miss Butrint, the most spectacular of Albania's archaeological sites, just 4km south.

Beach Bliss

Ultimate beach guide

Ksamil has beaches unlike anywhere on the Albanian Riviera (and arguably anywhere in this part of the world), with white sand – a treat, since the rest of the coast has pebbles and rocks – and impossibly aquamarine water. The three wild islands of **Tre Ishujt** appear to be floating just offshore, adding to the splendour.

Throughout June, July and August, every beach is packed to the brim with umbrellas and chairs, with nowhere to put down a towel – you might get barked at by a waiter if you try. Chairs can run you as much as 1000L at some establishments, while some beach clubs block access unless you pay a cover of 2000L.

Your best views of the islands are from **Ksamil Beach**, and it's a short swim across to the first of two. Or head to lively **Bora Bora**, which is often bumping house music, and rent a

 EATING & DRINKING IN KSAMIL: OUR PICKS

Ftelea Fish Taverna: Only the freshest fish and seafood, grilled, fried or served tucked into pasta or risotto. A Ksamil highlight. *noon-11.30pm* €€

Vamos: Latin American vibes under colourful umbrellas with vibrant cocktails to match. Hookah available. *4pm-2am* €€

Guvat: On a hill's edge with some of the best views, and often live music for sunset. Just don't be in a rush, as service can be slow. *7am-11.30pm* €€€

Bianco: Rooftop bar lounge with an infinity pool and restaurant by day, dance club after midnight. *8am-2am* €€€

KSAMIL

● SIGHTS
1 Ali Pasha's Castle
2 Bora Bora
3 Ksamil Beach
4 Pema e Thatë
5 Pulëbardha Beach
6 Viewpoint

● ACTIVITIES
7 Mussel Sailing Tour

● SLEEPING
8 Arameras Beach Resort
9 Ksamil Caravan Camping
10 Meta Hotel
11 Sunway

● EATING
12 Ftelea Fish Taverna
13 Guvat
14 Mussel House

● DRINKING & NIGHTLIFE
15 Bianco
16 Vamos

SEA ESCAPE

During 45 years of dictatorship, spies, fences and dogs kept Albanians trapped in their country, and when they tried to swim across to Corfu from Ksamil – just 70 minutes for a strong swimmer – they were shot dead by Greek or Albanian soldiers. But when communism fell in 1991, Albanians rushed to escape. An estimated 20,000 refugees hijacked an Italian ship in Durrës and sailed across the Adriatic. Others swam to Corfu, where they were met with a mix of fear and acceptance. More moved elsewhere in Europe, the Americas and Türkiye. Since 1991, an astonishing 40% of Albanians have left their country.

kayak or pedal boats (500L to 1000L). You'll also see plenty of boats you can hire (per person 1500L) for the 10-minute trip to the islands. You won't find much on the islands except trees, a few rocky beaches and a single bar, and it's perfect that way.

Outside the town centre, **Pema e Thatë** is a more peaceful, private beach, but you'll have to take a taxi or drive on dirt roads to get here. **Pulëbardha Beach** is similarly difficult to get to and not walkable from the centre, but it has a wilder, more natural coastal energy, as it's sheltered by a steep rock face.

Mussel Farming
Boat tour of Lake Butrint

Ksamil is known for its mussels. Lake Butrint, behind the seafront, is well known for its mussel farms – Ali Pasha used to bring his queen here to impress her. Hop in a boat and see for yourself with a 2½-hour **Mussel Sailing Tour** *(068 387 3305; per person 3900L)*. You'll learn how mussels are farmed, get a chance to prepare them yourself by removing 'the beard', then eat your haul for lunch with white wine, grapes and fresh bread. Alternatively, you can simply eat the blackish crustaceans with views over the lake at **Mussel House**.

Baptistry

TOP EXPERIENCE

Butrint

Early in the morning, before the tourist buses arrive and when the rocks are still tinged in the yellow dawn light, you might just imagine that the ancient walls of **Butrint** are whispering secrets to you of long-past lives. Easily the most romantic and beautiful – not to mention the largest – of Albania's ancient sites, Butrint, 4km south of Ksamil, is worth travelling a long way to see.

DON'T MISS

A 2600-year-old theatre

Great Basilica

Roman mosaics

Venetian tower and castles

Lake Butrint views

Butrint Museum's marble sculptures

Hellenistic (Greek) Theatre

Humans have occupied this precious landscape between brackish Lake Butrint and the Ionian Sea for 50,000 years, but excavations carried out in the 1920s found remnants of an ancient city inhabited by a wide swath of empires for a period spanning 2800 years. In the 8th century BCE, Hellenist tribes built the first *polis* (city). They built a **Temple** dedicated to Asclepius, the Greek god of medicine, and attracted worshippers from across the Balkans looking for healing.

PRACTICALITIES
- butrint.al
- 8.30am-8pm (last entry 6pm) Apr-Oct, 9am-5.30pm (last entry 3pm) Nov-Mar
- adult/child 12-18 800/500L

Later, they constructed the city's first ramparts, a **Lake Gate** at the eastern edge and the administrative Agora, which was later renovated by the Romans to become a **Forum**. Most enticingly for visitors today, the Hellenists built Butrint's marquee site: the **Theatre**.

It's a special experience to stand in the middle of the theatre, which the Romans expanded to seat 2500 spectators. Go ahead and shout: you'll hear an amplifying effect.

Roman Baths & Palace

The Romans conquered the Greek region of Epirus in 167 BCE, where the city of Butrint was located, officially turning it into a settlement for war veterans in the 1st century BCE under Julius Caesar's command. During this period, the Romans drained marshes to extend the city south and built several aqueducts, one of which can still be seen today.

Close to the entrance is the **Triconch Palace**, a grand Roman villa that was expanded in the early 5th century under the Byzantines following their split from Rome. It's usually much quieter than the ruins around the Theatre.

Nearby, look for the Roman thermal **Baths** with their mosaic wall patterns and the **Gymnasium**, later transformed into a church in the middle of the city. A **Nymphaeum** (fountain) dedicated to female divinities can be seen next to the Byzantine's Great Basilica.

Byzantine Basilica & Baptistry

The **Great Basilica**, a remnant of the Byzantines' eighth-century rule over Butrint, was constructed during the reign of Emperor Justinian I in the 6th century. The building is one of Butrint's most photogenic sites, with imposing arches and colonnades. The Byzantines also built a paleo-Christian **Baptistry**, which, in its heyday, was the largest such building between Rome and Constantinople. The circular building has a double colonnade and one of Albania's finest mosaics, featuring peacocks, stags and hares. Unfortunately for visitors, it's covered with sand for its own protection most of the year.

Venetian Tower & Castles

Butrint changed hands frequently during centuries of invasions by the Slavs, Normans and Angevins before the Venetians took control in 1386. See their 16th-century **Tower** straight ahead of the entrance. The Venetians also built a hilltop **Castle**, now the site of the **Butrint Museum**. Inside, learn more about the ancient city's fascinating history and see a wide collection of artefacts discovered on the grounds and arranged in chronological order. You'll find some of Albania's best pottery displays, as well as a striking collection of marble sculptures. Above the museum, climb up to the tower for the best views over Butrint, the surrounding parkland and out to Corfu.

FASCIST PAWN

When Italian archaeologist Luigi Maria Ugolini arrived in Butrint in 1927, the city was abandoned. The ruins seen today were mainly excavated by Ugolini and his team between 1928 and 1939 – but not as a favour to the newborn Albania. Italy wanted to assert its historic claims to the region – claims that became useful when the Fascists took over the country in 1939.

TROJAN REFUGE

In the epic poem *Aeneid* (19 BCE) by Roman poet Virgil, Butrint (Buthrotum in Latin) was founded by the Trojans, who fled Troy in the 12th century BCE after that famous horse incident. While it's a nice story, this was more likely a fabrication to earn the city favour with the Roman elites, who saw themselves as fellow ancestors of the Trojan refugees.

UNESCO

In 1992, Butrint became a UNESCO World Heritage Site – Albania's first. The ruins and the surrounding national park are also protected by UNESCO's Ramsar and the Albanian government. Expanding development in Ksamil is a concern for the site's protection.

To see another Venetian structure, leave Butrint and pay to use the mini cable **ferry** (*pedestrian 75L, car from 500L*). You can't miss the **Triangular Castle** on the left. It was built in the 15th century to protect the Butrint Canal against Ottoman and pirate attacks. You can walk around the castle walls, but it's rarely open.

Ali Pasha's Castle

Butrint's importance dwindled under the Venetians, and in 1797 the area was handed over to the French after the Serenissima's defeat. The Ottomans, with the help of the Russians, quickly took the Butrint area and slotted it into the Ottoman Empire. However, when Lord Byron visited the area in 1809, he found nothing but 'a land of ruins, desolation, and beauty' – Butrint's time as an important city under the control of various empires was over.

In the 1810s, the so-called Ottoman Napoleon, Ali Pasha, seized Butrint, using it for farmland and draining the marshes to feed his soldiers. **Ali Pasha's Castle**, on an island west of Butrint, was armed to protect trading routes. The only way to visit it is by hiring a small boat *(2500L 30 minutes)* on the other side of the cable ferry. Or you can observe it through the trees from a **Viewpoint** outside Butrint, on the road to Ksamil.

Gymnasium (p89)

Alternative Walking Tour

Many people whizz straight to the Greek Theatre, but save the best for last by ignoring the signs and turning right at the fork after the ticket booth. Soon you'll reach the comparatively modern Venetian Tower. Carry on along a narrow forest path to the atmospheric and often quiet ruins of the Roman Triconch Palace. Along the same path and deeper in the forest is the paleo-Christian Baptistry with its amazing mosaic floor (see what it looks like in the brochure). To the left is a wall with Greek inscriptions and the Gymnasium with visible mosaics. Turn back towards the water to the impressive arches of the Great Basilica and the Nymphaeum fountain. Then follow the massive Cyclopean wall (dating back to the 4th century BCE) along the lake shore until you get to the Hellenist Lake Gate. Duck under the imposing Lion Gate, a medieval addition built as an obstacle to slow down invading forces; it features a relief of a lion killing a bull. By slowly following the shady path to the top of the hill, you'll come to the Venetian Castle, which today houses the informative, artefact-filled Butrint Museum. Climb up the tower and admire the view, then leave through the castle's courtyard to marvel at Butrint's show-stoppers: the 4th-century-BCE Theatre, Temple, Forum and Roman Baths.

NATIONAL PARK

Butrint is more than just ruins. The site is part of a nearly 100-sq-km national park highlighted by wetlands, coastal islands and more than 1000 species of flora and fauna, including nearly 250 types of birds.

TOP TIPS

● Hourly buses come and go from Sarandë (200L, 30 to 75 minutes) and Ksamil (100L, 20 minutes) throughout the day.

● The drive here is lovely once you get past Sarandë's traffic. Parking is free.

● Allow a couple of hours for your visit.

● Bring a bottle of water and possibly snacks, as there are no restaurants inside. The lone restaurant/hotel outside the gate is subpar.

● Wear good shoes, as the terrain is rough and there are few places to sit.

● Sunscreen is a must.

● International visitors enter for free four days of the year: 18 April, 18 and 21 May, and 29 September.

Himarë

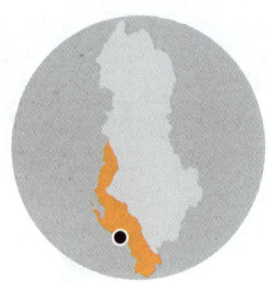

BEACHES | CAMPING | CITADEL

☑ TOP TIP

Hire a boat captain on the promenade to take you to isolated beaches, where it'll be just you and the murmuring waves. **Boat tours** *(from 3000L)* can drop you at a beach and pick you up in the afternoon, or shuttle you around to several.

Himarë (Himara) is the biggest town between Sarandë and busy Vlorë, with less of a bougie vibe than some other beach resort towns along the coast. It's attractive to all types of travellers, but those on a budget will feel especially at home here with the ample selection of backpacker hostels and campgrounds. The main reason to visit is for – what else? – the beach. Himarë has strong contenders for some of the coast's finest beaches, including an idyllic cove and a well-equipped, family-friendly beach. Up the hill, a castle towers over the city, with the decayed ruins making for a stunning backdrop for photos.

Historically, Himarë had strong connections with Greece and Corfu, which is visible on the horizon. Its early inhabitants were Chaonian tribes, and some in Himarë continue to speak a Greek dialect called Himariote. You'll also find a particularly strong collection of Greek-inspired eats such as moussaka and tzatziki here.

Beautiful Beaches

Some of the coast's finest

You don't need to go far to find a beach in Himarë. **Himarë Beach** is directly beneath the promenade and has the turquoise-tinged water the Ionian coast is famous for, along with a lively atmosphere when combined with the boardwalk bars.

GETTING AROUND

Himarë is little more than a couple of restaurant- and hotel-lined streets, so you'll be fine on foot once you're here. However, to see the best beaches and historic sites, you'll want your own vehicle (there are several car-hire companies in Sarandë) or taxi (of which you'll find plenty in the town centre). Hiking is doable, though ambitious. Himarë Castle, for instance, is a 2.7km, 200m climb from the promenade along the side of the highway. It's also possible to hike to the beaches from Livadi Beach if you follow the trail and 4WD tracks marked with red and white signs.

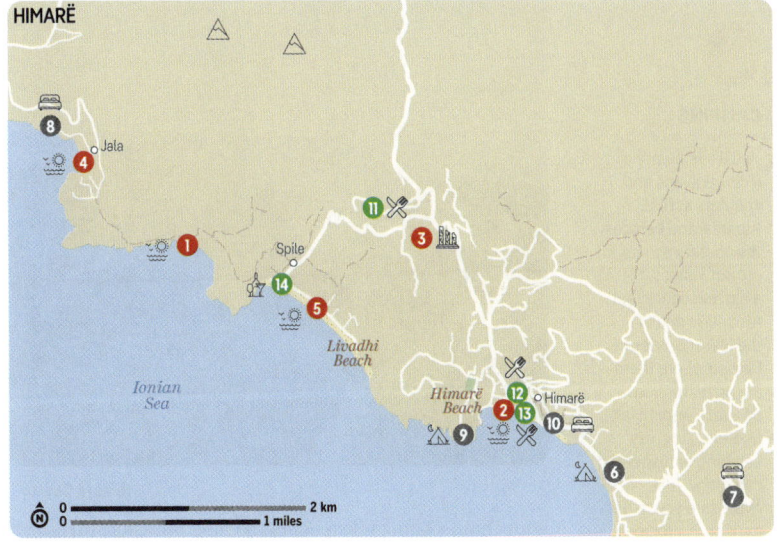

HIMARË

● **SIGHTS**	5 Livadhi Beach	9 Pine Side Camp	13 To Steki sti Gonia
1 Aquarium Beach	● **SLEEPING**	10 Vila Kosteli	● **DRINKING**
2 Himarë Beach	6 Camping Himara	● **EATING**	**& NIGHTLIFE**
3 Himarë Castle	7 Eléa Guesthouse	11 Fig and Olive	14 Manolo Beach Bar
4 Jalë Beach	8 Folie Marine	12 Taverna Lefteri	

Alternatively, the lineup of beaches north comprise some of the coast's finest. A 10-minute drive takes you to **Livadhi Beach**, a long curving pebble beach lined every summer with umbrellas and restaurants. It's a good option for families as it has plenty of amenities.

Or walk 40 minutes on the 4WD road from Livadhi Beach past Camping Himara (p107) to **Aquarium Beach** *(Plazhi i Akuariumit)*, a tiny cove with crystal-clear water that gently splashes into a cave. The beach is small, so it can easily fill up with campers and beachgoers in the summer, some of whom leave their trash behind (don't be one of them).

If you continue along the 4WD road, you'll eventually reach the southern edge of **Jalë Beach**, home to the snazzy Folie Marine (p107) resort. While the beach is an Ionian wonder, it has been consumed with development in the last few years,

 EATING & DRINKING IN HIMARË: OUR PICKS

Taverna Lefteri: This town is rich in delicious seafood, but Lefteri stands out for the care put into its presentation and quality. *noon-4pm & 7pm-midnight* €€

To Steki sti Gonia: Himarë's Hellenistic heritage shines at this restaurant on the seafront. The menu ventures beyond its excellent souvlaki. *11.30am-midnight* €€

Fig and Olive: With views over Livadhi Beach and twinkly lit evening meals, this place has a romantic vibe to go along with the quality seafood dishes. *5.30-10pm* €€

Manolo Beach Bar: Tried and true beach bar without the trendiness of some of the others. Open year-round. *7.30am-3am* €€

Himarë Castle

CAMPING

You'll see plenty of RVs, caravans and vanlifers across Albania, and besides the country's inherent attractiveness, there's a big reason for that. Albania is one of the few countries in Europe where there are no restrictions on wild camping (aka boondocking, dry camping or dispersed camping). Just make sure you're not parking in a national park or reserve, near government buildings or on private property.

Himarë is particularly attractive for campers, with campgrounds aplenty. Many have hookups for campers and ready-to-sleep tents already set up so you won't even need your own gear. Popular spots include the rocky seafront just northwest of town and around Livadhi (p93) and Aquarium (p93) beaches.

with chunks being taken out of the mountainside, turning it into one big construction site. Another reminder to come to Albania soon, before its scenery is destroyed.

Hilltop Citadel

The views are something else...

High on the hills above the seafront, a 45-minute walk or 10-minute taxi uphill, are the ruins of **Himarë Castle** *(300L)*. The enchanting citadel has existed in some form for 3500 years, with the earliest fortifications dating back to the Hellenistic Chaonians. Inhabited under rule by the Romans, the Byzantines and the Venetians, the castle was abandoned in the 16th century in favour of the port area.

Walking around is a delight. Despite the castle being a ruin, some people live in the houses within its walls, and the sea views are superb. You're going to want to bring your camera, as the pictures of the sea through the castle walls will surely be keepers.

TOURISM'S IMPACT

In a matter of a few decades, Albania has gone from isolated dictatorship to tourism hot spot. Visitors have undoubtedly had an impact on the country's economy, but they are also having dire consequences for the environment. Learn more in our **tourism essay** (p200).

Beyond Himarë

Peel yourself off the beach and visit two of the most intriguing historical sites on the Ionian coastline.

A short drive south of Himarë are two of the finest stops on the Albanian Riviera. In just 15 minutes, you'll reach a menacing pentagonal fortress that was run by Albania's infamous, semi-autonomous despot, Ali Pasha. From there, it's another 15 minutes to Upper Qeparo, a former ghost town with an adorable cluster of stone structures and restaurants surrounded by olive groves. Both deliver spectacular views and photos, and combined, they make for a lovely day trip. You'll also find some beaches and restaurants along the way, so there'll be no need to pack a lunch.

The sites beyond Himarë can just as easily be done as a day trip from Sarandë, or as stops between the Sarandë and Himarë.

Places
Porto Palermo p95
Qeparo p96

Porto Palermo

TIME FROM HIMARË: **15 MINS** 🚗

Ali Pasha's fort

Jutting out into a picturesque bay just south of Himarë is the triangular fortress, of **Porto Palermo Castle** *(300L)* – don't miss it if you're road tripping the coast. Construction on this island, later joined to the mainland, likely dates back to the Venetians, who built a triangular fortress across from Butrint (p88). However, the man attributed most to this castle, and the one who hired French architects to build it (and then killed them), was Albanian-Ottoman ruler Ali Pasha of Tepelenë. According to legend, Ali Pasha had the castle built as a gift for his wife, Kyria Vassiliki, whom he married after kidnapping her from Greece at the age of 15. It's well worth paying the entrance fee to wander around the castle and climb up to the rooftop for superb sea views.

The fortress itself is eerily dark inside, with limestone walls that rise 15m high and 1.6m thick on the perimeter. Simple signage indicates the room's use, including the prison cell used by King Zog I and the Italians during WWII. The fort and its bay, which has a small beach, were later used by Enver Hoxha's regime as a warehouse and parking spot for Soviet submarines.

Relax at Llamani Beach

If you're looking to soak up the sun without so much as lifting a finger, **Llamani Beach** is a well-developed small strip of

GETTING AROUND

These sites are best accessed as stops on a coastal road trip with your own vehicle, or in a taxi from Himarë. Frequent buses run from Himarë to Sarandë, but there's no set schedule. Ask the driver to let you off at Porto Palermo, Llamani or Qeparo – you'll then need to hike a steep 2.5km to get to the ghost town of Upper Qeparo (p96).

Upper Qeparo

ALI PASHA

Ali Pasha (1740–1822), also known as Ali Pasha of Ioannina, of Tepelenë, or the Ottoman Napoleon, was a powerful, semi-autonomous Albanian leader both feared and respected until his assassination. Born in Tepelenë to a minor Ottoman *bey* (lord) family, he rose to rule a vast area that included Albania and parts of Greece, Montenegro and North Macedonia. Though officially an Ottoman servant, Ali Pasha ran his territory like a kingdom, using spies, prisons and violence to crush dissent. At the same time, he is credited with unifying the region through religious tolerance and building roads, bridges, schools and fortresses. In 1820, Sultan Mahmud II ordered his assassination. After resisting for two years, Ali Pasha was shot dead, and his head was displayed in Istanbul as a warning.

pebble beach covered by macramé and thatched umbrellas. This beach is easily accessible from the highway and there's ample parking.

Qeparo

TIME FROM HIMARË: **30 MINS**

Enchanting ghost town

Drive up a narrow, winding hill over the modern town of Qeparo to reach the enchanting old town of **Upper Qeparo**. As soon as you arrive, you'll feel transported to another era – or at least to a small town in Greece. Qeparo dates back thousands of years, to the time of the Greek Chaonian tribes, and it was inhabited as late as the 19th century before it was abandoned and eventually become a ghost town. Well, it *was* a ghost town. Nowadays, the tiny alleys just wide enough for mules to carry materials around (they still do), the stone walls covered with flowers, and the truly awesome sea views out to Corfu have attracted investors, who've opened B&Bs and restaurants. But don't worry – Upper Qeparo still feels incredibly charming.

Walk around, snap photos and stop for a meal or stay the night. **Te Rrapi në Qeparo** is a friendly, family-run restaurant that makes Albanian specialities like stuffed aubergine, *fasulë* (white bean soup), and fish and meat grilled on the terrace. Or eat at **Ida & Xhorxhi**, another excellent Albanian restaurant with views north to **Ali Pasha Tower** *(Sarajet e Ali Pashës)*.

Built under the Ottoman era's rule, the few high-altitude buildings partly connected to the tower were both a defensive outpost and a summer retreat. To get to the tower, walk 200m along a footpath northeast of the parking lot beside Ida & Xhorxhi. The path weaves past olive groves – Qeparo has long been known as an olive-oil producer.

Dhërmi

FESTIVALS | BEACH CLUBS | OLD TOWN

Move over Ksamil. Dhërmi is becoming the new *it* spot on the Albanian Riviera. Historically linked with Greece as a mountain refuge for Hellenistic tribes for centuries, Dhërmi (Drymades in Greek) has a charming old town with some 30 churches – an astonishing number for its size. Every summer, the action is down on the coast, where the long strip of beaches buzzes with cool bars and hotels, many just constructed within the last few years. Come for one of Dhërmi's electronic music festivals, which attract thousands of revellers to a fun festival alternative on the European summer circuit.

Around Dhërmi, you'll also find a 'secret' beach that many call the Riviera's most stunning, as well as a mountain road that zigzags up to a wooded national park where you can go hiking, or dine on lamb with locals in the company of panoramic views.

☑ **TOP TIP**

If your aim is the beach, be careful not to book accommodation in the old town. It's about 2km between the two, and a steep walk. Disregard this advice if you don't mind taking a taxi or driving.

Dhërmi's Buzzworthy Beaches

Party spots

Dhërmi Beach is well and truly under the tourist trance in summer – expect booked-out accommodation, loud music and half of Tirana sprawled on the stones. Despite this, there is fun to be had, and as the beach is so long, it's possible to find

GETTING AROUND

Dhërmi's main beaches are located about 1.5km down from the highway. If you're taking a bus, ask the driver to stop before the beach turnoff just north of the village. Or walk from the highway trailhead down the well-marked **Mill's Trail** (3km). Gjipe Beach is 4km from the highway or a 20-minute walk from its car park. The road down from the highway is a single lane, so you'll have to pull over to let cars going the other direction pass you by – it's a nightmare in summer. Opt for a taxi to save yourself the headache.

Drivers should prepare themselves mentally for the hairpin turns on the Llogorë Pass (p99) – it's beautiful but treacherous. Thankfully, the road is well maintained.

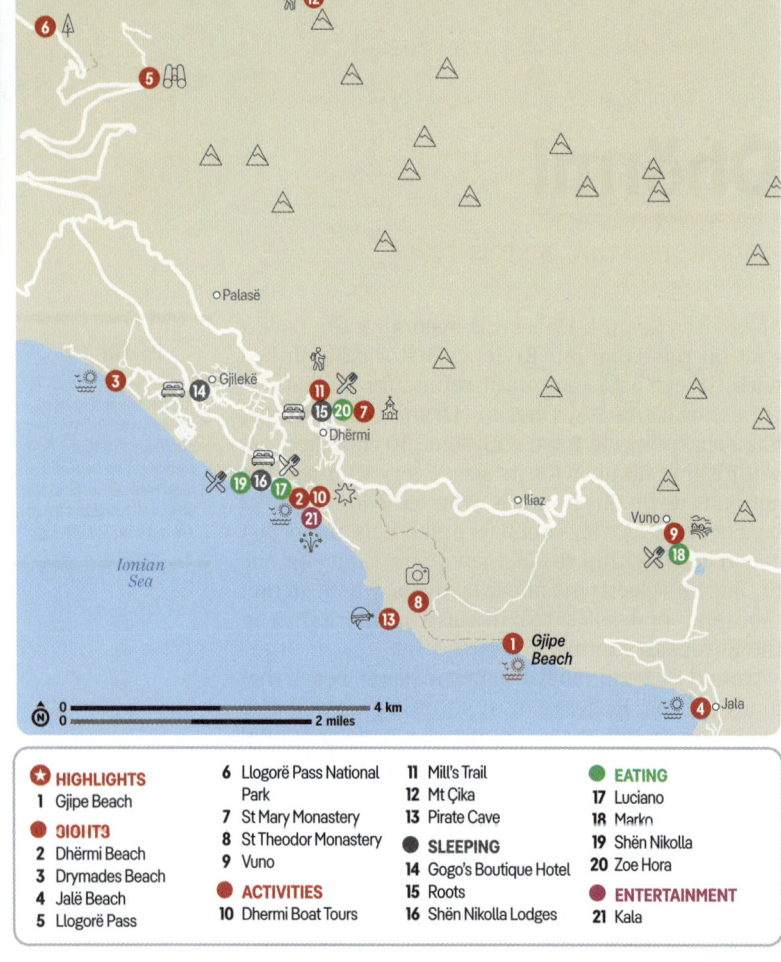

HIGHLIGHTS
1 Gjipe Beach

SIGHTS
2 Dhërmi Beach
3 Drymades Beach
4 Jalë Beach
5 Llogorë Pass
6 Llogorë Pass National Park
7 St Mary Monastery
8 St Theodor Monastery
9 Vuno

ACTIVITIES
10 Dhermi Boat Tours
11 Mill's Trail
12 Mt Çika
13 Pirate Cave

SLEEPING
14 Gogo's Boutique Hotel
15 Roots
16 Shën Nikolla Lodges

EATING
17 Luciano
18 Markn
19 Shën Nikolla
20 Zoe Hora

ENTERTAINMENT
21 Kala

quiet, unspoiled parts to lay down a towel and relax, even in high summer.

The same can be said for even longer **Drymades Beach**, which has been developed more recently with sparkling hotels, resorts and beach bars. Keep an eye out for summer music festivals like Kala that hit the beach throughout the summer.

Albania's Favourite Hidden Beach

Isolated sands

While **Gjipe Beach**, 15 minutes south of Dhërmi, isn't necessarily silent as there are beach umbrellas in summer (though it's refreshingly empty the rest of the year), it's arguably the most stunning of Albania's Ionian beaches. Cradled by cliffs and gracefully free of major development (for now), Gjipe's relative isolation is thanks to the fact that you can't park in front of the beach. To access it, you'll have to walk 20 minutes down an easy trail from the car park (400L). From the car park, you may also visit the 14th-century **St Theodor Monastery** (*Manastiri i Shën Theodhorit*), though it's usually closed to visitors.

Another way to visit Gjipe is via a full-day boat tour with **Dhërmi Boat Tours** (*dhermiboattours.com; 2500L*). The tour leaves at 9am, stopping at a **Pirate Cave** on the way before returning at 3.30pm.

Greece-like Stone Towns
Historic hilltop villages

About 200m above sea level, the old stone town of Dhërmi is worth wandering during your breaks from the beach. Alternatively, spend the night in one of its rustic B&Bs and look out at the sea from your window. Old Dhërmi draws firm links with Greece – it shares a common history and culture, and some locals speak Greek and similar dialects. It also looks a lot like a Greek village, especially the white-washed and blue-door **St Mary Monastery** (*Manastiri i Shen Merise*) at the top of town. The Orthodox church dates to the 16th century and features beautiful wall-to-wall 18th-century frescoes. The village has about 30 more churches, some of them active chapels, others ruins.

About 15 minutes' drive away, **Vuno** is another old stone village worth checking out. It's a quick stop on the way to the 'secret' Gjipe Beach or the resortified Jalë (p93).

Zigzag up a Mountain
Mountain pass and hiking

The peak of any Albanian Riviera road trip is, quite literally, the **Llogorë Pass**. Located 1043m above the coast and accessed via the highway road that zigs and zags at hairpin turns to the top, the views throughout are stunning, and it feels thrilling, akin to climbing up a roller coaster. Of course, you won't drop from the top (please don't), but there is a viewpoint with parking at the top for sweeping views of the Riviera.

Ninety-nine per cent of travellers simply continue driving from here, but the adventurous may choose to stick around the top and explore **Llogorë Pass National Park** – it's

ELECTRONIC MUSIC FESTIVALS

Dhërmi has become Albania's unofficial electronic music festival capital. **Kala** (*kala.al*), which lasts a week and is held on Dhërmi Beach in early June, has asserted itself as a fixture on Europe's summer electronic festival circuit. Tickets are limited to 3000 and go on sale in October.

The following week, **Anjunadeep** (*anjunadeep.com*) is a wellness-focused festival on Dhërmi and Gjipe with electronic music on the beach, 'poolside sessions', massages, yoga, HIIT workouts and six-course Albanian tasting menus.

These festivals can be a lot of fun, but if you want a quieter vacation, avoid Dhërmi altogether during the first two weeks of June, as accommodation prices skyrocket and the town sees thousands more visitors arrive.

EATING IN DHËRMI: OUR PICKS

Luciano: A mainstay on the Dhërmi coastline for two decades, Luciano's serves fresh seafood on a wooden terrace overlooking the sea. *8.30am-11.30pm* €€

Shën Nikolla: Refined beachside restaurant serving breakfast, pizza and fish with minimalist plating. Great location for sunset. *7am-11pm* €€

Zoe Hora: Upscale old-town restaurant with sea views, perfect for a romantic evening. Steak cuts, duck, salmon and pasta. *8am-10.30am, noon-3.30pm, 7-10.30pm* €€€

Marko: On the highway between Dhërmi and Himarë, this restaurant serves grilled meat, including spit-cooked lamb, on its panoramic terrace. *7am-midnight* €€

CAESAR'S SLOG

In the 1st century BCE, political tensions in Rome pitted two former allies, Julius Caesar and Pompey, against each other in a civil war. One of the most pivotal battles of this war took place on the modern Albanian coastline. Bound for Rome, Caesar took his army through Epirus, the Roman name for Albania at the time, and sought to surprise Pompey's forces in Durrës (then called Dyrrhachium) by climbing the Llogorë Pass in winter. But with Caesar's army weary from the mountain slog, he suffered a humiliating defeat.

Yet Caesar didn't stop there. He regrouped, recruited more soldiers and beat Pompey at the larger Battle of Pharsalus in Greece, paving his way to be named *dictator perpetuo* (dictator for life) in 44 BCE.

Mt Çika

free and great to roam through. On the northern (cooler and wetter) side, the park is thick with windswept forest, including black and Bosnian pines, Bulgarian firs, oaks and ash trees. It's a stark difference from the desert-like Dhërmi-facing side.

Inside the national park, which was preserved in 1966 under Enver Hoxha's regime, there are around 100 animal species, including Chamois mountain goats, European wildcats, otters, wolves and golden eagles. Most locals come to enjoy a roast lamb lunch from one of the many roadside restaurants here, but there are also hiking trails. The most obvious one is the 13.2km round-trip to **Mt Çika** (Maja e Çikës; 2045m), but that relatively short distance doesn't mean it's easy. The hike gains nearly 1500m in elevation. The trail starts from the parking area at the pass itself and is vaguely signed. Bring a GPS tracking system if you want to climb the mountain. There are some shorter and much easier signed trails as well, though signage is limited.

Vlorë

INDEPENDENCE TOWN | BOAT TOURS | LAGOON

Vlorë was Albania's first capital when homegrown hero Ismaïl Qemali declared independence from the Ottomans in 1912. In the century that followed, Vlorë was little more than an unattractive port city and an unavoidable stop on the way to the Albanian Riviera's beaches. But this bustling city is on the upswing thanks to increased investment from Tirana and, controversially, abroad.

Since 2014, major renovations have been made to Vlorë's waterfront, streets and tiny historic district, which was painted in attractive pastel colours. The biggest developments were still to come at the time of writing: a new international airport opening in 2025 that hadn't launched its first commercial flights yet, and major resorts planned on Sazan, Albania's biggest island and uninhabited coastland, by a company linked to Donald Trump's son-in-law, Jared Kushner.

In Vlorë, go on a boat trip to see the island and pirate's cove, walk to mosques and monuments, and drink at trendy bars with locals through gritted teeth, in the hope that all this development doesn't have deleterious effects.

Stroll around Town

Adorable historic centre

If you do one thing in Vlorë, stroll its cafe-lined seafront promenade and see if you can spot the difference in the colour of the water where the Ionian and Adriatic seas meet. If you have more time, walk up Blvd Ismaïl Qemali to find a tiny historic centre and some national history monuments. Check out the stone and red-brick **Muradie Mosque** *(Xhamia Muradie)*, built in 1542 by Mimar Sinan – a top architect of the time – and the 12m-tall **Independence Monument**, featuring a statue of a man waving an Albanian flag, with various patriots, including national hero Ismaïl Qemali, at his feet. Qemali

☑ **TOP TIP**

For panoramic views over Vlorë, drive or taxi up to Kaninë Castle (p104) and walk along its long ramparts. Covering more than 30,000 sq metres, the castle was an ancient settlement and a medieval fortress. From the top, you can see as far as the summit of Mt Çika.

GETTING AROUND

New roads in Vlorë have done little to ease traffic congestion, as the city tends to be bumper-to-bumper, with few places to park. A municipal bus (40L) runs frequently along the main thoroughfare, Blvd Ismaïl Qemali, but not at scheduled times. The promenade is an enjoyable stroll, though deceptively long. Take a bike if your accommodation has one. Taxis are everywhere and they're your best bet to get to Nartë Lagoon (p103), unless you join a tour.

VLORË

SIGHTS	8 Nartë Lagoon	16 Albania Fly Tandem	**EATING**
1 Grama Bay	9 New Beach	17 Haxhi Ali Cave	21 Labëria
2 Independence Monument	10 Old Beach	**SLEEPING**	22 Novus
3 Kaninë Castle	11 Radhimë Beach	18 Arial Lofts	23 Vani 2
4 Karaburun Peninsula	12 Sazan Island	19 Bohemian Boutique Suites	**DRINKING & NIGHTLIFE**
5 Kristera Beach	13 St Mary Monastery	20 Vlora Backpackers Hostel	24 Komiteti
6 Muradie Mosque	14 Zvërnec Bridge		25 Saint Tropez
7 Nartë Beach	**ACTIVITIES**		
	15 3 Fiori Boat Trip		

declared Albania's independence here in 1912 and served as prime minister until 1914.

Now continue down cobblestone Rr Justin Godar, Vlorë's tourist-primed historic centre. It might not look as it did during the 15th century when it was a merchant hub during the Ottoman Empire – renovations in 2014 spruced it up with pastel-coloured painting and a strip of bars and boutique hotels – but it is quite charming.

Wild Boat Trips

Ghost island and pirate cove

Visible off Vlorë's shoreline are two wild, windswept destinations well worth visiting on a motorboat trip. Many agencies offer similar boat tours – some actually are the same owners with different names – but an experienced outfit that operates year-round is **3 Fiori Boat Trip** *(vloraboattrips.com; tours €23–59)*. Don't expect a tranquil experience though – drivers usually blast music the whole way (you can ask them not to, but it's actually a lot of fun).

Tours bounce along the waves where the Adriatic and Ionian seas meet due west to **Sazan Island**, Albania's largest. This 5.7-sq-km island was once a submarine and chemical-weapons base used by the Soviet Union during the Cold War. The island maintains an Albanian-Italian military base used to combat narcotics smuggling, but it's otherwise abandoned. That may soon change, as the Albanian government accepted a proposal by the investment firm of Jared Kushner, Donald Trump's son-in-law, to turn it into a resort. For now, boat tours can still take you up close to Sazan Island to see the apartment buildings and bunkers that were abandoned when communism fell; in summer only, the tours dock at the beach and allow visitors to walk around.

Tours also go to the **Karaburun Peninsula**, where you'll battle waves to reach **Haxhi Ali Cave**. According to legend, pirate Haxhi Ali would hide in the cave and pop out to loot incoming ships. It's eerie inside, and the water is an unbelievably bright blue. Tours can also take you snorkelling in a cave and along the peninsula's coastline to beaches and **Grama Bay**, where there are rock inscriptions dating back over 2400 years.

Flock to an Island Monastery

Make a bird-watching pilgrimmage

About 20 minutes' drive northwest of Vlorë is the country's second-largest lagoon, **Nartë Lagoon**. Popular with bird-watchers, the protected area is home to more than 100 bird species, including greater flamingoes and rare Dalmatian pelicans (famously painted by English artist Edward Lear). But the best reason to come here is to cross the 400m winding wooden **Zvërnec Bridge** to a tiny island home to one of Albania's best-preserved churches: **St Mary Monastery** *(Manastiri i Shën Mërisë)*. The church was built in the 14th century and is an excellent example of an Eastern Orthodox prayer site,

ALBANIAN INDEPENDENCE

In the First Balkan War (1912), armies from Serbia, Montenegro, Greece and Bulgaria gave the Ottomans the boot after more than 500 years. But with Balkan armies in Albania (who had sided with the Ottomans), questions arose about what to do with the territory. Albanian independence activist Ismaïl Qemali took action, travelling to Vlorë and uniting Albanian delegates in a congress to declare Albanian statehood. Without much firepower, Albanian statehood certainly wouldn't have been sustained if not for a meeting of the Great Powers weeks later at the London Conference, where Albania's national borders were drawn as part of the Treaty of London. But it wasn't all good news for Albania, who lost territories populated with its ethnic kin, including Kosovo to Serbia (later Yugoslavia), and Chameria and Ioannina to Greece.

LOCAL ADVENTURES

Neart Meminaj, owner of **3 Fiori Boat Trip** *(@boattripvlore)*, shares his favourite trips around his hometown:

Kristera Beach I love relaxing at this great and quiet place with crystal-clear water.

Nartë Lagoon (p103) Book an off-road 4WD tour to Zvërnec Bridge and St Mary Monastery for an unforgettable ride through the forest

Paragliding There are two or three companies, such as **Albania Fly Tandem** *(albaniaflytandem. com)*, that will fly you over the city and the sea.

Brataj Bridge Go by car or guide to this bridge and have a small picnic near the river.

Kaninë Castle You can visit the castle and at the same time you see all of Vlorë like it's in your hand! Sunset time recommended.

St Mary Monastery (p103)

with detailed paintings on its wooden iconostasis, pillared archways and lovely red shingles. The monastery was used as a prison under Enver Hoxha's regime and was renovated in the 1990s. No photos allowed inside.

Spend Time at the Beach

Nearby beaches

If you're itching for a beach and can't make it farther south along the Riviera, Vlorë has some that are several steps from the port. Northwest of the port is **Old Beach** *(Plazhi i Vjeter)*, a 2km strip of fine sand, while southwest is **New Beach** *(Plazi i Ri)*, home to volleyball tournaments every summer. Both might not have the cleanest water, so if you want to go swimming, head farther north to **Nartë Beach** with its deep blue Adriatic water, or south to **Kristera Beach** or **Radhimë Beach** for turquoise Ionian dips.

Radhimë is lined with modern hotels, often with their own private beaches, and is home to **Labëria**, a destination restaurant that's renowned for its roast lamb.

 EATING & DRINKING IN VLORË: OUR PICKS

Vani 2: Local secret tucked off the promenade, with kind service and heaped plates of seafood at fair prices. *noon-10pm* €€

Novus: Taste local favourites like stuffed peppers and moussaka served cafeteria-style, just steps from the port. *noon-9pm Mon-Sat* €€

Komiteti: Tirana's awesome, vibey *raki* bar has a branch in Vlorë's old town, and it's as gorgeous as ever. At the very least, come for the home decor inspiration. *7.30am-midnight* €€

Saint Tropez: This airy seafood restaurant and bar on Vlorë's northern beachfront fills up every summer. Join the cool crowd for sunset sips. *7am-midnight* €€€

Beyond Vlorë

North of Vlorë are a couple of road-trip stops for history lovers and an up-and-coming destination for kitesurfers.

Off the highway north of Vlorë are two fascinating archaeological sites that remain slightly off the beaten track for most travellers. The more famous of the two is Apollonia of Illyria, which first broke ground in 588 BCE and went on to have as many as 70,000 inhabitants. The other, Ardenicë Monastery, is a 13th-century hilltop monastery with an amazing fresco-and-gold-filled interior.

Even more off the radar – though viably a popular future attraction considering the sport's growing popularity – is the kitesurfing school situated on the long, windy and sandy Seman Beach. Consider spending a few days in the bungalows on this less-visited beachfront to learn or master the sport.

Fier

TIME FROM VLORË: **40 MINS**

Apollonia Archaeolgical Park

The evocative ruins of the ancient Greek colony of **Apollonia** (*600L*), set on a windswept hilltop formerly occupied by Illyrians, is among Albania's most important archaeological sites, though much of the city remains buried. Within roughly 4km of defensive walls and an 0.8-sq-km site, you'll find a **Theatre** and the elegant pillars of the restored facade of a 2nd-century-BCE administrative centre known as the **Monument to the Agonothetes**.

Founded by Greeks from Corinth and Corfu in the first half of the 6th century BCE, Apollonia quickly flourished into a powerful city state, minting its own currency and thriving off trade – including of enslaved people – and housing a population of 70,000. Under Roman control from 229 BCE, the city became a noted centre of learning with a renowned school of philosophy. Octavian (later Emperor Augustus) was studying here in 44 BCE when he learned of Julius Caesar's assassination.

Don't miss the **Apollonia Archaeological Museum**, housed inside a Byzantine monastery, which features stone gargoyles outside, and faint frescoes and impressive Roman mosaics inside.

Apollonia is located about 12km west of Fier.

GETTING AROUND

Furgon (shared minibuses) head to the ruins and monastery from Fier – ask locals for the correct bus.

If driving to Apollonia, ignore Google Maps, which, at the time of research, was getting thrown off by a new road, and take the road from Pojan instead.

Water levels can sometimes cover the sandy roads on the way to Seman Beach, making it impassable by car. You may need to park and walk the last 20 minutes or so.

QUEEN TEUTA

One of the most iconic figures in Albanian history is Teuta (231–228 BCE), the pirate queen of Illyria. After her husband King Agron's untimely death, and with his heir too young, Teuta took charge of the kingdom and ruled with an affinity for a particular Illyrian tradition: piracy.

Ticked off that their ships were getting robbed in the Adriatic, Rome sent two envoys to talk to the queen. Insulted, Teuta killed one and seized their ship, setting off a war that led to the Illyrian queen's death (allegedly by throwing herself off a mountain).

For Roman record-keepers, Queen Teuta was an arrogant pirate ruler. But for Albanians, she's a badass female leader who resisted encroaching empires.

Ardenicë Monastery

Be impressed by a remote medieval monastery

Beautiful **Ardenicë Monastery** *(Manastiri i Ardenicës; 100L)*, dating from the 13th century, is rarely visited by self-guided travellers, yet this magnificent little church is mighty fine to look at, both inside and out. Particularly remarkable is the Orthodox monastery's iconostasis of saints and sinners, dragons and angels. Equally impressive is the golden pulpit, which positively heaves with adornments, not to mention the frescoes of the Zografi brothers that can be seen on display upstairs.

The Orthodox monastery is remotely located on a hilltop between the towns of Lushjë and Fier. An attendant will let you in and show you around.

Kitesurfing

Long **Seman Beach** isn't the most popular among Albanian beachgoers for a simple reason – it's windy. But where some avoid windy beaches, kitesurfers' ears perk up. Seman Beach has steady thermal winds that don't exceed 45 knots, shallow water and a sandy beach (a rarity in Albania), making it perfect for both beginners and experienced riders. **Kitesurf Albania** *(@kitesurf_albania; full gear rental/ lesson per hr €120/75)* rents equipment and teaches courses led by the eccentric Artur Sulejmani, who has more than 15 years' experience in the sport. Beach bungalows are available on-site.

Places We Love to Stay

€ Budget €€ Midrange €€€ Top End

Sarandë p81

Central Boutique Hostel € Everything's fresh in this backpacker spot that opened in 2025 – new bathrooms and beds with curtains, and a kitchen that serves a simple breakfast.

Titania Hotel €€ Fairly priced hotel above the boardwalk with modern, sea-facing rooms that feel like a giant goldfish bowl.

Harmony Hotel €€ The minimalist Mediterranean decor and distance from the loud promenade make this hotel a great pick for couples looking for a romantic retreat.

Vila Kalcuni €€€ Watch the boats pass this white mansion, four-star hotel located on a beachy corner close to Sarandë's port.

Ksamil p87

Ksamil Caravan Camping € Save some cash for the beach by parking your van or pitching a tent at this campground. Open year-round.

Sunway €€ Snag a room at this solid roadside hotel that, unlike many in Ksamil, manages to stay fairly priced.

Meta Hotel €€ The closest you'll get to the beach at a midrange price point. The stone-shaped headboard cushions might have you feeling like you've woken up in a comfier version of Butrint.

Arameras Beach Resort €€€ Go all-out at this beach resort on the far side of Ksamil; it has an infinity pool and its own private beach.

Himarë p93

Pine Side Camp € Like a backpacker hostel, but with ready-to-sleep tents that cascade down towards a rocky seafront, where you can cannonball into the sea.

Camping Himara € Set up a tent under the olive trees at this chilled-out camping ground across the main road from Livadhi Beach (p93). Best access to Aquarium Beach (p93) cove.

Vila Kosteli €€ Cliffside apartments run by a friendly couple. Sandwiched between Himarë's two beaches, some rooms have terraces with sun loungers overlooking the sea.

Eléa Guesthouse €€ Escape the coast's hustle at this hilltop retreat. The on-site restaurant is one of the best dining experiences in the area.

Folie Marine €€€ Don't lift a finger at this luxury resort on turquoise Jalë Beach. It comes with its own spa, shops and nightclub.

Dhërmi p98

Roots €€ Charming stone and wooden guesthouse with plenty of character in Old Dhërmi's stone town (about 3km uphill from the beach).

Shën Nikolla Lodges €€ Instead of a cookie-cutter hotel, stay in air-conditioned wooden cabins steps from the beach.

Gogo's Boutique Hotel €€ This one's close to Drymades Beach (p98) and pays homage to Dhërmi's ancestors with its Greece-like white, curved walls. A relaxing retreat.

Vlorë p102

Vlora Backpackers Hostel € Throwback to backpacker days gone by, with a small bar and a caring, English-speaking owner who's more than happy to help.

Arial Lofts € Family-sized rooms with kitchenettes in a quiet area between the city and Nartë Lagoon. Steps from the Old Beach (p104).

Bohemian Boutique Suites €€ Don't let the fact this was the city brothel in the early 20th century deter you; this B&B in the heart of the historic centre has been adorably decorated with boho flare and serves a pleasant breakfast on its back terrace.

Above: the Valbonë to Theth Loop (p120); Right: Mesi Bridge (p119)

Albanian Alps & Northern Albania

NATURE AT ITS PEAK

You didn't come to the Balkans to miss Albania's most Accursed Mountains, did you?

Names don't come much more evocative than the Accursed Mountains (Bjeshkët e Namuna), also known as the Albanian Alps. But the dramatic peaks of northern Albania truly live up to the wonder in their name. Sure, at under 3000m they might not be as tall as the Swiss Alps, but the snow-sprinkled mountain pinnacles, deep green valleys and thick forests northeast of the area's only major city, Shkodër, are nothing to scoff at. Mountain villages here feel graciously stuck in time, where crops are cultivated with sickles, yoghurt and cheese are eaten from chiming cattle and horned sheep, ancient Kanun traditions are commemorated and happy hospitality remains strong, despite the swell of visitors from June through September.

Many come to hike from Valbonë to Theth, a nifty circuit that also includes a three-hour ferry ride. But this popular hike is far from the only hiking option, and if you ask in-the-know locals, it's not even the best. So find your own favourite mountain trail and plunge into a turquoise blue-eye pool near Theth, and leave time to cycle around Shkodër: it's a lovable, colourful city with historic architecture and a carp-filled lake. Around Shkodër, you'll find Albania's most foundational agrotourism spot, Adriatic beaches far quieter than those down south, and an unforgettable drive that snakes up to the country's northern boundary. Just be warned: the north might become your favourite Albanian region.

THE MAIN AREAS

SHKODËR
Colorful, cyclable city and historic sites. **p112**

THETH
Village base for mountain hikes. **p128**

Find Your Way

Massive mountains and few roads make much of the Albanian Alps inaccessible to heavy traffic – and that's for the better. Let locals take you over paved roads, and go on a boat trip along Lake Koman.

Shkodër, p112
The ancient Illyrian city has attractive streets both walkable and cyclable, plus plenty of historic sites, tasty restaurants and quality accommodation.

Theth, p128
Spend a day or two hiking here for that real Alps feel, with stone and wooden buildings lining a riverbank surrounded by huge mountains.

FURGON
Let the experts do the driving by hopping on a local *furgon* (shared minibus). Ask your accommodation to book private transfers, or go to the bus stop and wait for a public *furgon* to arrive (there's no fixed schedule).

CAR
Your own vehicle is best for a quick trip to Theth – you'll be able to leave whenever you want rather than wait for the twice daily buses. A car is also necessary for road trips north.

Rozafa Fortress (p115)

Plan Your Time

Most travellers come north to hike in the Albanian Alps, particularly the Valbonë to Theth loop, which involves taking the Koman Ferry. But there's plenty more to explore if you have time.

Two Days in the North

● Wander **Shkodër** (p112). Visit the **Marubi National Photography Museum** (p112) and the **Site of Witness & Memory Museum** (p115), a former communist prison. Then rent a bike and cycle to **Rozafa Fortress** (p115) and back. Dine on carp at **Aleksi** (p114).

● Bus to Theth for some Albanian Alps, with a hike to **Grunas Waterfall** (p128) and the **Blue Eye Kaprre** (p128).

Long Weekend in the Alps

● After your first day in **Shkodër** (p112), do the **Valbonë to Theth Loop** (p120). A 6.30am *furgon* will take you to Koman for the three-hour ferry to Fierzë, then another minibus will take you to Valbonë for the night. Rise early to hike the 1795m **Valbonë Pass** (p121) to Theth. On your last day, hike to **Grunas Waterfall** (p128) and the **Blue Eye Kaprre** (p128) before taking the 5pm *furgon* back to Shkodër.

SEASONAL HIGHLIGHTS

SPRING
The Albanian Alps can have snow as late as June, so be sure to check conditions and consult a local guide if planning to hike.

SUMMER
Peak season for hiking. Consider Valbonë (p121) or Theth (p128) – the Blue Eye (p128) is refreshing this time of year.

AUTUMN
With warm temperatures and fewer crowds, this is a terrific time to hike, and to visit Albania in general. Some guesthouses will be closed.

WINTER
The road to Theth shuts when there's heavy snow, and hiking can be very dangerous. Stick to Shkodër.

Shkodër

CYCLING | PHOTOGRAPHY | GRILLED CARP

☑ TOP TIP

Plan for at least two nights if you're hiking in the Albanian Alps, including the ever-popular **Valbonë to Theth Loop** (p120), where you'll spend one night in Valbonë after taking the Lake Koman Ferry and another in Theth. Allow more days for a blissful escape from society, and a couple more to explore Shkodër.

Dating back to Illyrian times, Shkodër (Shkodra) is one of the oldest cities in Europe. It's a lively spot, enriched by its students and bike culture – you'll be hard-pressed to find another city in Eastern Europe with this many locals whizzing around on two wheels. Its colourful architecture is reminiscent of Italy, though don't mistake it for elsewhere: this is a proud Albanian city. It was harshly repressed due to its critical-thinking intelligentsia during Enver Hoxha's reign, and it sparked the country's first pro-democracy protests in 1990.

Located about 100km from Tirana and close to the Montenegro border, many travellers rush through Shkodër en route to the Albanian Alps, but it's worth spending a couple of nights soaking up this pleasant and welcoming city. Check out the interesting photography and communist-era prison museums, and rent a bike to see an ancient hilltop fortress or stand-up paddleboard through a carp-filled lake that's the biggest in the Balkans.

Albania's History in Photographs

Treasured Marubi photo gallery

In the heart of Shkodër, on its pedestrianised Rr Kolë Idromeno, is a photo gallery vital to understanding Albania's history and culture. The **Marubi National Photography Museum** *(Muzeu Kombëtari i Fotografise Marubi; marubi.gov.al; 700L)*

 GETTING AROUND

The best way to get around Shkodër is on foot, especially along and around the main tourist road, Rr Kolë Idromeno. There's plenty of art, interesting architecture, and lots of cafes and bars to look at. Otherwise, get around like a local on a bicycle. Most accommodations rent them, and there are plenty of small shops around town that rent them out, including **Shkodra Rent Bikes** *(@shkodrarentbikes; per day 400–600L)*. Official taxis and public buses (40L), many of which stop at Democracy Sq (p116), can take you to the lake or the castle.

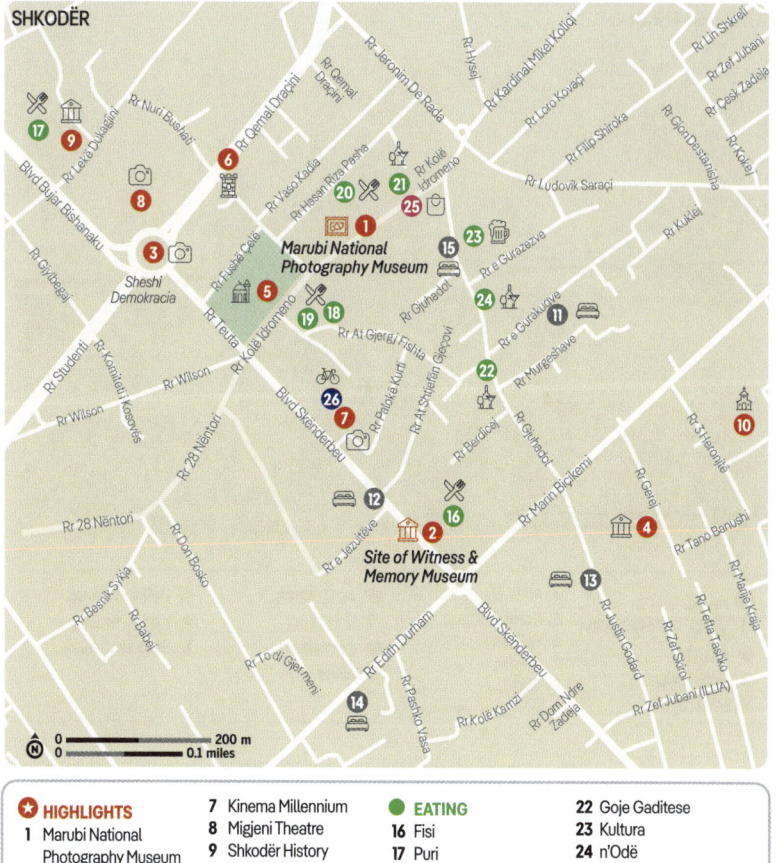

SHKODËR

HIGHLIGHTS
1. Marubi National Photography Museum
2. Site of Witness & Memory Museum

SIGHTS
3. Democracy Square
4. Diocese Museum
5. Ebu Bekr Mosque
6. Englishman's Clocktower
7. Kinema Millennium
8. Migjeni Theatre
9. Shkodër History Museum
10. St Stephen Cathedral

SLEEPING
11. InTown
12. Mi Casa Es Tu Casa
13. Rose Garden Hotel
14. Tradita Hotel
15. Wanderers Hostel

EATING
16. Fisi
17. Puri
18. Stolia Coffeehouse
see 14 Tradita Hotel
19. Traditional Food
20. Vila Bekteshi

DRINKING & NIGHTLIFE
21. Bam

22. Goje Gaditese
23. Kultura
24. n'Odë

SHOPPING
25. Margjelo Filigran Jewelry

TRANSPORT
26. Shkodra Rent Bikes

celebrates the work of Pietro Marubi (1832–1903) and his heirs, who documented Albanian life in the late 19th and early 20th centuries.

Born in Italy, Marubi travelled to Albania and decided to settle in Shkodër, where he opened the country's first photo studio in 1856. Marubi documented life across the country as a foreign correspondent for French, Italian and British magazines, collecting 40,000 glass-plate negatives, which are held at the museum. He passed his knowledge to an heir, Kel Kodheli (1870–1940), who took the Marubi name and carried on his photography tradition, capturing

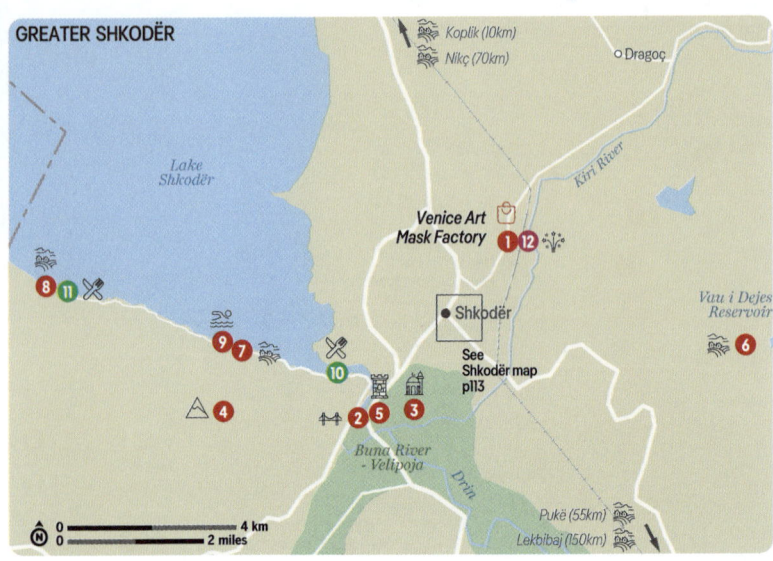

GREATER SHKODËR

HIGHLIGHTS
1. Venice Art Mask Factory

SIGHTS
2. Buna Bridge
3. Lead Mosque
4. Mt Tarabosh
5. Rozafa Fortress
6. Rragam
7. Shiroka
8. Zogaj

ACTIVITIES
9. Drini Times

EATING
10. Aleksi

11. Pelikani Kaçurrel

ENTERTAINMENT
12. Shkodër Carnival

---

images that displayed the country's rich cultural heritage, particularly in the north.

The museum's 1st floor is a temporary exhibit. Upstairs in the permanent exhibit is a geometric exhibition of the Marubis' work, including Kel's son, Gege. Look out for the first-ever photographs taken in Albania in 1858, as well as fascinating portraits, and an interesting exhibit of vintage camera equipment displayed inside a makeshift darkroom.

EATING IN SHKODËR: OUR PICKS

MAP P113 & P114

Traditional Food: It won't win any design awards, but this spot does delicious Albanian food, including *qofte* (meatballs) and stuffed peppers at rock-bottom prices. *7am-11pm €*

Stolia Coffeehouse: Western-style brunch – delicious smoothie bowls, stuffed croissants and avocado toast with ice coffees. *7am-7pm Mon-Fri, to 4pm Sat & Sun €*

Puri: Come try their 'Father's Rice', a well-spiced meat patty, *goulash* (meat stew) and *fasulë* (white bean soup). *6.30am-11pm €*

Fisi: Hearty portions and fair prices for mixed grilled meat as well as friendly service. A Shkodër classic. *11am-10.30pm €€*

Vila Bekteshi: All white tablecloths, potted flowers and timber floors, along with tasty pasta, pizza, and grilled surf'n'turf. *8am-11pm €€*

Aleksi: Slice into a fresh carp steak while overlooking its former home, Lake Shkodër. *10am-10pm €€*

Pelikani Kaçurrel: Make this your cycling destination: a lovely fish restaurant and beach on Lake Shkodër. *8am-11.30pm €€*

Tradita Hotel: Delivering one of the city's finest restaurant experiences, this painstakingly restored 17th-century mansion once belonged to a famous local writer. *€€*

Enter a Communist Prison Cell
Shkodër's fascinating history museums

During the communist period, the **Site of Witness & Memory Museum** *(Vendi i Dëshmisë dhe Kujtesës; 200L)*, which started life as a Franciscan seminary, was officially used as the Shkodër headquarters of the Ministry of Internal Affairs. What does that actually mean? It was an interrogation centre and prison for political detainees. Over the years, thousands of people spent time in the prison – some never to re-emerge. The museum is a chilling memory of the horrors that took place here.

Inside, there are walls of photos of the victims who died here, and testimonies from survivors. Walk through the museum's red-painted tunnel and inside the prison cells used to hold political detainees. There are also signs discussing Shkodër's role in overthrowing communism when it became the site of student protests in January 1990.

Another museum to visit to understand this city's past is the **Shkodër History Museum** *(Muzeu Historik i Shkodrës; 200L)*. Housed in a gorgeous 200-year-old Ottoman-era residence, the museum has a collection of archaeological discoveries dating back to the Neolithic period on the 1st floor, and an ethnographic museum upstairs with traditional Albanian costumes from the north, including a UNESCO-recognised *xhubleta* (long woollen dresses often adorned with metals that chime with movement).

Finally, the **Diocese Museum** *(100L)*, located behind the beautiful St Stephen Cathedral (p117), is a small non-profit dedicated to the north's proud Roman Catholic tradition. The museum collection includes paintings, sacred art, vestments and liturgical objects.

Sweeping Fortress Views
Climb up to Rozafa Fortress

With spectacular views over the city and lake, **Rozafa Fortress** *(400L)* is the most impressive sight in Shkodër. The main reason to visit is for its sweeping views over Shkodër's waterways and brightly painted homes, though it's also peaceful to walk within the fortress walls.

Founded in the 4th century BCE – during Illyrian times – and rebuilt much later by the Venetians and then the Turks, the 36,000-sq-metre fortress takes its name from a woman who was allegedly walled into the ramparts as an offering to the gods so that the construction would stand, as a curse allegedly caused the walls to fall down every night. The story goes that Rozafa, the unfortunate woman chosen to be walled-up in the fortress for good luck, asked that two holes (one for her arm, the other for her breast) be left in the stonework so that she could continue to breastfeed her baby.

The fortress also has a small, rather disappointing museum, with some artefacts, old weapons, a large model of the entire fortress and northern Albania's only 3rd or 4th-century mosaic.

Close to Rozafa, see Shkodër's more than 250-year-old **Lead Mosque** *(Xhamia e Plumbit)*, which reopened in 2025

THE FALL OF COMMUNISM

As word spread across Lake Shkodër that the Berlin Wall had fallen, a few hundred people, mostly students, took to the streets to topple the bust of Joseph Stalin in Shkodër. The January 1990 protests, about five years after the death of Enver Hoxha, quickly spread to Tirana and across Albania, and the country voted in favour of a parliamentary democracy in national elections in March 1992. But the transition was not smooth. Finally free to leave, Albanians fled to neighbouring countries and across Europe, even swimming to Corfu and hijacking a ship. Organised crime families filled the power vacuum and a pyramid scheme in 1996–97 emptied Albanians' savings, leading to violent protests. (To read more about the pyramid scheme crisis, head to p83.) Albanian politics has calmed down since then as the country vies for European Union membership.

CYCLE TO LAKE SHKODËR

Do as the Shkodrans do and cycle along the biggest lake in the Balkans.

START	END	LENGTH
Democracy Sq	Zogaj	17km; 2 hours

With an estimated 30% of Shkodrans cycling regularly, it's time to join in with the locals. Many guesthouses rent bikes for around 500L per day, and several shops around town do as well. Scooters and electric bikes are also often available.

Start in ❶ **Democracy Square** *(Sheshi Demokracia)*, Shkodër's central roundabout, and check out its Soviet-style Migjeni Theatre and Englishman's Clocktower. Then join the popular cycling route south from the square to ❷ **Rozafa Fortress** (p115) which dates back 2400 years – to Illyrian times. You'll probably have to walk your bike to the top of the hill to reach the fortress (don't forget to lock it).

Cycle back down to the Buna riverfront and cross the pedestrian ❸ **Buna Bridge**, an Ottoman construction from the late 15th century. Now cycle along the road that lines Lake Shkodër, looking out for birds before you get to the town of ❹ **Shiroka**, which has several restaurants and hotels.

The paved, slightly hilly road continues along the lake, with many restaurants along the way serving grilled carp, a Lake Shkodër catch. The town of ❺ **Zogaj** is a good target for your ride, as it has the excellent seafood restaurant Pelikani Kaçurrel (p114), which even has its own little beach if you want to take a dip.

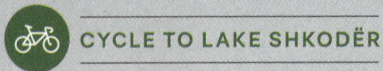

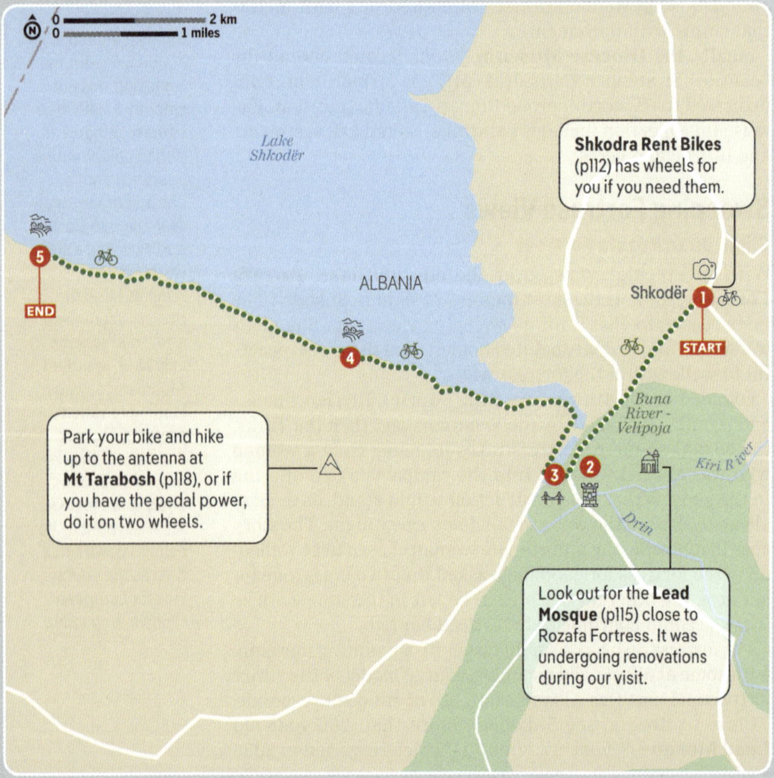

Shkodra Rent Bikes (p112) has wheels for you if you need them.

Park your bike and hike up to the antenna at **Mt Tarabosh** (p118), or if you have the pedal power, do it on two wheels.

Look out for the **Lead Mosque** (p115) close to Rozafa Fortress. It was undergoing renovations during our visit.

after it was damaged by flooding. The 18th-century mosque was also the first in Albania to reopen after the fall of the dictatorship.

Historic Buildings

From religious sites to Soviet-era theatres

There are two religious sites of historical note in Shkodër, of different denominations: **Ebu Bekr Mosque** in the city centre actually dates from the 18th century but was fully renovated and refaced in 1995 with donations from Saudi Arabia, and Mother Teresa came to **St Stephen Cathedral** in 1991 to reopen this beautiful church after it was turned into a sports hall during Albania's communist era.

Turning to more recent history, **Kinema Millennium** is a bold, Soviet-era cinema still active today, and **Migjeni Theatre** is another interesting communist-era building that still holds performing arts shows.

And then there's **Englishman's Clocktower**, the former residence of English nobleman Lord Alfred Paget while he was trying to convert Shkodër's residents in the late 19th century; it remains an interesting, odd city feature.

Shop for Silver & Carnaval Masks

Proud artistic traditions

Fun fact: the mask worn by Tom Cruise in *Eyes Wide Shut* (1999) – you know, the one where the clueless doctor argues with a high Nicole Kidman and goes to a bougie cult sex party – was made by Albanian artist Edmond Angoni, founder of **Venice Art Mask Factory** *(veniceartmask.eu)* in Shkodër. Located 1.5km from the city centre, the factory opened in 1996 and is the leading producer of the papier-mâché masks used at Venice's Carnival. Each mask takes at least five days to make, some as long as three weeks, with each design passing through several ladies for acrylic painting, feathers and more decorations. The masks are wild and wonderful, and they make for great souvenirs even if you don't have any carnivals or cult parties coming up.

Take your pick from hundreds in the shop – prices start at €25 and go up to €3500 for more elaborate pieces. If you're there between Monday and Friday, pay €3 for a 20-minute tour of the factory to see the experts at work. For an extra €30, the ladies can show you how to make your own mask (reserve ahead).

GREATER ALBANIA

Despite the border, Albania and Kosovo share one culture and one ethnicity. They were separated by lines drawn by Western powers at the 1913 Treaty of London. Thus, since the fall of communism in both countries, many have called for joining under one red and black flag as Greater Albania. The proposal would be particularly advantageous for Kosovo, which could use both the coastline and the military help (due to persistent threats from Serbia).

But talk of a Greater Albania has died down recently as both countries aim to join the European Union, which would effectively eliminate the border. It's also clear that while being ethnically related, varying 20th-century rule has changed the two culturally, with Albanians left more traumatised under Hoxha than Kosovars under Tito.

DRINKING IN SHKODËR: OUR PICKS ──────MAP P113

n'Odë: A bohemian spot that gets everyone singing on Saturday nights when a live band plays smack in the centre. *7am-11pm*

Kultura: This pub comes to life at night when it turns into a loud club. It's quieter, and fun to people-watch, when seated on the street tables. *7am-midnight*

Goje Gaditese: Have a cocktail at this trendy bar and restaurant, mostly frequented by those in their late 20s and 30s. They usually have DJs at weekends. *7am-11.30pm*

Bam: Sip an espresso, smoke some hookah or have a cocktail at this lounge on Shkodër's main pedestrian street. *7am-11pm*

AVOID THE CROWDS

Alma Bazhdari Naraci, owner of Shkodër's first hostel, **Mi Casa Es Tu Casa** (@shkodra backpackershostel), shares her favourite quiet escapes.

Pukë In summer, it's 40°C in parts of Albania, but if you go to this small, not busy mountain village, you'll feel refreshed.

Koplik Why do people go to France? Every June, the land north of Shkodër, outside Koplik, is filled with lavender, a spiritual plant that brings you calm.

Nikç Go to this village in the mountains, and you'll enter a world without modernity.

Rragam A village near an artificial lake that's quiet, without any construction around.

Lekbibaj Take a small boat, follow the Albanians, and you're in a wild hiking region that feels like another world.

Venice Art Mask Factory (p117)

But you don't need to head to Italy or Hollywood to see Venice Art masks in action. Every February or March, **Shkodër Carnival** celebrates the last days before Lent (when Catholics give up something pleasurable for 40 days), and it's complete with elaborate costumes and street parades. It's great fun, though it can be chilly at that time of year.

Another place to do some shopping is at **Margjelo Filigran Jewelry** on Shkodër's main pedestrian street. The small shop carries on the long tradition of silver thread filigran jewellery, which dates back to Mesopotamian times (3000 BCE). Filigran, or filigree, remains a speciality among just a few artisans in Shkodër. Prizren in Kosovo is also known for its filigree if you go that way.

Paddle the Lake

Great city to be active

Lake Shkodër is the biggest lake in the Balkans, and it's filled with plenty of life, including some 200 bird species, such as Dalmatian pelicans and whiskered terns. Get out on the lake to see them on a stand-up-paddleboard trip with **Drini Times** (*drinitimes.al; self-guided per hr €10, guided from €40*). Guided tours can take you around the lake and/or down the Buna River, or you can rent your own board. A full-day tour involves 19km of paddling, with the possibility of being pulled by boat if you get too tired. You can also inquire about kayaking trips.

If you aren't into getting wet, the best views of the lake, along with the Alps, the city and even the Adriatic, are from the top of **Mt Tarabosh** (593m). Hike or mountain bike up to the antenna at the summit via the 4WD Rr Kazenës – it takes about six hours on foot.

Beyond Shkodër

Bathe in the shadow of towering peaks, a hidden turquoise river and the sparkling Adriatic Sea.

Make Shkodër your base for adventure, with action-packed activities in every direction. Of course, the gargantuan, snow-streaked Albanian Alps are a must. They're most commonly tackled via a three-day circuit that includes a hike over the 1795m Valbonë Pass and a riverboat trip to a hidden turquoise beach that will make you feel like you've arrived in Thailand.

But there's plenty more, including Albania's longest Ottoman bridge, its most influential agrotourism outfit and Adriatic beaches with deep blue water and bird-filled wetlands. If you have your own wheels – preferably a motorcycle – road trip north to see one of the few remaining off-the-beaten-track stretches of land in this enchanting country, where a zigzagging motorway will take you to turquoise pools and waterfalls.

Places
Boks p119
Fishtë p119
Lezhë p122
Shëngjin p123
Lumi i Shales p126

Boks
TIME FROM SHKODËR: **20 MINS**

Longest Ottoman bridge

If you only have time for a quick trip from Shkodër, **Mesi Bridge** (*Ura e Mesit*) is one of the most beautiful Ottoman bridges in Albania, and the longest, at 108m. Built in 1768 under the command of Mehmet Pashë Bushati, it spans the Kir River and is replete with 13 stone arches, the central one being 14m high. The bridge has been retired from use – a new bridge now crosses the river, but you can still admire it from the town of Boks. Get here by bike or via the hourly minibus from the **Rus Bus Stop** in Shkodër.

Fishtë
TIME FROM SHKODËR: **45 MINS**

Farm-to-table feast

Before chef Altin Prenga opened **Mrizi i Zanave** (*mrizizanave.al*) in his hometown in 2010, you would have been hard-pressed to find traditional Albanian cuisine served in the country's restaurants. After the fall of communism, Albanians were more hungry for foreign cuisine and not so interested in what was made in their own kitchens: foreign food had been kept from them during the dictatorship, and they were forbidden

continues on p122

GETTING AROUND

The northern mountain roads can be rough, windy and covered in snow or black ice as late as June, so take public or private minibuses from Shkodër whenever possible. The two exceptions to this rule are the northern Albania road trip (p124) and agrotourism destination Mrizi i Zanave, where organised transport is neither simple nor useful.

HIKING TOUR

Hike the Valbonë to Theth Loop

Many come to the Albanian Alps for the spectacular 14km hike from Valbonë to Theth that traverses the 1795m Valbonë Pass. A section of the Peaks of the Balkans Trail (p123), it takes between five and seven hours, depending on where in either village you start or end. The rest of your time will be spent winding through mountains in a *furgon* (shared minibus), floating on a Drin River ferry boat, and relaxing in alpine tranquility.

1 Shkodër

Ditch the car (if you have one) and let the experts do the driving as you hop on a *furgon* for the trip from **Shkodër** *(€8, 1½ hours)* to the Koman Ferry Terminal. The drive is a narrow, winding mountain road with dramatic scenery along the way. Guesthouses in Shkodër can book your minibus and ferry tickets (€10), or book them yourself via the ferry website *(komanilakeferry.com)*.

The drive: The *furgon* will pick you up at 6.30am and arrive at Koman Ferry Terminal at 8am, with an hour to relax and have a snack before the 9am ferry.

2 Koman Ferry Terminal

From the **Koman Ferry Terminal**, hop on the Lake Koman Ferry. The trip from the artificial reservoir of Lake Koman to Fierzë is a fun, sociable affair, with many buying beers on board and sharing snacks. But don't get too caught up in the fun – the scenery along the Drin River is simply spectacular. Reserve ahead, as spots fill up. Arrange a smaller boat if you plan to stop along the way or want to visit Lumi i Shales (p126).

The cruise: It's a three-hour ride to Fierzë. The ferry trip only operates from 15 April to 5 November.

Grunas Waterfall (p128)

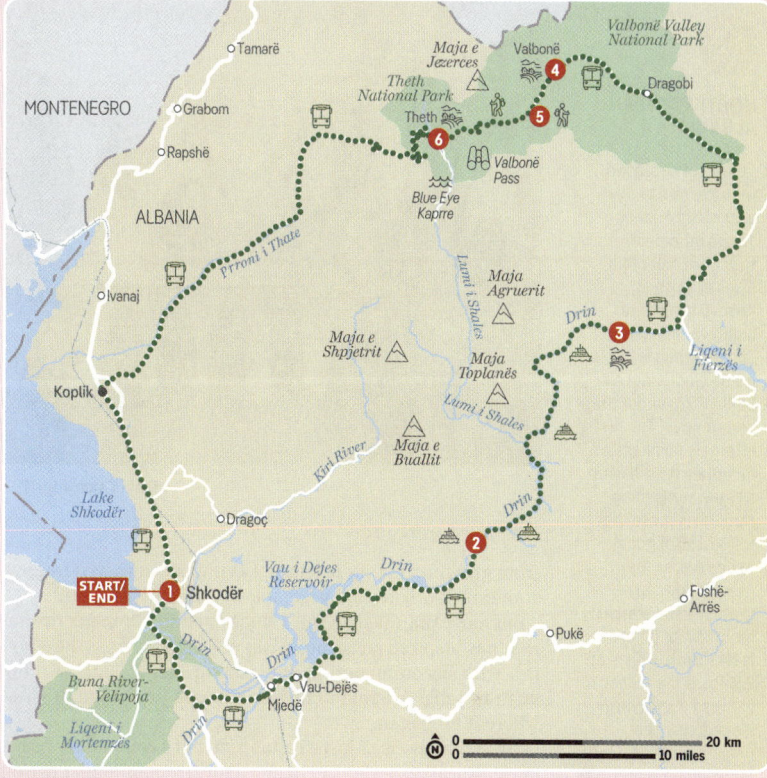

3 Fierzë

Get off the Lake Koman Ferry at **Fierzë**. Then, catch a *furgon* to Valbonë (€8).

The drive: It takes about an hour to reach Valbonë.

4 Valbonë

Valbonë isn't much but a long strip of guesthouses, many owned by the Selimaj family. When you arrive from Fierzë at 1pm, you'll have plenty of time and little to do but hang out at the guesthouse until you wake the next morning for your hike. Local **Erenik Selimaj** *(067 323 0951)* can advise and connect you with professional guides for alternative hikes to surrounding peaks and villages.

The hike: The trailhead is at the end of the road in Valbonë. Get a lift from your guesthouse to the trailhead to avoid the monotonous walk over a dry, stoney riverbed.

5 Valbonë Trailhead

The main event, the 14.7km hike from Valbonë to Theth over the **Valbonë Pass** (1795m), is marked with red and white signs. The trail is mostly underneath the beaming sun, but you'll be rewarded with spectacular views from atop Mt Valbonë, 7.5km from the village.

The hike: The hike down to Theth is steep, with a lot of loose dirt, but it's mostly under the shade of old-growth forest. In autumn – a quieter and cooler time to hike – these trees are ablaze in reds and oranges.

6 Theth

The hike ends slightly north of the traditional village of Theth (p128). Walk from the trail to the village, which has become a hub of the Albanian Alps, with guesthouses lining the river. See its famous Grunas Waterfall (p128) and Blue Eye Kaprre (p128) before taking the *furgon* back to Shkodër (€12). The *furgon* from Theth takes 2½ hours and departs twice daily at 11am and 5pm.

Mrizi i Zanave (p119)

NORTHEASTERN ALBANIA

There's little reason for travellers to drive east of Shkodër or Tiranë other than to access mountain hikes or to go to Kosovo (which we highly recommend!). The main hub is Kukës, a small industrial city built in 1976 under the dictatorship. The rest is largely uninhabited mountain terrain with a highway slashing through (stick to the tolled E851 if going to Kosovo, as the other roads can be sketchy). The starkest mountain of them all is **Mt Korab**, which, at 2764m, is the tallest in Albania and North Macedonia. The marked route up it is between 19km and 24km, with no special technical portions requiring extra gear. You'll likely need a couple of days to do it.

continued from p119

from growing quality produce, having been ordered to grow standardised fruit and vegetables for quantity instead.

But more than two decades since opening, Prenga's restaurant has inspired an agrotourism movement across the country, with accommodation and restaurants proudly serving farm-to-table Albanian cuisine. You can (and should) go to where it all began.

Mrizi i Zanave isn't just a restaurant, but a community-based agricultural powerhouse. Inside a former communist prison (don't worry, it's all nice and clean now), it produces tempting cheeses with cow's and goat's milk brought from 90 nearby family farmers. Below the prison are the cellars where Mrizi i Zanave makes six types of wine and *raki* (fruit brandy) using Albanian shesh and kallmet grapes. Outside are the vineyards and fields lined with rows of cabbage, pumpkins, potatoes and garlic – ask for a free tour.

But this restaurant isn't just for looking at. Come for a full-on feast at breakfast (8am to 10am), lunch (noon to 4pm) or dinner (6 to 10pm). Portions are beyond generous, featuring about a dozen cheeses, piles of pickled vegetables, and plate after plate of delicious (and traditional) meat or vegetarian dishes, all paired with wine, and all for between €20 and €30. *Je bëftë mirë!* (Bon appétit!)

Lezhë

TIME FROM SHKODËR: **45 MINS**

Hero monument

Gjergj Kastrioti (1405–68), aka Skanderbeg, the Albanian national hero who heroically united local tribes and fended off the Ottomans for 25 years, died in the small, windy northern city of

VALBONË TO THETH LOOP

You can hike over the **Valbonë Pass** (p121) from either Valbonë or Theth. The majority go from Valbonë, as this knocks out the hotter, more gradual part first and is more frequently offered by tour operators. From Theth, it's steeper but shadier.

Lezhë in 1468. This is also where he united Albanian and Montenegrin princes to form the League of Lezhë, with himself, the bearded general, as its fearless leader.

Skanderbeg converted from Islam to Roman Catholicism as part of his defiance, and the Christian mausoleum where he was buried in 1468 sadly looks a far cry from what it once did. At the time, it was a cathedral, which was destroyed almost immediately by the Ottomans and converted into a mosque. Later, it became a Bektashi *teqe* (shrine), which was destroyed in 1967 by Enver Hoxha's secular regime and turned into a stone monument with a glass roof. Nowadays, the hero's remains are housed beneath the **Skanderbeg Memorial** *(Vendvarrimi i Skënderbeut; 200L)*, where there's a bronze bust of the rebel, a mosaic depicting the Albanian eagle and copies of the weapons he used (the originals are in Vienna).

Lezhë's castle

While you're in town, drive up to **Lezhë Castle** *(Kalaja e Lezhës; 300L)*, which was first built in the 4th century BCE and subsequently used by various empires, including the Greeks, Mesopotamians, Illyrians and Byzantines. At 186m above the city, the castle has commanding views, though the ramparts are in rough shape.

Shëngjin

TIME FROM SHKODËR: 1 HR

Adriatic beaches

Shëngjin Beach, the strip of beach as Albania curves north, has long been a popular summer retreat for Tirana residents, as it's just an hour from the city. Its well-aged resorts and hotels are a far cry from the Ionian hubs in the south, and the water isn't nearly as clear or turquoise – up here in the Adriatic, it's a heavy, deep blue. But there's always a refreshing breeze, and Shëngjin has all the amenities for a pleasant day at the seaside, including restaurants, umbrellas and lounge chairs. While in the area, make a reservation to try **Rapsodia** *(@rapsodia_restorant)*, one of Albania's top destination restaurants, with Chef Alfred Marku making a name for himself with his contemporary, seafood-focused small plates.

Northwest of Shëngjin's main development, the wind blows the sand northwards, causing the dunes to pile up on the mountainside, a phenomenon called **Rana e Hedhun** (Thrown Sand). The resulting sandy beach is becoming a popular spot for vanlifers and those looking for a wilder beach strip. Park your vehicle if you've got one, then park yourself at **Bar Ledh** *(@bar_ledh)* for a drink or some fresh catch.

A straight-shot south of Shkodër is another strip of sand on the Adriatic that doesn't see nearly the amount of foot traffic as down south. At **Velipojë Beach**, there's plenty of space to spread out, and a wide range of hotels. Much

PEAKS OF THE BALKANS TRAIL

The hike between Valbonë and Theth (p120) is part of the recently developed **Peaks of the Balkans Trail**, a 192km transnational loop trek that spans Albania, Montenegro and Kosovo. The hype-worthy trek has 10 stages and can be done in sections. It takes between seven and 12 days to do the loop, depending on your fitness and how much you plan to stop, and it's considered moderately difficult.

Several companies offer tours, or you may do it self-guided, but just make sure you receive border permits to travel between the three countries before you set off.

Visit *peaksofthebalkans.info* for more info, as well as maps and options for local guides.

SKANDERBEG'S IMPACT

Learn more about Skanderbeg and his influence on Albania in our **Skanderbeg essay** (p198).

continues on p126

DRIVING TOUR

Northern Albania Road Trip

For many, Shkodër and Theth are as far north as Albania goes, but don't just stop there. Farther north is perfect road-trip territory, particularly beloved by motorcyclists who adore its well-maintained highway that zigzags at impossible angles up several mountains. Equally enticing are the area's turquoise natural pools, waterfalls and hikes, which make for a driving day you won't forget. Vermosh, Tamarë and Lepushë have hotels if you'd like to stay the night.

1 Keq Marku Tattoo Art Studio

From **Shkodër**, drive north on SH1/E762, past the town of Koplik for 21.5km, to reach the unique roadside **Keq Marku Tattoo Art Studio** *(@keqmarkuart)*. Albania is filled with more than 170,000 bunkers built during Enver Hoxha's paranoid dictatorship, but as far as we know, this is the only one that does tattoos. The artist escaped Albania on foot in his youth, spent 13 years in prison and has been doing tattoos for more than two decades. Reserve ahead to get tatted.

The drive: Turn left off the highway before the town of Ivanaj to get to Syri i Sheganit. The country road is shoddy but should be fine for all vehicles.

2 Syri i Sheganit

Before you reach the village of Kosan, turn left off the highway onto Rr Nrece. Make another left on the main road, Rr Gashaj, and finally another left on a shoddy dirt road to end up at the striking **Syri i Sheganit**, a little-known blue-eye spring with turquoise water that pours out of a 30m-deep karstic

Syri i Sheganit

chimney. Around the corner, have a coffee at **Bar Restorant Syri i Sheganit** and spot Dalmatian pelicans from the terrace.

The drive: You'll cross two serpentine roads that slither up the mountainside. Take it easy, as black ice is common.

3 Tamarë

Surrounded by imposing mountains, **Tamarë** is an idyllic place to stop for lunch. The town has a few quality restaurants, including **Sofra e Kelmendit**. On your way to Tamarë, look out for the **Kryqi i Krishtit** cross carved into the mountain above Brigjë, and stop for photos at **Rrapsh Viewpoint**, ahead of Grabom.

The drive: Selcë Cemetery, which leads to Tarraca e Gërçes, comes up quickly at the bend, so don't miss it. It's right after the schoolhouse.

4 Tarraca e Gërçes

Pull off the road at **Selcë Cemetery** and park. The attraction here isn't the cemetery but the series of turquoise natural springs up the hill. Follow the red and white markers up the rocks for a few minutes to see **Tarraca e Gërçes**. Hiking farther will take you to a waterfall, **Ujëvara e Selcës**.

The drive: Be especially careful on the roads up here. Again, black ice is likely.

5 Vermosh

This northern stretch is the highest altitude of the road trip. It's cold and will most likely be snowy if you go outside of summer. Many come up here for the jaw-dropping hike from **Lëpushë** over **Mt Vajushë** (2057m) and into Montenegro. (Getting to Lëpushë involves detouring onto a road that's less maintained.) But if you continue on the highway, you'll reach **Vermosh**, a verdant valley along a river with waterfalls and a canyon within walking distance. There are hotels here if you'd like to stay the night before returning to Shkodër the next day.

LAKE KOMAN

Lake Koman isn't really a lake at all, or at least not a natural one. It's actually a reservoir that stretches for 34km, created as a result of the damming of the Drin River in the 1970s during Enver Hoxha's dictatorship. The creation of the reservoir necessitated changing the water level and displacing thousands of villagers, with no compensation or rehousing offered.

Some moved to Shkodër or Tirana, while others moved higher into the mountains and fended for themselves – look out for the makeshift boats owned by these savvy locals when travelling on the Lake Koman Ferry (p120) to Fierzë. Also look out for **Paqe Island**, where, according to local legend, rival families resolved Kanun blood feuds. Learn more about the ancient **Kanun** code on p128.

continued from p123

of the action tends to revolve around the restaurant-cafe **La Maroja** (*@lamaroja.restaurant*).

Explore forest and lagoon on a bird-watching reserve

South of Shëngjin, **Kune-Vain-Tale Reserve** *(free; parking 200L)* is a 44-sq-km lagoon and coastland with protected deciduous forest and more than 340 animal species, including nearly 200 birds. Bird-watchers come for self-guided tours to spot Dalmatian pelicans, greater flamingos, pygmy cormorants and common kingfishers, though larger Divjakë-Karavasta National Park (p68) south of Durrës is larger and has better amenities.

Kune-Vain-Tale is also a popular spot for cyclists and mountain bikers, though you'll need your own ride, as there's nowhere to hire bikes here.

If you're curious to check it out, a good target is **Trëndafili Mistik** (*@trendafilimistik*), a seafood restaurant on the lagoon with a lovely terrace and gorgeous stone architecture.

Lumi i Shales

TIME FROM SHKODËR: **4 HRS**

Hidden river beach

Nestled deep in the Albanian Alps, and accessible only by riverboat, is a dramatic canyon sliced by crisp, crystal-clear turquoise water with a beach-like atmosphere. Known straightforwardly as **Lumi i Shales** (Shala River), it's called 'Thailand of the Albanian Alps' on social media. This paradise is well

Lumi i Shales

worth the day trip from Shkodër, even though it's not quite as hidden as it once was.

Hotels in Shkodër can reserve a minibus for a 7am departure to arrive at Koman for 9.30am, or contact **Ndue Molla** *(068 585 4169)* to book your return trip for €40, or €25 for just the boat if you find your own way to Koman – there are several guesthouses in town, as well as the cute A-frame cabins at Agora Farmhouse (p131), 45 minutes away.

From Koman, you'll take a small riverboat on a beautiful trip up the river until the water is low enough for you to walk on the rocks and order a drink at one of the beach bars.

You can walk along the river from here, but make sure to arrive back at the bottom for your scheduled departure time. Or consider staying the night, as it's much more peaceful when the day-trippers leave.

Theth

HIKING | MOUNTAINS | UNIQUE CULTURE

KANUN

Isolated by geography, northern Albanians lived by the Kanun, a legal and moral code first codified in the 1400s and written down in the early 20th century, though it could be much older. This extensive code – consisting of 12 books and over 1200 articles – governs everything from what to do when your goat crosses into a neighbour's yard to avenging family murders through blood feuds. The Kanun also created the role of 'sworn virgins' – women who pledged celibacy to gain men's social privileges. Despite being made illegal under the Ottomans and Enver Hoxha, the Kanun endures to an unknown extent today: as of 2022, around a dozen sworn virgins remain, and thousands have sought asylum in Europe over the last two decades to escape blood feuds.

The unique mountain village of Theth easily has the most dramatic setting in Albania. Even the journey here is quite incredible, whether you approach over the mountains on foot from Valbonë or by vehicle over the recently paved mountain road from Shkodër. Both a sprawling village along a riverbed set amid an amphitheatre of slate-grey mountains, and a national park containing stunning landscapes and excellent hiking routes, Theth is now the capital of Albanian Alps tourism, welcoming thousands of international tourists a year – a far cry from its days of Kanun law and families settling blood feuds. Come here to see Theth's historic church and tower, and explore the mountainous national park on foot, home to a natural pool and waterfall. You can easily spend a few nights here, cosying up in one of many stone and wooden guesthouses.

Climb Mountain Peaks

Explore peaks, pools and forests at Theth National Park

Theth is located within the 26.3-sq-km **Theth National Park** *(Parku Kombëtar Alpet e Shqipërisë)* – a high-altitude preserve with peaks reaching 2567m (Mt Radohima), thick forests, alpine bluegrass, gushing waterfalls and mysterious blue-eye natural pools – yes, there's more here than at the over-visited Blue Eye (p84) near Sarandë. There are even populations of brown bears, as well as chamois, lynx, wild goats, grey wolves and golden eagles.

The national park is probably the best base in Albania for hiking. The most popular hike is over the Valbonë Pass (p121).

Otherwise, **Grunas Waterfall** is a fun little hike from town. You'll get there in about half an hour depending on where you start in town, and it's an ideal swimming spot. Consider making it a stop on a longer (six- to seven-hour) round-trip hike to **Blue Eye Kaprre**, an electric-blue natural pool that emerges from an underground well. The Blue Eye is well known by now, but definitely worth it. See directions for the hike from Grunas Waterfall to the Blue Eye on p130.

There are other trails around Theth, though they are less well known, meaning their level of signage is limited, if there at

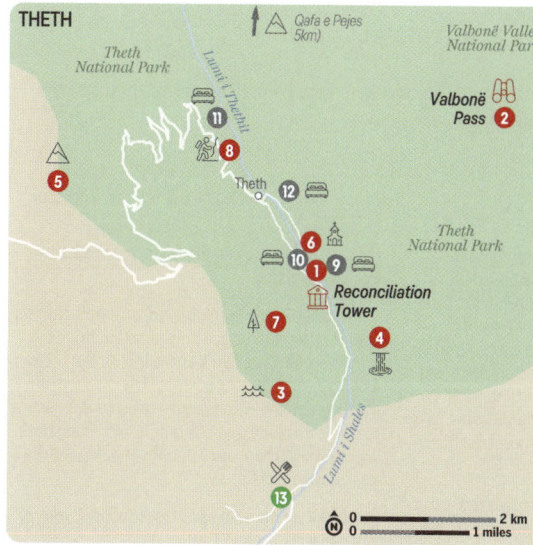

- **HIGHLIGHTS**
  1. Reconciliation Tower
  2. Valbonë Pass
- **SIGHTS**
  3. Blue Eye Kaprre
  4. Grunas Waterfall
  5. Shtegu i Dhenve
  6. Theth Church
  7. Theth National Park
- **ACTIVITIES**
  8. Theth Zipline
- **SLEEPING**
  9. Dreni
  10. Marashi
  11. Molla
  12. Vila Zorgji
- **EATING**
  13. Blue Eye Dostanisha

TOP TIP

If you're around in July, check out **Zâ Fest** (@zafestival), a celebration of Albanian music, poetry and film. There's a good mix of traditional folk songs and electronic beats, along with yoga and group hikes.

all. Options include hikes to the **Shtegu i Dhenve** and **Qafa e Pejes** mountain passes. There are also hikes in the Bogë Valley west of Theth. WhatsApp **Erenik Selimaj** (067 323 0951) for tips and to be put in touch with professional guides.

Also, ask your accommodation about a 4WD excursion, or fly along the 1110m **Theth Zipine** (@thethizipline; 2000L).

Blood Feud Tower & Church

Fascinating northern traditions

You'll see plenty of stone *kullas* (tower houses) across Albania – every village in the north had at least one before King Zog I had many of them destroyed in an effort to 'modernise' the country. But the one in Theth has a particularly fascinating story. The **Reconciliation Tower** (Kulla e Ngujimit; 150L) dates back 400 years and was used as a 'lock-in tower' during blood feuds, obligated by an ancient code of conduct known as the Kanun. Dating back at least as far as the 15th century, one aspect of Kanun law stated that a murder must be met by death, and men who refused to kill a rival's family could be subject to humiliation.

If you climb in and up the stairs of the tower, you can picture the life led by those condemned by their family ties to wait in the tower as a safe haven to avoid being killed in the blood feud. Ask the great-grandchildren of a tower judge outside to open it up and tell you some stories in English. If you're lucky, costumed guides will recount stories of Kanun days (in Albanian).

Another interesting historic building is the stone-and-shingle **Theth Church** (Kisha e Thethit), which was built in 1892, though it looks much older. Topped with a rustic wooden cross, the church was used as the village hospital during the communist era, meaning that many locals over the age of 35 were born in the quaint structure. It should be open for service on Sundays.

GETTING AROUND

Theth is very spread out along the riverbed, so expect a long walk to reach either end (depending on where you're staying) if you've hiked from Valbonë. Taxis are available to get to and from the Blue Eye trailhead in Nderlysaj, and there are often shared buses waiting there at the end of the day. Or just walk. Keep in mind that there are just two daily buses that travel from Theth to Shkodër (€12), at 11am and 5pm.

THETH BLUE EYE & WATERFALL LOOP

Combine Theth's top two natural attractions in one hike, or shorten the trip by taxiing to and from the village of Nderlysaj.

START	END	LENGTH
Theth	Theth	18km; 6–7 hours round-trip

Leave ❶ **Theth** at the trailhead on the road before the Reconciliation Tower (p129). Walk along the eastern bank of the river and turn left up the mountain instead of crossing the red bridge. Then hop over a slippery cascade and up to ❷ **Grunas Waterfall** (p128) for a dip. It's just about 30 minutes to the waterfall, which can be visited on its own, and it's a marvellous spot to go for a swim – you may see an afternoon rainbow if the sun hits it right.

Returning from where you came, cross the red bridge this time and follow the river, which may be dry during summer. Follow signs for the village of ❸ **Nderlysaj** and cross the bridge. Stop for a coffee, snack or to use the restroom at ❹ **Blue Eye Dostanisha**.

It's about 2.5 km from Nderlysaj on a well-trodden path (and a treacherous bridge) to the bright turquoise ❺ **Blue Eye Kaprre** (p128). The water's a chilly 7–10°C (it gets warmer downhill), but we highly recommend jumping in on a hot day. Unlike the Blue Eye (p84) near Sarandë, swimming here is permitted. There are a couple of cafes nearby if you need to fuel up.

Return along the same path to Nderlysaj, where you can walk back to Theth.

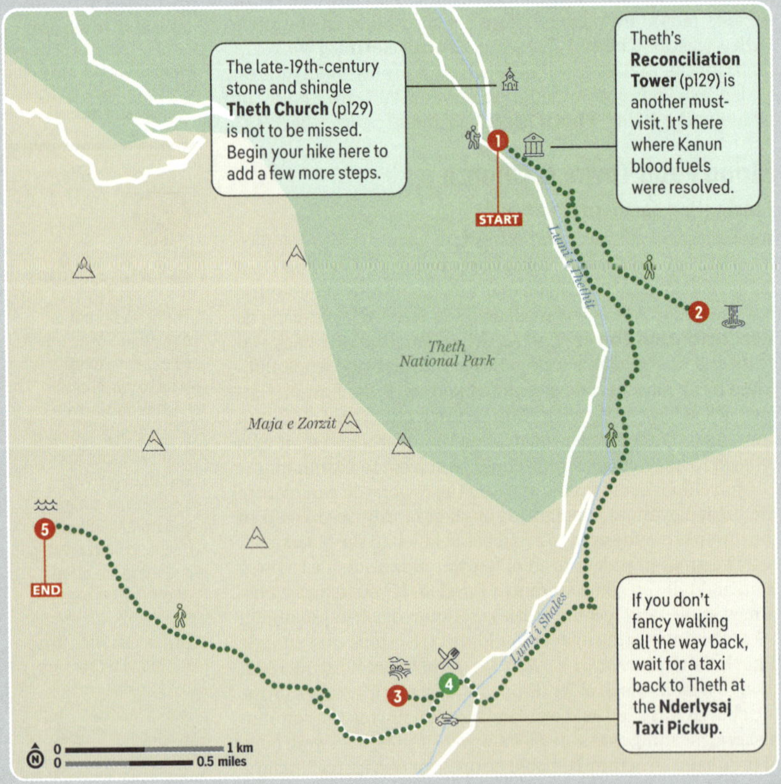

> The late-19th-century stone and shingle **Theth Church** (p129) is not to be missed. Begin your hike here to add a few more steps.

> Theth's **Reconciliation Tower** (p129) is another must-visit. It's here where Kanun blood fuels were resolved.

> If you don't fancy walking all the way back, wait for a taxi back to Theth at the **Nderlysaj Taxi Pickup**.

Theth National Park

Maja e Zorzit

Places We Love to Stay

€ Budget €€ Midrange €€€ Top End

Shkodër

Mi Casa Es Tu Casa € Beautiful mansion, once the former home of Peter Marubi, now a chill, colorful backpackers hostel for all ages (without the party vibe).

Wanderers Hostel € Make travel friends in the garden before embarking on organised trips to the Albanian Alps. Note that some dorms are a few minutes away from the main building.

InTown € Behind the bright orange facade is a lovely B&B with freshly renovated rooms and a tranquil garden steps from the action.

Rose Garden Hotel € Mix of modern decor and Victorian-style furniture around a lovely hidden courtyard that has roses and plenty of other flowers growing.

Tradita Hotel €€ Painstakingly restored 17th-century mansion that once belonged to a famous Shkodran writer, now a museum-like boutique hotel with comfortable rooms and locally woven bed linen.

Around Shkodër

Clandestino € Spend a few days camping between a lagoon and the Adriatic at this hippie-ish campsite south of Shkodër. The staff are great and the shared meals delicious. Bring mosquito repellent.

Mrizi i Zanave €€ Stay for (included) breakfast the next morning at the agrotourism powerhouse in Fishtë. The architecture at their guesthouse is a marvel, with glass meeting stone next to an Ottoman-style villa.

Highlander House Vermosh €€ Doze off to an out-of-this-world show – the stars – in one of the glass-roof A-frame cabins in Vermosh. Also known as 'Under Stars House'.

Agora Farmhouse €€ If you have your own vehicle, this is a lovely retreat, with adorable A-frame cottages along the water between Shkodër and Koman.

Theth

Dreni € Mansion with shareable dorms and meals served outside in the field in front of the building. Camping available.

Molla €€ Have your breakfast in front of a grand mountain amphitheatre and sleep on comfy, modern beds in a cozy wooden guesthouse: what the Albanian Alps are all about.

Vila Zorgji €€ Gorgeous stone guesthouse, camping and a shady restaurant terrace offering respite from the heat.

Marashi €€€ Recently renovated guesthouse facing the water with an Instagrammable standalone tub in the penthouse suite.

Valbonë

Rilindja €€ This fairy-tale wooden house has been a traveller favourite since opening in 2005. It's 3km from Valbonë's centre.

Jezerca €€ Freestanding pine cabins that sleep two, three or five people, and guesthouse rooms.

Villa Dini €€ Well-maintained guesthouse with simple decor and excellent food for dinner and breakfast. Ask English-speaking owner Erenik for some local tips.

Tradita Hotel

Southeastern Albania

CULTURAL CAPITALS

Fascinating Ottoman-era architecture and adventures await in this large, crucial region of the country.

Just because this is the book's final chapter doesn't mean you should skip southeastern Albania or leave it for last. Southeastern Albania is *the* place to be if you love culture, architecture, art and history. Both of Albania's two UNESCO-protected cities, Berat and Gjirokastër, are here, and each city resembles an open-air museum with well-preserved Ottoman-era architecture. In fact, during Enver Hoxha's dictatorship (1944–92), both cities were declared 'museum cities' and thus worthy of protection, despite the communists' affinity for secularism.

In Berat, wander stone alleyways to marvellous mosques, churches and a town-sized castle, stopping finally at a romantic restaurant to taste award-winning wine grown in the region that surrounds the city. Gjirokastër was built in the same period but looks strikingly different, with stone houses covered by thick rock slabs cosied up to Ottoman-style villas formerly inhabited by some of the country's most noteworthy 20th-century figures.

Less visited, though critical for thrill-seekers, Përmet is a growing adventure hub on the shore of Europe's largest wild river, successfully protected as a national river park in 2023 after an international campaign. Don't miss Përmet's hot springs and slow food.

Near Lake Ohrid, Korçë is a charming, educated city with colourful French-influenced architecture and a rich tradition of vibrant medieval art and photography. Visiting at least one of these southeastern destinations is a must on any Albania itinerary.

THE MAIN AREAS

BERAT
Preserved Ottoman neighbourhoods and castle. **p138**

GJIROKASTËR
Stone city with stories to tell. **p147**

PËRMET
Rafting, hot springs and slow food. **p156**

KORÇË
Catholic art and colourful streets. **p159**

For places to stay in Southeastern Albania, see p169

THE GUIDE

SOUTHEASTERN ALBANIA

Left: Mangalem (p141), Berat; Above: Resurrection of Christ Orthodox Cathedral (p160), Korçë

Find Your Way

A car is particularly key in this expansive, under-visited area of the country. If taking public transport, you'll need to rely on taxis and tours to visit more remote destinations.

THE GUIDE

SOUTHEASTERN ALBANIA

Berat, p138
UNESCO-recognised city known for its picturesque windows, Ottoman-era neighbourhoods and hilltop castle. Also Albania's wine capital.

Gjirokastër, p147
Another UNESCO city with striking stone houses and a castle. Some of Albania's most important 20th-century figures were born here.

CAR

Your own vehicle will give you the best access to uncharted adventures over the mountains to remote villages. Many roads, including Përmet to Korçë, Tepelenë to Nivicë, and the coast, have been recently paved.

FURGON

Albania's old-school *furgons* (shared minibuses) travel along the main highways at unscheduled intervals, stopping at makeshift terminals in Berat, Gjirokastër, Përmet and Korçë. A *furgon* can also take you up the steep hill to Gjirokastër's old town.

TAXIS

Southeastern cities don't have rideshare apps or electric taxis, but they do have metered taxis. Private transfer taxis like **DayTrip** *(daytrip.com)* are useful for getting between cities, with English-speaking drivers also able to stop for sightseeing.

Korçë, p159
City that's home to cute architecture inspired by France and Italy, and an amazing collection of medieval art and churches.

Përmet, p156
Adventure hub close to hot springs, wild river rafting and a canyon. Also a gastronomic hub known for its slow food.

Plan Your Time

A flat map of this area is deceiving – while the destinations look close, they're obscured by huge mountains and connected by mostly winding highways. Allow plenty of time to travel between them, especially if you don't have your own wheels.

Gjirokastër (p147)

Weekend in Berat

● If you only have a couple of days, travel south from Tirana's international airport to **Berat** (p138), an outdoor museum of Ottoman-era architecture. The UNESCO city's centrepiece is **Berat Castle** (p138), which has an excellent collection of Catholic art at the **Onufri Museum** (p140). Then, time travel to the 16th, 17th and 18th centuries with a walk around the **Mangalem** (p141) and **Goricë** (p141) neighbourhoods and have dinner with the friendliest host ever at **Lili** (p141; reserve ahead).

● The next day, book a rafting tour through the **Osum Canyon** (p145). When you get back to the city, shower, change and head for a romantic dinner with Berati wine at **Amalia** (p141).

SEASONAL HIGHLIGHTS

You don't have to be picky – cultural sites are still visit-worthy whether rain or shine, hot or cold. Be careful driving in the winter.

JANUARY
Go skiing at Albania's only ski resort in **Dardhë** (p164) and get cosy in one of its charming stone-and-wood guesthouses. Be sure to have winter tyres or chains, as rural roads are icy.

MARCH–MAY
The most thrilling time to raft the wild **Vjosa River** (p156), with more water and waves than in the summer. There are also fewer tourists and, unlike the coast, most sites are open.

JUNE
Go swimming with locals instead of international tourists in the huge and ancient **Lake Ohrid** (p165) near Korçë. Pogradec, Tushemisht and Drilon on the lake shore are terrific lakeside bases.

Five Days to Explore

● After you've seen Berat, take the highway down to **Gjirokastër** (p147), another UNESCO city with architecture that's also Ottoman, though with completely different vibes. Wander Gjirokastër's **Bazaar** (p149), visit its **Castle** (p149) and enter **house museums** (p150) formerly inhabited by some of Albania's most well-known figures, including Enver Hoxha, Ismail Kadare and Musine Kokalari.

● If you can manage it, take a day trip to **Përmet** (p156) to soak in the **Benjë Hot Springs** (p158), hike the **Langarica Canyon** (p158) and, if you didn't go to Osum Canyon, raft the **Vjosa River** (p156), Europe's first wild national river park. Don't miss trying out some of Përmet's reputable slow-food restaurants; **Te Culi** (p157) comes recommended.

Time for Adventure

● Instead of starting with Berat, take the scenic route east to **Lake Ohrid** (p165) and see the **Lin Mosaics** (p168) and **Drilon National Park** (p165), where dictator Enver Hoxha used to holiday. Then it's time to witness Korçë's colourful **art and architecture** (p159) before checking out the remarkable concentration of churches in **Voskopojë** (p163). Drive south on the **wild mountain road** (p166) to the **Melesin Distillery** (p166), one of the 'World's Greatest Places' (according to *TIME* magazine). You'll then reach **Përmet** (p156) for **Benjë Hot Springs** (p158), **Langarica Canyon** (p158) and river rafting with **Vjosa Rafting Albania** (p157). Drive south to **Gjirokastër** (p147) before looping up to **Berat** (p138) via the Albanian Riviera.

THE GUIDE

SOUTHEASTERN ALBANIA

JULY
Combine your beach vacation with a trip up to **Gjirokastër** (p147), which is slightly cooler and less rainy at this time of year. Gjirokastër's **National Folk Festival** (p150) also happens in July, but only once every five years (the next is in 2028).

AUGUST
Head to Korçë for **Beer Fest** (p162) and **Lakror Fest** (p162) to celebrate local beer and doughy pies, respectively. The beer fest attracts thousands of visitors every year.

SEPTEMBER
This is the best time to travel to Albania in general, with milder temperatures and fewer crowds. This is especially helpful in **Gjirokastër** (p147) and **Berat** (p138), which fill up in summer.

OCTOBER
Taste local wine and dance to DJs and local concerts at Berat's **Wine & Stories** (p162) festival. Berati red wine is perfect for warming up as the temperatures get cooler.

Berat

MOUNTAIN TOWN | ALLEYWAYS | RUINS

☑ TOP TIP

While most Albanians are only nominally religious, there is one tradition that nearly everyone practices: *xhiro*. Simply meaning 'walk', a *xhiro* is a post-dinner stroll often taken with friends and family. In Berat in summer, you'll see dozens of locals out for their sunset *xhiro* on Blvd Republika and along the river. Join them.

Punch the numbers into your time machine and get transported back to life under the Ottoman Empire in beautiful Berat. With a story that dates back 2400 years, this UNESCO World Heritage city is a mountain town in central Albania with a very special kind of magic. Berat started as an Illyrian settlement around the 4th century BCE, when it was crowned with a town-sized fortress more than 200m up. Cascading down from the castle are preciously preserved Ottoman-era neighbourhoods with winding stone alleyways. Berat's white facades and rectangular windows have earned the city the name *Qyteti i një-mbi-një Dritareve*, translated as either 'One Above the Other Windows' or 'Town of a Thousand Windows' (as it's more commonly known). But the bare stone facades are deserving of their place in your photo albums, too.

Expect crowds in high season in the historic centre – locals live in the modern and crumbling communist neighbourhoods nearby.

Explore a Town-Sized Castle
Dozens of prayer sites

Look up and you can't miss **Berat Castle** *(Kalaja e Beratit; 300L)* peeking out over the mountain. The castle is a town in and of itself, with more than 100 residential buildings, dozens of towers and church ruins, two mosques and a stone wall

---

GETTING AROUND

Berat Bus Terminal is nearly 3km from the historic centre, and occasional public buses run from here into town, or you can take a taxi. Berat is walkable, though the steep alleyways may be difficult for those with mobility issues. If you require a taxi to the door, stay outside the old districts of Mangalem or Goricë. If you have your own car, know that parking is a headache in Berat, and quite pricey – find a spot outside the centre and leave your car there for the entirety of your stay.

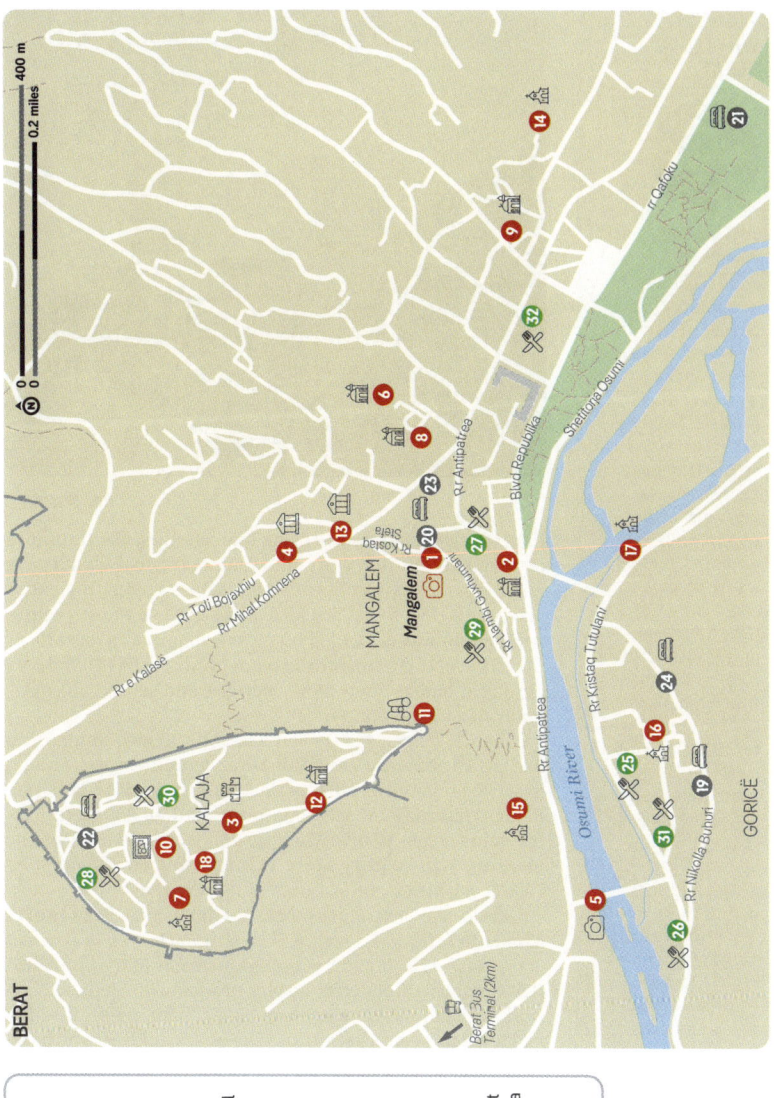

BERAT

★ HIGHLIGHTS
1. Mangalem

● SIGHTS
2. Bachelors' Mosque
3. Berat Castle
4. Ethnographic Museum
5. Gorica Bridge
6. Helveti Teqe
7. Holy Trinity Church
8. King Mosque
9. Lead Mosque
10. Onufri Museum
11. Panoramic Viewpoint
12. Red Mosque
13. Solomoni Jewish Museum
14. St Demetrius Cathedral
15. St Michael Chapel
16. St Spyridon Church
17. St Thomas Church
18. White Mosque

● SLEEPING
19. Berat Backpackers
20. Bujtina Kodikët
21. Colombo Hotel
22. Klea Hotel
23. Mangalemi Hotel
24. Vista

● EATING
25. Amalia
26. Eni
27. Friendly House
28. Klea
29. Lili
30. Temi
31. Tradita e Beratit
32. Zgara Zaloshnja

WHY I LOVE BERAT

Joel Balsam, Lonely Planet writer
Berat might only occupy a day or two on your trip, and it's clearly not off the beaten track, but it's a guaranteed highlight. There was a chance that under secular Hoxha and the communists, poly-religious Berat could have been destroyed – but it wasn't, which is a huge win for humanity. I love wandering through Berat's stone alleyways, picturing what it might've been like 300 years ago. No matter how many times I do, I always notice something different. And while I can appreciate a bare stone wall as much as the next world traveller, seeing the Ottoman villas painted as they were in white, and with those enchanting wooden windows and roofs, really makes Berat feel like you've been transported back in time.

Red Mosque

that stretches 1.4km. In spring and summer, the fragrance of chamomile is in the air (and underfoot), and wildflowers burst from every gap between the stones, giving the entire place a magical feel. The castle dates back to the 4th century BCE and was expanded by various empires as recently as the 19th century – under the reign of Ali Pasha (p96). In its heyday, it had as many as 42 churches and several mosques, many of which remain today.

From the entrance, turn left and walk 10 or 15 minutes to find the **Panoramic Viewpoint** over Berat. Turn back around to see the remaining pillar of the 15th-century **Red Mosque**, Berat's first mosque. Holding to the wall on your left, pass the ruins of the **White Mosque** and walk down to see the amazing 14th-century **Holy Trinity Church** *(Kisha Shën Triades)*, which is, unfortunately, usually shut.

Back in the centre of the castle, don't miss the **Onufri Museum** *(Muzeu Kombëtar Ikonografik Onufri; muzeumet -berat.al; 400L)*, a gallery located inside St Mary Cathedral (1797). It has a wonderful display of some 200 medieval artworks, including a 6th-century codex, bone relics of saints and a magnificent iconostasis. The audio guide is worth the extra 100L.

Although the fortress is open 24 hours, all visitors have to purchase an entry ticket from the main gate; the ticket

EATING IN BERAT: OUR PICKS

Eni: Small spot jutting out of the cliffside (the mountain rock is visible) on the Goricë side with an affordable menu, made with heart. *11.30am-10.30pm* €

Zgara Zaloshnja: Trinket-filled alleyway spot. Try Berati speciality *vienez* (beef Wellington–like fried meat and cheese roll). *8am-10pm* €

Klea: Castle-top restaurant with a lovely courtyard and fresh Albanian dishes. Breakfast for guests only. *noon-10pm* €

Temi: Taste Albanian favourites like *fërgesë* (dip made with red peppers and ricotta cheese) within the castle walls. *noon-4pm & 6-10.30pm* €

booth here is only open between 9am and 6pm in high season. The castle has souvenir shops, restaurants (lunch and dinner only) and guesthouses inside the castle walls, as well as terrific views, so leave at least an hour to explore or spend the night. For your safety and for the longevity of the castle, don't climb on the ancient structures.

Wander Ottoman Neighbourhoods
Mangalem and Goricë

On either side of the river that cuts through this beautiful UNESCO city are two historic neighbourhoods that transport you back to life under the Ottoman Empire.

Below the castle is **Mangalem**, a maze of winding stone alleyways typically inhabited by Muslim residents, with most buildings being constructed in the 18th and 19th centuries. It's fun to get lost between its cool stone walls and admire the intricate doors and windows, though not so much if you're looking for your accommodation (ask for clear directions when you book). On the eastern edge of the neighbourhood, check out the tiny **Solomoni Jewish Museum** (200L). On display is a photo collection that tells of Berat's once-thriving Jewish community (very few remain today), which included over 600 Jews sheltered here during WWII.

Mangalem continues on the other side of Rr Mihal Komnena (the road that leads up to the castle). Wander the airy alleyways here to find more beautiful architecture, none more so than the **Ethnographic Museum** (muzeumet-berat.al), an 18th-century residence turned museum that was closed for renovations during our last two research trips.

You'll get the best views of Mangalem's famous windows on the other side of the Osum River in **Goricë**, which was mostly built in the 16th century and typically inhabited by Christians. Only a few stone thoroughfares and a couple of pretty churches remain. Having dinner here at restaurants like Amalia or Tradita e Beratit, or staying at one of its lovely guesthouses, is particularly atmospheric.

RELIGION IN ALBANIA

While Christianity arrived during Byzantine times, many Albanians converted to Islam when the Ottomans moved in. During communism, Albania was declared a secular state, and then it banned religion altogether in 1967 – some say dictator Enver Hoxha was the country's only sanctioned god. Today, religion is accepted in Albania, with the majority identifying as Sunni (Islam), followed by Catholic, Eastern Orthodox Christian and Bektashi (an Islamic Sufi sect).

In daily life, though, many Albanians are only nominally religious, and you'll rarely see religious clothing and symbols, such as hijabs and crosses, around. When a religious holiday like Easter or Eid hits, Albanians will happily take the day off to celebrate, even if the tradition isn't their own.

EATING IN BERAT: OUR PICKS

Friendly House: Conveniently off the main drag, with an ambient interior and busy outdoor terrace. *noon-midnight* €

Amalia: Candlelit Goricë alleyway restaurant with an Albanian cuisine tasting menu (€28 for two). *11.30am-11.30pm* €€

Lili: Leave with a smile on your face, a full belly and a new friend in English-speaking owner Lili. Reserve ahead. *5.30-10pm Mon-Fri* €€

Tradita e Beratit: Romantic restaurant in Goricë that's the perfect setting for tasting Albanian wine. *noon-10.30pm* €€

BERAT MOSQUE & CHURCH WALK

To see Berat's many Muslim, Bektashi and Christian prayer sites is to understand its history – or at least to try.

START	END	LENGTH
St Demetrius Cathedral	Goricë Bridge	2km; 1 hour

Start from a square you'll only find in Albania – one that's bordered by both a church and a mosque. After the fall of communism, modern ❶ **St Demetrius Cathedral** *(Katedralja e Shën Dhimitrit)* was built over a mid-19th-century basilica that was destroyed during the dictatorship. It's across from ❷ **Lead Mosque** *(Xhamia e Plumbit)*, the city's former main mosque, opened in 1554.

In Berat's medieval centre, see the 16th-century ❸ **King Mosque** *(Xhamia e Mbretit)* and, behind it, ❹ **Helveti Teqe** *(Teqeja e Helvetive)*, a prayer site for the Helveti, who, like the Bektashi, are a dervish order of Muslim mystics. Ask a groundskeeper if they can open the doors to visit inside.

Walk down and enter the 19th-century ❺ **Bachelors' Mosque** *(Xhamia e Beqarëvet)*, which was built for unmarried shop assistants and junior craftsmen (the door is in the back). Walk backwards along Berat's newer suspension bridge to admire the famous windows of the Mangalem district. Hop up to tiny ❻ **St Thomas Church** *(Kisha e Shën Thomait)*, a recent creation built on the ruins of an 18th-century church, with a lovely garden. There are beautiful views of the windows from here, too.

Wander through magnificent Goricë to the 19th-century ❼ **St Spyridon Church** *(Kisha e Shën Spiridhonit)* and finish at ❽ **Goricë Bridge** *(Ura e Goricës);* the original, built in 1780, was wooden.

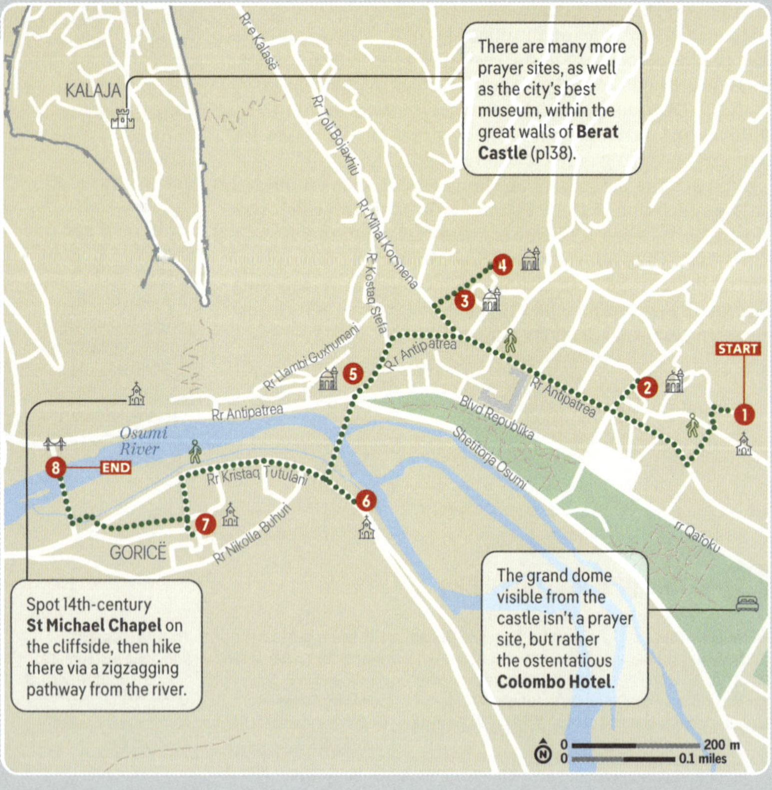

There are many more prayer sites, as well as the city's best museum, within the great walls of **Berat Castle** (p138).

Spot 14th-century **St Michael Chapel** on the cliffside, then hike there via a zigzagging pathway from the river.

The grand dome visible from the castle isn't a prayer site, but rather the ostentatious **Colombo Hotel**.

Beyond Berat

Leave time to explore the hilly terrain around Berat, which has Albania's best wineries, along with rafting, hiking and an important archaeological site.

Allow at least a day or two to explore the exciting hills around Berat. Albanian wine is making a name for itself on the international oenology circuit, and the wine made in the fertile Berat region is leading the charge. You'll be saying *gëzuar* (cheers) to Albanian wines with grape varieties only found at vineyards located a 30-minute drive from Berat's historic centre.

The adventurous should plan a rafting trip in between the stark limestone cliffs of Osum Canyon, or hike Mt Tomorr – a spiritual mountain – for expansive views. On the way to or from Gjirokastër, stop off at Byllis, an important archaeological site that dates back 2400 years.

Places
Ura Vajgurore p143
Roshnik p143
Osum Canyon p145
Byllis p146

GETTING AROUND

Rather than negotiating the winding mountain roads and bold drivers, leave the driving to the experts and pay for a tour or taxi from Berat. There are no useful bus routes for Osum Canyon (p145) or Byllis (p146), though you may be able to get to Roshnik or Ura Vajgurore by *furgon* (shared minibus). Driving between Osum Canyon and Gjirokastër isn't really possible – unless you want to trash your vehicle on shoddy, unpaved roads (as this writer did). Instead, backtrack north from Berat on SH 7.

Ura Vajgurore
TIME FROM BERAT: **20 MINS**

Taste Albanian wine
On the way into Berat, just off SH 72, **Çobo Winery** *(cobowine.com; standard/premium €25/€45)* does tastings inside its beautiful family-built cottage and in its peaceful garden, surrounded by chirping birds and the smell of fruit and flowers. Try a tasting or bring home a bottle of wine made from Albanian grapes, including shesh i zi (black grape that's often barrel-aged) and pulëz (white wine grape from Roshnik near Berat). The showstopper is the Shendeverë label, meaning 'joyful' in Albanian. It's a sparkling wine made in the Champenoise method.

Standard and premium tastings come with fruit, olives, cheese and crackers, and you may visit the cellar underground to learn how Çobo's wine is produced and aged. A 10-minute documentary about how the winery was founded in 1998 is on loop inside (and on YouTube). Organised bus tours are available from Berat if you don't have a car.

Roshnik
TIME FROM BERAT: **30 MINS**

Agrotourism winery
Alpeta Agrotourism *(alpeta.al; tastings 2000L)*, located in Roshnik village, is one of the first agrotourism operations in Albania, with vineyards tumbling down a verdant hillside

ALBANIAN GRAPES

Elion Fiska of **Alpeta Agroturism** (@alpeta_agroturizem) explains the different grape varieties grown in Albania.

Pulëz: Authentic white grape first cultivated in Berati-region vineyards. Known as the 'gold of Roshnik', it produces fresh, aromatic white wine with citrus and floral notes.

Kallmet: Red grape grown in northern Albania that has a unique taste, deep colour, soft tannins and red-berry flavours.

Vlosh: Grape grown mostly in the Vlorë region. Rarer among Albanian wines, with spicy and herbal undertones.

Shesh i zi and shesh i bardhë: Black and white grapes in the same family that are widely grown in Albania and frequently blended with international varieties. Shesh i zi offers dark fruits and spice, while shesh i bardhë brings freshness and stone-fruit aromas.

that ranges from 300 to 700m in elevation. The winery, set on 37,000 sq metres of land received from the government after the fall of communism, is home to many picturesque vineyards, and the wines have been awarded various medals at the Decanter World Wine Awards.

As well as tastings, visitors can choose to stay the night and eat in Alpeta's marvellous restaurant, which features the farm's proud goat meat, cheese and butter (it's bright white, as opposed to the yellow of cows' butter), as well as dried figs. You can also learn to cook traditional dishes with a three-hour **cooking class** *(per person €50)* using fresh ingredients from the farm.

Climb Mt Tomorr

Towering over the Berat region, **Mt Tomorr** *(Maja e Tomorrit)* is considered a spiritual site for Albanians of various faiths, including Muslims, Bektashis and Christians. Some even believe that the 2416m mountain vibrates with a mysterious energy that's been picked up by satellites. It's also a protected 260-sq-km national park with coniferous forest that's home to bears, wolves, wild goats and various birds of prey. Entrance to the park is free.

Book a 4WD tour or a guided hike with Alpeta Agroturism *(alpeta.al/tours; €89)* or tour operators in Berat, or tackle Mt Tomorr on your own as a day hike that's a 12.4km round-trip.

If going it alone, you'll need the help of a hiking app such as **Wikoloc** *(wikiloc.com/outdoor-navigation-app)*, as the

Çobo Winery (p143)

trails aren't well signed. Start from the village of **Ujanik** and hike up to the summit, which has a Bektashi *teqe* (shrine). You'll be able to see as far as Italy and Greece's Mt Olympus on a clear day.

Osum Canyon

TIME FROM BERAT: 1½ HRS

Raft the canyon

South of Berat, the Osum River snakes down to become the most impressive gorge in southern Albania. **Albania Rafting Group** *(albrafting.org; day tour with transport €85)* hosts fun whitewater rafting excursions through **Osum Canyon** *(Kanionet e Osumit)*. Day tours generally last 3½ hours on the water plus time factored in for the two-hour drive from Berat (if you don't have your own off-road vehicle).

The experience is both peaceful and exhilarating, as tall limestone cliffs tower up to 80m on both sides, narrowing in points to barely fit the size of the raft. Look out for the oddly shaped rocks that resemble a nose and a dragon, and be prepared to get soaked (perhaps while kissing your love) in gushing waterfalls.

Rafting season lasts from February through June, with the highest rapids following the winter rains. In May and June, the rapids dial down to Class I or II, and by the end of the season, you may have to jump up and down to move over the rocks.

It's worth paying for the day tour with transport included, as this gets you the van ride from Berat (and lunch in Skrapar) – the drive is a challenging zigzag, even for the

Osum Canyon (p145)

ALBANIA'S COOLEST CASTLES

Petrelë Castle: Cool castle close to Tirana, with a little cafe and a zipline nearby.

Krujë Castle: See where Albania's national hero faced several sieges by the Ottomans – and won.

Lekursi Castle: The best spot for sunset snaps in Sarandë. The restaurant is just OK.

Porto Palermo Castle: Ali Pasha's prized triangular fortress, built for one of his wives. Find it near Himarë.

Berat Castle: This castle atop the historic Ottoman city dates back to the Illyrians and is the size of a town.

Gjirokastër Castle: See a downed US plane and military weapons in this castle, once used as a base by invading Italians.

most experienced drivers. It's also worth re-emphasising that you cannot drive south from the canyon to Përmet or Gjirokastër unless you have an off-road vehicle or feel like destroying your car.

If you're not into rafting, it's possible to tour the canyon for the views and to jump in the turquoise water. Albania Rafting Group and your accommodation in Berat can organise tours.

Byllis

TIME FROM BERAT: 1½ HRS

Ancient Illyrian ruins

With a commanding view over a hilltop 500m over the Vjosa Valley, **Byllis** (*Parku Arkeologjik Bylis; 400L*) dates back to the 4th century BCE and was once a critical fortress under the rulership of the Illyrian 'pirate' Queen Teuta (p106), as well as the Romans and the Macedonians. Unfortunately, the city has been pretty much destroyed for the last 1400 years, leaving little but crumbling stone remains on the hilltop. Still, there's a mystical nature to being on the hilltop, and there's an on-site cafe if you want to take it easy before your next stop.

Spread out within the 2.2km city walls are numerous structures with limited signage. The most important of these is the theatre. Built in the middle of the 3rd century BCE, the 40 rows of seats could seat up to 7500 people.

Byllis is off E853, on the way to Gjirokastër.

Gjirokastër

STONE ARCHITECTURE | BAZAAR | CUISINE

On a mountain range overlooking the fertile Drin Valley, Gjirokastër (Gjirokastra), aka Stone Town, is a UNESCO World Heritage Site and, along with Berat, an Albanian 'museum city'. Its massive castle, inhabited by plenty of leaders over more than five centuries, stands commandingly over the old city – home to some 600 Ottoman-style houses with extremely heavy rock-slab roofs – and the shoddily built new town in the floodplains.

Wander the quaint Bazaar alongside enticing traditional restaurants, souvenir shops and, since the pandemic, hip cocktail bars. As you walk around, be sure to stay on the lookout for archways with metal doors – they're probably bunkers built by Gjirokastër-born dictator Enver Hoxha.

Gjirokastër is a popular day trip from Sarandë, especially for the cruise-ship crowd, but plan to spend at least a couple of nights here, as there's plenty to see and do.

☑ TOP TIP

There isn't a tremendous amount to do in Gjirokastër, but there's a charm here that beckons visitors to stay a few days or longer and meander the Bazaar and explore the surrounding goat paths. If you're a backpacker, Gjirokastër is home to some terrific hostels.

Stone City Stroll

So many historic sites to see

Go for a walk around Gjirokastër to see its metre-thick stone walls holding up roofs layered with heavy stone slabs. Also spot the oddly shaped metal fences made from the moulds of a now-defunct cutlery factory, harking back to the time when

GETTING AROUND

Intercity buses from cities like Sarandë, Berat and Korcë stop on the highway in the newer town at the bottom of the hill. From there, you can walk up (warning: it's a workout!) or take a local public bus. Times vary. There are also taxis. Consult with your accommodation before arriving about the best way to get up the hill, or if driving, ask your accommodation where to park in the Bazaar. Be careful not to trip over the cobblestones or slip on rocks when walking around the Bazaar.

Gjirokastër was an industrial hub during communism. Just be careful not to slip in the rain – it rains quite frequently here.

Start at the **Bazaar** *(Qafä e Pazarit)*, located at a five-point intersection at the top of Gjirokastër's old town. The commerce hub dates back to the 17th century – before that, shopping was done within the castle walls, and it's only been in the last few years that it's become this busy, with trendy bars and restaurants opening all around following the lull of the pandemic. Pop into one of them for a fancy cocktail or a *raki* (fruit brandy), or for live music on most weekend nights. Feel free to shop for souvenirs here as well, but know that the goods are usually foreign-made.

Close to the Bazaar, find the 18th-century **Bazaar Mosque** *(Xhamia e Pazarit)* outside of prayer time (you'll be asked to cover up). Beneath it is the atmospheric stone-walled cafe, **Te Kubé**, that's so much more than a place for an espresso. Inside, you'll find a unique mini-museum dedicated to Albanian iso-polyphony music. The museum also transforms into a communist bunker tunnel that was once connected to the castle. It's a sensory experience that lights up to the sounds of traditional Albanian folk songs as you walk. There's also an interactive display outside the tunnel.

Outside the Bazaar, you'll find many more stone houses connected by tiny, confusing alleyways. The neighbourhood northwest is not to be missed, as it has several engrossing house museums (p150). **Dunavat**, a neighbourhood southwest of the Bazaar, is quieter and, if you're up for a slog uphill, it ends at **Ali Pasha Bridge**, a 19th-century crossing at the edge of town. The bridge was originally part of an aqueduct that fed the castle's cisterns.

Commanding Castle & Folk Festival
Stones etched with history

The hilltop where **Gjirokastër Castle** *(Kalaja e Gjirokastrës; 400L)* overlooks the valley has been inhabited since as far back as the 4th century, though much of what you can see today was built about 500 years ago. Since that time, this strategic complex has been a medieval fortress, a base for Ottoman Ali Pasha before he challenged the sultan (and ended up losing his head), a prison during Albania's monarchic and communist periods, and an Italian army barracks during Italy's WWII occupation of the country.

Today, the castle – 500m long, 75m wide – is a refreshing respite from the summer heat. It's filled with antique artillery

ISO-POLYPHONY

Registered on UNESCO's Intangible Cultural Heritage List in 2008, Albanian iso-polyphony is an unforgettable, chilling style of folk music. Do yourself a favor and YouTube a video of it right now.

Iso-polyphony is typically defined by two singers: one sings the melody while the other sings a counter melody with a quivering choral drone, similar to an echo in a church. Iso-polyphony, after all, has its origins in songs sung in Byzantine churches.

Today, this form of singing is dying out, but you might be lucky enough to hear it here in Gjirokastër (as we did on a recent visit), since it's historically been linked with the south. You'll certainly hear it if you come for the National Folk Festival (p150), though this only occurs every five years.

EATING IN GJIROKASTËR: OUR PICKS

Odaja: Delightful, honest Albanian cooking since 1937; in an upper-floor restaurant with plenty of vegetarian options. *10am-11pm* €

Kardhashi: A tad pushy, though eminently generous, top-of-the-hill restaurant with plenty of outdoor seating. *8.30am-10.30pm* €

Furra: Recently opened spot in the Bazaar with top-quality Albanian casseroles and pizzas. Good vibes, too. *noon-10.30pm* €€

The Barrels: Farm-to-table cuisine beside a vineyard at this wildly popular agrotourism destination across the valley. Reservations required. *noon-11pm* €€

Gjirokastër Castle (p149)

ISMAIL KADARE

Born in Gjirokastër in 1936, Ismail Kadare is Albania's greatest author and one of the most renowned scribes of the 20th century.

Both celebrated and threatened during communist times, prompting an escape to France in 1990, Kadare has written more than two dozen books, many of them translated into English. His novels usually have a grotesque and surrealist bent, and often touch on the history of Albania, including *Chronicle in Stone* (1971), which is about his hometown during WWII. Other locations are also covered, such as ancient Egypt in *The Pyramid* (1996). Kadare won the first Man Booker International Prize in 2005 and was nominated 15 times for the Nobel Prize in Literature. He continued to publish until his final days in 2024.

and a sprawling terrace that hosts a clock tower and a recovered US fighter jet with an interesting backstory. The castle is also home to two museums.

The **Army Museum** (*Muzeu i Armëve; 200L*) contains dozens of communist weapons and tools (though no English explanations), and cells where political prisoners were kept between 1929 and 1968. Look for the seven windows that face the town here – 'You'll be sent to the seven windows' was a common local threat throughout the communist era.

The second museum, **Gjirokastër Museum** *(200L)*, is a wonderful exhibition delivering the most thorough history of Albania in English you'll find in the country.

Every five years, the castle's terrace also hosts the **National Folk Festival**, where Albanians from far and wide sing quivering iso-polyphony songs and dance in choreographed performances. The last event was held in 2023, so the next should be in 2028.

Fascinating House Museums

Inside the stone walls

Gjirokastër was home to some of the most memorable Albanians in recent history, and their former homes, or at least versions of them, have been transformed into museums. **Kadare**

DRINKING IN GJIROKASTËR: OUR PICKS

Gallery: Sit at the bar for a pint or a colorful cocktail and meet fellow travellers at this Irish pub, just off the Bazaar intersection. *9am-1am*

Black Rose: Slightly older crowd, with live Albanian music, jazz and acoustic music, as well as DJs in the summer. Makes its own *raki* (fruit brandy). *8am-2am*

Babameto 2: Sit on a bench facing the small promenade out front, where a DJ plays every Saturday in summer. *8am-1am*

Komiteti: *Raki* bar and restaurant with outstanding museum-like decor. Also found in Tirana, Korçë and Vlorë. There's a DJ on Saturdays. *8am-midnight*

House (*Shtëpia e Ismail Kadaresë; 500L*) celebrates the life of Ismail Kadare (1936–2024) – Albania's most famous writer – in the house where he grew up. Expertly renovated, the modern exhibition showcases Kadare's writing over several rooms, including the family's air raid shelter, which could fit up to 90 people. There's little context about who Kadare was, but if you've done some research beforehand and are a fan of his writing, it's a thrill.

Albania's infamous dictator Enver Hoxha (1908–85) was also born in Gjirokastër, though his former home, or at least the Ottoman-style residence built in its place, has little mention of him. Instead, Gjirokastër's **Ethnographic Museum** is a worthwhile place to visit to learn about the city and its vibrant culture. There are plenty of objects to see, including a fine collection of traditional clothing and furniture, along with plenty of information to keep you busy for at least a couple of hours.

Muza Ime Musine Kokalari *(500L)* is dedicated to Musine Kokalari (1918–83), a Gjirokastër-born feminist writer and social democrat. Kokalari was one of the few women to be educated under the Ottomans, and she went on to lead Albania's Social Democratic Party. Her competition after the war, as it turned out, was her distant cousin Hoxha, who arrested and imprisoned her before the 1943 election, after which his communist party was elected. She was imprisoned for three decades under Hoxha. Muza, which opened in 2024, is a loving ode to the activist, with some of her possessions and quotes on display, as well as a 15-minute projection-mapping documentary that provides a short biography of her tragic life.

Two more house museums demonstrate life in Gjirokastër during the Ottoman era. High above the old town in a three-storey building with twin towers and a double-arched facade, **Zekate House** *(250L)* dates from 1811 and has a luxurious interior, especially the upstairs galleries, which have carved wooden ceilings, stained-glass windows and detailed wall frescoes.

Similarly, **Skenduli House** *(300L)*, built in 1700 and renovated in the late 19th century, is still in the hands of the same family that has owned it for nine generations. A male member of the family can give you a spirited tour of the home's features (he speaks Albanian, Italian and French), including its cold storage, 300-year-old taps, hole toilet and, much more impressively, the room used only for wedding ceremonies that has 15 mostly stained-glass windows.

Cool down in Communist Bunker Tunnels

Cold in various ways

When Albania found itself isolated after leader Enver Hoxha cut ties with the Yugoslavs, the Soviets and the Chinese, it built tens of thousands of small mushroom-shaped bunkers across the country in case of attack. It also built bunker tunnels, some of which hosted frequent drills, where residents were forced to wait on cold, damp benches before commanding comrades told them they were free to return home.

STOPS AROUND GJIROKASTËR

Wouter de Rooij, owner of **Stone City Hostel** (@stonecityhostel), has lived in Gjirokastër for more than a decade. He says that visitors often miss out on these interesting spots close to the city.

Nivicë Canyon and Peshturë Waterfall Spectacular canyon (p167) and the tallest waterfall (p167) in Albania (over 200m).

Zagori Valley One of our favourites, with Ottoman bridges, cute remote villages, waterfalls and good hiking.

Libohovë and Labovë e Kryqitë Villages with the oldest church in Albania and a cool castle from Ali Pasha.

Hadrianopolis Archaeological site easy to get to with a regular car. They only excavated a tiny bit of it, but there's a beautiful Roman theatre and remnants of a bathhouse.

Cold War Tunnel

ALBANIA'S GRANNY CHEFS

Under Hoxha's dictatorship, the banning of emigration and the repression of food with any religious significance created a sort of culinary amnesia in Albania, where dishes that had lasted centuries were on the brink of being lost. Then, the grannies stepped in. Grandmother Tefta Pajenga started a TV show in 2004, where she taught younger Albanians how to cook traditional dishes. The concept caught on, and in 2018, an event in Tirana paired 12 grandmothers with 12 top chefs to teach them their recipes. Since then, age-old Albanian dishes like *flia* (layered crepes) and *mishavinë* (cheese fermented in animal fat) have flourished, and the traditional cuisine is as popular as ever. During research, Albanian top chef Bledar Kola was planning to open Mullixhino, a traditional Albanian restaurant in Gjirokastër.

Locals understandably have little interest in hanging around this grim slice of communist history, but there are a few abandoned bunker tunnels around Gjirokastër that you can explore (claustrophobes, beware). The most visitor-ready is the **Cold War Tunnel** *(200L)* above Çerçiz Topulli Sq. There, a municipality tour guide will take you around the tunnel's 80 rooms, built by prisoners housed in the castle through the 1960s. See the decaying conference room, kitchen and generator, and learn about Albania's communist period. Even if you've been to Tirana's Bunk'Art 1 (p55) and Bunk'Art 2 (p51), the history comes alive here, especially if you're lucky enough to be hosted by the guide with the deadpan humour. Tours are led every hour during high season.

Cook Albanian Cuisine

With a sprinkle of grandmother's love

Albanian cuisine might share similarities with its neighbours, but it's clearly it's own thing – and now that you've tasted it, you should probably learn how to make it at home. With **Për drekë tek Marjeta** *(@marikaragjozi)*, Marjeta Karagjozi invites guests to her home terrace in Gjirokastër to cook traditional dishes, just as she makes for her grandkids.

In the **cooking classes** *(vegetarian/meat per person €30/40)* with Marjeta, you'll make dishes such as *qifqi* (rice-and-egg balls fried in a 105-year-old specialised pan) and *qofte bobollaqe* (meatballs in yoghurt), plus *asullde* (caramel pudding) for dessert.

But don't worry, you won't have to make everything – salad, bread, wine and *raki* are provided. It's a cute, local experience, especially as Marjeta's daughter or grandkids hang around to translate. *Ju bëftë mirë* (Bon appétit)! Book via Instagram.

Beyond Gjirokastër

Go off the beaten track to explore mountain villages, historic sites and jaw-dropping nature.

Save for visiting the Blue Eye on the road to Sarandë, few people explore the area around Gjirokastër – but that's a mistake. These hills are some of the most beautiful in Albania, and they're filled with beautiful sites, though you have to know where to look. Opposite Gjirokastër is a verdant hillside, perfect for exploring on horseback, where you'll see ancient ruins and one of Albania's most beautiful Byzantine churches. North, Ali Pasha's hometown is a site of the ruins of a grim communist prison and castle. But the real treat is found in the Kurvelesh Highlands, where you'll see gushing waterfalls and giant canyons. You can finish your explorations on the coast.

Places
Asim Zeneli p153
Tepelenë p155
Libohovë p155
Labovë e Kryqitë p155

Asim Zeneli
TIME FROM GJIROKASTËR: **20 MINS**

Horse-riding tours to viewpoints
After all that walking in Gjirokastër, let another mammal do the work, this time on a horse-riding tour with **Visit Gjirokastra** *(visit-gjirokastra.com)*. Formerly known as Caravan Horse Riding Albania, the experienced operator offers a few different rides from its stable in the village of Asim Zeneli, located on the verdant hill opposite Gjirokastër.

Rides from the village may go up to a viewpoint *(€40, 1½ hours)*, or to the Drino Valley *(€50, 3 hours)* so the horses can have a sip in the artificial Lake Çini. You can also embark on weeklong riding journeys that include yoga and meditation. Trips are intended for those who've ridden before and restricted to over-14s.

Hike to the ruins of an ancient city
Some men buy their wives rings, others build them cities. Or at least that was the case for King Pyrrhus of Epirus, Alexander the Great's cousin, who had the city of **Antigona** *(Parku Arkeologjik i Antigonës; 300L)* built for his wife, Antigone, in 285 BCE. Only a smattering of stone ramparts and portico columns remain since the city was destroyed by the Romans in the Third Macedonian War, but it's an interesting goal for a 1½-hour (unmarked) hike from Asim Zeneli village, and the views are stunning.

GETTING AROUND

You're all but hopeless around here without your own vehicle, save for getting to Tepelenë (p155), where you should be able to catch a *furgon* (shared minibus) from the highway at the bottom of Gjirokastër. Fortunately, cars are available for rent in Gjirokastër, and tours will take you to any of these sites.

HIDDEN CANYON DRIVE

While it's off the radar for most travellers, the road cutting through the Kurvelesh Highlands, between southeastern Albania and the Ionian coast, is a true delight.

START	END	LENGTH
Tepelenë	Himarë	70km; 2½ hours

From ❶ **Tepelenë**, the freshly paved road hugs the curvature of the mountains – the Kurvelesh Highlands, to be exact – and soon passes ❷ **Ali Pasha Aqueduct** (*Ujësjellësi i Ali Pashait*; p167) a 20-pillared, 19th-century water passage running over the riverbed. Farther along the road, park in the town of ❸ **Progonat** (p167). It's time to stretch your legs by hiking along the 20-minute trail to the base of ❹ **Peshturë Waterfall** (*Ujëvara e Peshturës*; p167), one of Albania's most wonderful waterfalls, which gushes from a height of 400m into a turquoise pool.

Heading back to the car, continue west past an imposing communist monument until you reach ❺ **Nivicë Canyon** (p167), a Garden of Eden if there ever was one. The giant canyon stretches for 40km between several gorges and drops as much as 700m. The main gorge – visible from ❻ **Bujtina Mbi Kanion**, the cafe and guesthouse on the ridge – drizzles with waterfalls and bursts with wildflowers every April. Spend the night here or in one of the other guesthouses around, then backtrack and take the steep road down to ❼ **Kuç** – the views of the coast from this part of the drive are absolutely stunning. Continue along SH 76 to reach ❽ **Himarë** (p92), a coastal hub.

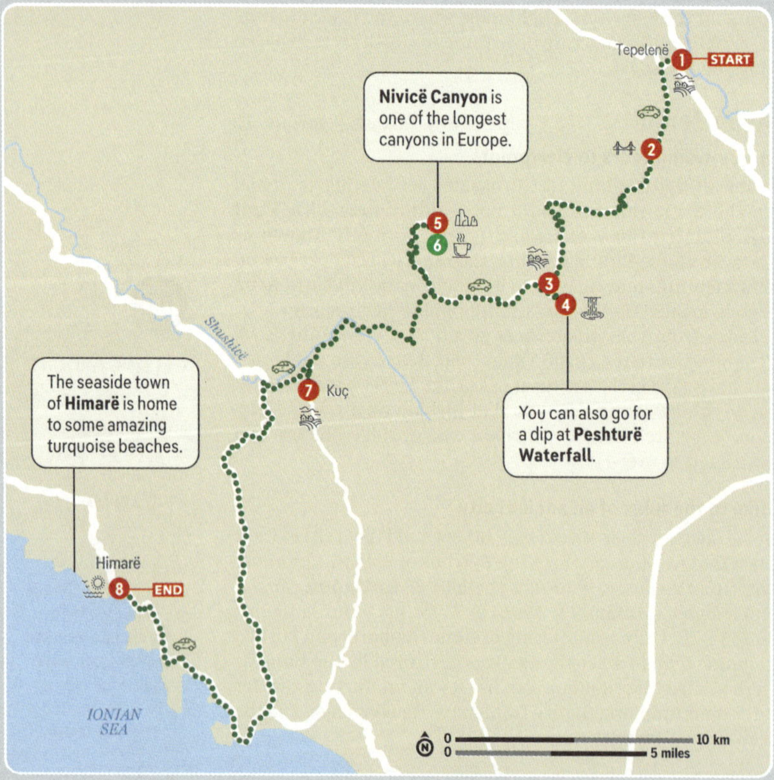

Nivicë Canyon is one of the longest canyons in Europe.

The seaside town of **Himarë** is home to some amazing turquoise beaches.

You can also go for a dip at **Peshturë Waterfall**.

Tepelenë

TIME FROM GJIROKASTËR: **30 MINS**

See a castle juxtaposed against a forced labour camp

North of Gjirokastër, the town of Tepelenë is known mostly as the home of Ali Pasha, the 19th-century Ottoman ruler who had plenty of imposing fortresses built or expanded across the country before he ended up being killed by a Turkish sultan. Indeed, in his hometown, there's the 40,000sqm **Tepelenë Castle** *(Kalaja e Tepelenës)*, which has impressive ramparts 10m tall and 5m thick.

But if you go *behind* the town, you'll find the notorious **Tepelenë Internment Camp**, where some 1500 families performed forced labour as prisoners during the communist regime, between 1949 and 1954. Prisoners were malnourished and the sanitation was horrid, leading to a typhus epidemic that killed hundreds of inmates, including at least 300 children. The high mortality rate of children in particular forced the government to close the camp, though other camps continued to operate across Albania. Today, you may walk around the perimeter of the camp's abandoned barracks for a grim reminder of the toll of Albania's dictatorship.

Libohovë

TIME FROM GJIROKASTËR: **30 MINS**

Cute village with fortress ruins

On the way to Labovë e Kryqitë (see below), stop in the quaint little of village of Libohovë. There, you'll find **Libohovë Castle** *(Kalaja e Libohovës)*, a fortress built between 1741 and 1822 for Ali Pasha's sister, who lived here until she died. Only the ramparts and corner towers remain. The village is also known for **Rrapi i Libohovës**, a giant, 50m-tall plane tree estimated to be more than 220 years old. There's a humble cafe beneath the tree, perfect for basking in its natural glory.

Labovë e Kryqitë

TIME FROM GJIROKASTËR: **35 MINS**

One of Albania's oldest churches

On the hill opposite and southeast of Gjirokastër, Labovë e Kryqitë village has one of the country's oldest, and most important, Byzantine churches. **St Mary Church** *(Kisha e Fjetjes së Virgjëreshës)* was founded by Emperor Justinian of the Roman Empire in the 6th century. Justinian is said to have built it in honour of his mother and kept a relic of the True Cross there. The relic has since disappeared, allegedly taken by Enver Hoxha's daughter.

The current church, with its remarkable dome and redbrick facade featuring white geometric designs, was built as early as the 10th century, which would make it one of Albania's oldest churches. However, other sources say it was built in the 13th century. Regardless, it's one of Albania's most beautiful Byzantine churches, with numerous frescoes and an iconostasis. To see inside, call the **janitor** *(069 545 9224)*, or look for him in the bar across from the church.

ALBANIAN GULAGS

Dictator Enver Hoxha was an admirer of Joseph Stalin and copied the Soviet dictator's system of gulags. From 1945, critics of the Communist Party, along with their families, were executed, exiled or imprisoned in internment camps under horrific conditions. As many as 200,000 people were subject to forced labour, torture, psychological abuse and neglect that led to starvation and disease. The most infamous internment camp was in Spaç, where nearly 2000 people were held at one time in cells so small that no one could lie down.

Yet, despite Hoxha's clear neglect for human rights, some in Albania feel nostalgic for the stability of his regime. According to a 2016 survey, half of Albanians viewed Hoxha's role as positive, with the largest percentage (55%) living in the south.

Përmet

RIVER RAFTING | HOT SPRINGS | GASTRONOMY

☑ TOP TIP

Hike from Përmet town up to **St Mary Church** and cemetery in Leus. Inside, this church is wall-to-wall with some of the finest Orthodox frescoes you'll find not just in Albania, but anywhere. To get the key, knock on the door to the house opposite the gate.

Përmet's slogan is 'We have everything but the sea'. We're not so sure about that, but this little valley town in the quiet south of the country does indeed have a lot going for it. Namely, its proximity to two of Albania's most talked-about adventures: Benjë Hot Springs, located next to a canyon; and Vjosa River, a wild body of water that was named Europe's first national river park in 2023. Përmet has also earned a reputation as a gastronomic hub thanks to its affinity for locally sourced ingredients and recipes registered within the Slow Food network (look for the stickers).

You can spend a day here rafting and soaking in the hot springs, perhaps also with a little hike along the rim of the canyon. But like Përmet's slow food, it's best to take your time and stay as long as you can to soak in this area's sublime tranquillity.

Battle river waves

Raft in Europe's only wild national river park

After years of campaigning from international environmental organisations, as well as the Patagonia clothing company and actor Leonardo DiCaprio, Albania's **Vjosa River** was declared a wild national river park in 2023 – Europe's first. Along with the main river basin, the park protects more than 400km of

---

GETTING AROUND

Përmet is most commonly accessed via Gjirokastër or Korçë. Don't attempt to drive here from Berat, as the road from the Osum Canyon is shoddy.

The town is small and walkable, though you'll need a car to get to Benjë Hot Springs (p158) and Langarica Canyon (p158), since there are no bus routes that travel the 14km to get there. You can also organise a tour.

For rafting the Vjosa River, guides can pick you up or meet you at their offices close to Përmet. If driving, beware of the narrow, cobblestone roads up the hill. The city's most charming and historic guesthouses are up here.

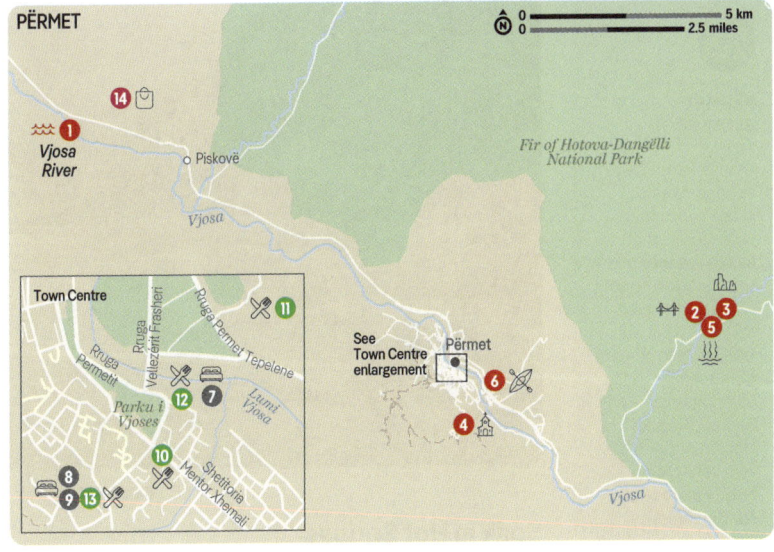

PËRMET

HIGHLIGHTS
1 Vjosa River

SIGHTS
2 Kadiu Bridge
3 Langarica Canyon
4 St Mary Church

ACTIVITIES
5 Benjë Hot Springs
6 Vjosa Rafting Albania

SLEEPING
7 Honey House Kastrioti

8 Mosaic House
9 Villa Përmet

EATING
10 Familjari
11 Sofra Përmetare
12 Te Culi

13 Villa Përmet

SHOPPING
14 Baxho Meshini

waterways and 1100 animal species from development, including hydroelectric dams.

What better way to celebrate this preservation win than to go rafting on the river? **Vjosa Rafting Albania** (raftingvjosa.al; €35) leads 2½-hour group trips twice daily. You'll bob along the river for 9km, past strange rock formations, birds, remains of Ottoman bridges bombed during WWII and sadly, plenty of trash – hopefully the park's status means that will be cleaned up soon. It's good fun, especially when the water's highest in spring (March to May). The season wraps up in October.

 EATING IN PËRMET: BEST SPOTS

Te Culi: Affordable, home-style food that adheres to Përmet's slow food principles, which emphasise local ingredients and recipes. *7am-10pm* €

Sofra Përmetare: This spot is well attuned to curious visitors hoping to try Albanian dishes; plenty of vegetarian options, too. *noon-10pm* €

Familjari: This slow food restaurant has been honing its skills since it opened as a state-run restaurant in the 1970s. *noon-11pm* €€

Villa Përmet: Try regional specialities like *gliko* and stuffed peppers, served inside a 200-year-old villa turned hotel. *12.30-3.30pm & 7.30-10.30pm* €€

PËRMET SLOW FOOD

Around Përmet, you'll see restaurants, shops and hotels with stickers that have a red snail and the title 'Slow Food'. This doesn't mean that your meal will take hours to prepare from scratch – well, hopefully not. Rather, this is to signal a partnership with Italy's **Slow Food Foundation for Biodiversity** *(fondazioneslowfood. com)*, which is active in more than 100 countries. The foundation supports businesses that believe in principles like sustainability, avoiding GMOs and cooking with local ingredients. In Përmet, slow food might be *kole* (smoked veal sausage with sour cabbage), *pastërma* (dried meat), jars of *gliko* (fruit or vegetable preserve in a sugar syrup), or cows' or sheep's cheese such as *kaçkavall*, made in a bunker at **Baxho Meshini**.

Benjë Hot Springs

Soak in Hot Springs
Thermal pools

Twenty minutes from Përmet, at the mouth of the 5km-long Langarica Canyon, **Benjë Hot Springs** *(Llixhat e Bënjës)* is a handful of mineral-rich thermal pools with healing properties. Back in the communist era, it was a therapeutic site to heal rheumatism and other ailments. These days, it's a nice place to warm up after a rafting trip, or to soothe some aching muscles, though don't expect the water to be piping hot – it's around 25°C year-round. Locals usually have a fire going nearby to warm up after the pools, and there'll be someone selling drinks and snacks (in summer only). Don't stay in the water too long, as the sulphur can be bad for your skin. The pools are alongside the Ottoman **Kadiu Bridge** *(Ura e Kadiut)*, built under the command of Ali Pasha in 1760.

See a Wild Canyon
Limestone cliffs

If you follow the river past Kadiu Bridge, you'll enter **Langarica Canyon**, a marvellous slice in the quiet landscape, with limestone cliffs that climb up to 150m on either side. From June to October, the water is low enough to walk through (water shoes are a good plan though, as it's stony below), passing a waterfall at the end of the canyon. In April, May and November, when water levels are high, walk above the canyon along the ridge, looking for pigeon-filled caves and more hot springs. Rafting companies offer guided tours, but it's safe enough to go on your own.

Korçë

MEDIEVAL ART | COLOURFUL ARCHITECTURE | BEER

Arriving in Korçë (Korça) might prompt a double-take: is this still Albania, or have you been transported to France or Italy? Occupations from both countries in the 20th century prompted Korçë to build rows of charming, colourful villas along cobblestone boulevards, particularly in the north side of town. The city also has remnants of its Ottoman rulers, with a central bazaar that has recently been renovated to be a tourist hub rather than a commerce centre, and the Byzantines, who inspired a dizzying number of churches and a museum with Albania's best collection of medieval art.

There are just a few traditional sites in this city, but don't be surprised if you feel like staying at least a couple of days in a cosy guesthouse, spending your time wandering Korçë's charming streets, drinking local beers with the city's particularly stylish residents and exploring the variety of *plein air* adventures nearby.

Bright & Beautiful Medieval Art

Not your typical gloomy Catholic art

In many countries, Catholic art consists of drab, dark portraits of church figures, rich people and war – but not in Albania. Here, Orthodox artwork bursts with pinks, turquoise, reds and blues, always with the shiny backdrop of gold to signify a spiritual halo. See the best collection of Albanian Orthodox artwork at Korçë's best museum: **Medieval Art Museum** (*Muzeu Kombëtar i Artit Mesjetar; adult/youth 700/210L*). Housed in a former church (Korçë had plenty to spare) and opened in 2016, the museum has roughly 7500 pieces ranging from the 14th to the 20th century. It's an impressive collection, especially considering so much was destroyed during the Ottoman and communist periods.

Grab a phone with an audio guide from the front desk or ask for the link to download the app, and prepare to spend a couple of hours going from one hypnotising piece

☑ TOP TIP

Don't miss Korçë's old **Bazaar** *(Pazari i Korçës)*, once home to hundreds of traders in the 19th and early 20th centuries. It was renovated in 2015 to become a square with cafes, souvenir shops and bars. A little south is the city's main mosque, **Xhamia e Iljaz Mirahorit**, built in 1496.

GETTING AROUND

Korçë is a lovely city to walk around in, with wide boulevards, parks, churches and cute cobblestone streets. There's no formal municipal bus network in the city – *furgons* (shared minibuses) drive the main thoroughfares spuriously. Hail a local taxi if you need one; they'll also take you to neighbouring villages and wait around if you don't have your own car.

KORÇË

★ HIGHLIGHTS
1. Medieval Art Museum

● SIGHTS
2. Archaeological Museum
3. Bazaar
4. Gjon Mili Museum
5. Museum of Education
6. Resurrection of Christ Orthodox Cathedral
7. Xhamia e Iljaz Mirahorit

● SLEEPING
8. At Home
9. Hani i Pazarit
10. Life Gallery
11. Vila Eden

● EATING
12. Antik
13. Le Paris
14. Shija e Saçit
15. Taverna Vasili

● DRINKING & NIGHTLIFE
16. Birra Korça

17. Kooperativa
18. Republika

● ENTERTAINMENT
19. GADK
20. Korça Beer Fest
21. Vila Cofiel

---

to another, as nearly every single one is explained in vivid detail. Highlights include the huge 19th-century iconostasis from the village of Rehovë and the icon of St Christopher with the face of a dog.

Find more Catholic art in the city's main church, the **Resurrection of Christ Orthodox Cathedral** (*Katedralja Ortodokse Ringjallja e Krishtit*). It was built in 1993, so the painted figures here didn't face the wrath of having their eyes and noses scratched out by Ottomans or secular adherents to the dictatorship. The dome and wooden chandeliers are particularly enchanting.

Behind the cathedral, Korçë's **Archaeological Museum**, in a 19th-century Ottoman mansion, was being renovated during research, but it traditionally has a collection of hundreds of pre-historical objects that were discovered in the area and two skeletons from an Illyrian burial site.

Unforgettable Photography
Portraits of Picasso by Gjon Mili

Albania is blessed with excellent photographers. Foremost among them is Gjon Mili (1904–84), a photojournalist who took portraits of some of the 20th century's most famous faces for *Life* magazine. As an electric engineer trained at the Massachusetts Institute of Technology (MIT), Mili was a pioneer in using stroboscopic and electronic flash to light his subjects. His work has also been featured in 17 exhibitions at New York's Museum of Modern Art.

MORE ALBANIAN PHOTOGRAPHY
Head to the one-of-a-kind **Marubi National Photography Museum** (p112) in Shkodër to see the photographic collection of the Marubi 'dynasty', Albania's first and foremost family of photographers.

See replicas of many of Mili's portraits (*Life* has the rights to the originals) at the **Gjon Mili Museum** *(200L)*. You'll see striking images of Salvador Dalí, Alfred Hitchcock, Adolf Eichmann, Edith Piaf, Miles Davis, and a particularly stunning set of portraits of Pablo Picasso that are bound to flash in your mind like the light in the photos for years to come.

To see how the mix of photography and technology has progressed since, catch an immersive show at **GADK** *(Galeria Arteve Digjitale; gadk.al; 600L)*. Twenty-minute shows have you standing in the centre of a room as images surround you. Recent exhibitions have featured Italian art, Van Gogh and socialist realism from Albanian painters including Vilson Kilica and Ismail Lulani.

Tour Albania's Oldest Brewery
See the process from grain to bottle at Birra Korça

Green bottles of Korçë beer are everywhere in Albania, with the blonde European pilsner still made where it was first brewed in 1928 by Italian entrepreneur Umberto Umberti.

Birra Korça *(birrakorca.com.al)* leads free tours in English from 10am to 3pm daily, where you'll hear the brand's interesting history when it was state-controlled during communism,

LITTLE PARIS

Korçë changed hands several times in the early 20th century, leaving a lasting impact on the city's attitude and architecture. Two years after Albanian independence, Korçë was taken by the Greeks, but it was lost to Allied France in 1916 during WWI in order to protect the Serbian army. France controlled Korçë until 1920, earning it the nickname 'Little Paris'; the French built a Lycée school that educated Albanian elites for decades, including dictator Enver Hoxha. In 1939, Fascist Italy took Korçë, followed by the Germans until 1944, though many in town had different ideas. The Albanian Communist Party was founded in Korçë in 1941. Perspectives changed after the dictatorship, with Korçe heavily supporting the Democratic Party in the free elections of 1990.

 EATING IN KORÇË: OUR PICKS

Shija e Saçit: Taste Korçan *lakror* (baked spinach pie) in an alley behind the bazaar. Expect to wait, as it's baked fresh. *10am-4pm & 7-11pm* €

Le Paris: Stop for a buttery croissant and stick around for a sumptuous meal at this cafe, owned by a French and Albanian couple. *8am-11pm Tue-Sun* €€

Antik: Ask a local, and they'll probably recommend this spot. The tasty Albanian and Italian food, all at fair prices, proves them right. *11.30am-11.30pm* €€

Taverna Vasili: Intimate steakhouse resembling a local's home, with a raised terrace for alfresco dining. There's live music at weekends. *12.30-11.30pm* €€

BEST SOUTHEASTERN FESTIVALS

Wine & Stories *(@wineandstoriesofberat):* Celebrate Albania's best wine region with tastings, live DJs, concerts and talks taking place in October/November.

National Folk Festival: Every five years in June/July, Gjirokastër hosts Albania's most important cultural festival with music, dancing and iso-polyphony singing in the castle. The next one is in 2028.

Korça Beer Fest *(@festaebirreskorce):* Cool off from the summer heat in August at Albania's largest beer festival, featuring more than 40 breweries and tens of thousands of visitors.

Lakror Festival: Women in Korçë and nearby villages, including Polenë, Voskopojë and Boboshticë, come together in August to bake *lakror,* the region's treasured savoury pie, cooked in a *saç* (large metal pan) on an open fire.

Museum of Education

and see the process from grain to bottle. This isn't your typical major brewery tour – you'll be able to drink a glass of unfiltered beer hosed straight from the tank – which is why it's great. Stick around at the bar for some of the cheapest pints you'll find anywhere, at just 80L.

First Albanian Language School
Wander the wooden school floors

For centuries of Ottoman rule (roughly from 1385 to 1912), the Albanian Shqip language was spoken but not taught. That all changed in 1887 with the opening of the first language school in an 1840 Korçë house owned by the patriotic Tërpo brothers. At the **Museum of Education** *(Mësonjëtorja e parë shqipe dhe Muzeu i Arsimit; 300L)*, walk along the old wooden floors of the school rooms (the first in Korçë to have boys and girls seated together) and see original photographs and textbooks.

 DRINKING IN KORÇË: OUR PICKS

Birra Korça: Have a pint for less than a euro at the expansive bar terrace of the brewery that makes Albania's most popular beer. *8am-midnight*

Republika: Sports bar meets gastropub meets cool cocktail club that's popular among Korçë's young, well-dressed crowd. *8am-2am*

Vila Cofiel: This cavernous bar and restaurant is one of the few places in Albania where you'll frequently hear traditional Albanian music. *8am-midnight*

Kooperativa: Tiny communist-themed cafe and bar terrace on the bazaar. Has a small but tasty snack menu, including *qofte* (meatballs). *7am-1am*

Beyond Korçë

This area is full of surprises: a beach in eastern Albania, the church-filled ghost town of Voskopojë, an unforgettable drive to the coast and great skiing.

Few international visitors will have heard of the destinations in this part of Albania, and that's the best thing about it. Explore the mountains west of Korçë to go horse riding and see Voskopojë, a ghost town that seems to have more churches than houses. Southbound is a ski town (yep, Albania has a ski resort) and a new mountain highway that can take you all the way to the Albanian Riviera. North, this side of Lake Ohrid has a few cute villages with a beach for swimming and pedal boating, as well as peaceful freshwater canals and some of the finest ancient mosaics in the Balkans.

Places
Turan p163
Voskopojë p163
Dardhë p164
Pogradec p165
Lin p168

Turan
TIME FROM KORÇË: **10 MINS**
Horse-riding journeys
House of Horses (*@shtepiaekuajve; per hr 2000L*), a hotel, restaurant and stable 4km from Korçë, is passionate about its horses and offers rides that are much more than a simple stomp around. They run one-hour trips along the river for beginners, along with three-hour jaunts up the mountains. But if you're an experienced rider, try one of their four- or five-day trips through the mountains; they run throughout the year.

Voskopojë
TIME FROM KORÇË: **30 MINS**
Church town nestled beside mountains
Due west of Korçë, Voskopojë, aka Moscopole, may be a tiny village surrounded by mountains today, but as recently as 1750, it was a commerce hub close to the Roman Via Egnatia (p65), which ran from Venice to Constantinople. With 50,000 inhabitants, many of whom were Aromanian Christians (a persisting minority in the Balkans), the village had a university, the region's first printing press and a whopping 26 churches, all but eight of which were destroyed by the end of the 18th century. A handful of churches and a monastery are still standing, prompting a plethora of new guesthouses to catch the influx of summer visitors.

The largest and most accessible surviving prayer sites are **St Mary Church** (*Kisha Fjetja e Shën Mërisë*), built between

GETTING AROUND

Pogradec is your best bet via *furgon* (shared minibus) – the rest of the towns and villages here will require your own vehicle or taxi from Korçë. Main highways are decently maintained, and the mountain road towards Përmet was recently paved – just brace for plenty of ups, downs and hair-raising turns. For an in-depth look at southern Albania, especially its unique foodways, consider an eight-day **Folklore Tour** (*agrotourism.gov.al/folklore-tour*).

MOTHER TERESA

Anjezë Gonxhe Bojaxhiu (1910–97), better known as Mother Teresa, is easily the world's most famous Albanian. Born ethnic Albanian in Skopje, North Macedonia, she moved to Ireland at 18 to join the Sisters of Loreto and left a year later for missionary work in Calcutta, India. Mother Teresa devoted her life to helping the poor, sick and disabled, most benevolently establishing a colony in India for people with leprosy. She was awarded the Nobel Peace Prize in 1979 for her humanitarian work and posthumously canonised as St Teresa of Calcutta in 2016.

Mother Teresa's connection to Albania was strong throughout her life, with her family moving to Tirana in 1934. She was prohibited from visiting during the secularist dictatorship and only managed to visit twice before her death.

MARISHA_SL/SHUTTERSTOCK

1694 and 1699; and **St Nicholas Church** (Kisha Shën Kolli), an early-18th-century church with frescoes by the Zografi Brothers, who were famous Albanian painters.

Outside the centre, there's **St John the Baptist Monastery** (Manastiri i Shën Prodromit), built in 1632 and located on a hilltop 30 minutes' hike from town; **St Athanasius Church** (Kisha Shën Thanasit), an 18th-century church with vivid gold and blue frescoes by the Zografi Brothers; and **Prophet Elijah Church** (Kisha e Profet Ilias), a basilica built in 1751 that was damaged in a 1960 earthquake.

If you're sticking around for a meal, you'll be fed well with lakror (baked spinach pie) and other shareables at **George** (@georgeboutiquehotel_restaurant).

Dardhë

TIME FROM KORÇË: **35 MINS**

Mountain village for winter skiing or a summer retreat

Despite being filled with mountains, the only place in Albania to go skiing is at **Ski Pista Begell** (@skipistabigell), located on the outskirts of the charming mountain village of Dardhë, 20km from Korçë. The resort has two lifts – dropping from a max elevation of 1663m – along with equipment for rent and a restaurant in the lodge. Make a weekend out of it by staying in the village: it gets blanketed in snow in winter and has cosy stone and wood B&Bs stacked on the hillside, along a winding cobblestone road. Be careful on the roads if you're driving. In summer, Dardhë is a growing destination as a fresh-air retreat from the heat.

Frescoes, St Nicholas Church

On the way into town, be sure to stop for lunch at the very welcoming agrotourism pioneer, **Antoneta** *(@taverna_antoneta_boboshtice)*, which has been open since 2000.

Pogradec

TIME FROM KORÇË: **45 MINS**

Ancient lake surrounded by boardwalks and villages

While two-thirds of ancient **Lake Ohrid** are in North Macedonia, a third of the 358-sq-km lake is in Albania, and its coast is a popular summer retreat for locals, though off the beaten track for international visitors. The first village you'll see if driving from Korçë is **Pogradec**, where there's a long beach that you can swim in or rent pedal boats. The boardwalk alongside the beach is perfect for an evening *xhiro* (after-dinner stroll), especially after tucking into the smoked duck at **Rosa e Tymosur** *(@rosaetymosur)*.

A 10-minute drive east along the water is **Drilon National Park** *(free)*, a cool forest along a freshwater stream crisscrossed by flat trails and 13 pedestrian bridges ranging from 7m to 44m long. Have a coffee or try fresh lake trout at one of the lakeside restaurants and watch the ducks, just like dictator Enver Hoxha used to when he vacationed here.

A few minutes farther along the lake, **Tushemisht** is one of Albania's cutest villages to meander through. It has a stone boardwalk lining a crystal-clear canal and a Byzantine-style church up the hill. If you're hungry, eat *tavë Koran* (lake trout cooked with tomatoes and onions) at **Ollga**.

DRIVING TOUR

Drive Korçë to the Coast

Take the road less travelled across southeastern Albania, where you'll traverse a serious mountain chain through the Vjosa Valley, then up to high-altitude Nivicë Canyon before dropping down the side of a mountain to the Ionian coastline. There are plenty of places to stop for gourmet food, and you'll find lots of cosy and/or luxurious guesthouses. A regular vehicle is fine, but a 4WD is key for the suggested detours.

1 Melesin Distillery

Beginning in Korçë (p159), drive southwest on SH 75. This is one of Albania's wildest mountain roads, with big climbs, steep drops and wild turns. Prepare your stomach accordingly. Your first stop is at what *TIME* magazine called one of the 'World's Greatest Places': the **Melesin Distillery** *(melesin.com)* in Leskovik. The state-of-the-art *raki* (fruit brandy) distillery is impressive, yet it feels strange to find this luxe establishment in such a quiet town.

The Drive: The highway to Përmet is less dramatic, and quite pretty along the river. Turn right on Rr Benjës to detour to Benjë Hot Springs (p158) – your muscles could probably use the relaxation after that drive.

2 Përmet

Follow the wild Vjosa River to the adventure base of Përmet (p156). This valley town is known for its slow food restaurants and rafting trips on the Vjosa River (p156), which was named Europe's first national river park in 2023.

Rafters, Vjosa River

The Drive: Continue north on SH 75, stopping along the highway for artisanal cheese at Baxho Meshini (p158) and at the (super touristy) Vjosa Waterfalls. If you have time and a 4WD vehicle that can handle atrocious potholes, detour to Teqja e Baba Aliut, a hilltop Bektashi *teqe* (shrine).

3 Tepelenë

You'll see the landscape change when you cross the narrow **Këlcyrë Gorge**. Turn right on SH 4 towards Tepelenë (p155), Ali Pasha's hometown. While you're here, visit the Tepelenë Castle (p155) and see where hundreds of political prisoners were held at the Tepelenë Internment Camp (p155).

The Drive: Leave Tepelenë on the road heading southwest towards Bëncë. Expect another amazing mountain drive, this time between the peaks. It's all well paved and easy-going, with few cars.

4 Nivicë Canyon

You'll pass the 19th-century **Ali Pasha Aqueduct** on your way to **Progonat**, where you can park and hike for 20 minutes to the amazing 400m-tall **Peshturë Waterfall**. Pass a bold Communist monument on your way to the 40km **Nivicë Canyon**, a natural paradise home to waterfalls and wildflowers. It's also one of the longest canyons in Europe.

The Drive: Backtrack from Nivicë and take the road opposite Sofra Labe Restaurant. This mountain road from Nivicë is a nifty way to get to the coast, with great views of the sea.

5 Himarë

Gaze at the Ionian Sea as you drop down to SH 76 just after Kuç. Turn left towards SH 8, a coastal road where there's plenty of stops, including the former ghost town of Upper Qeparo (p96), long Borsh Beach (p85) and Ali Pasha's Porto Palermo Castle (p95). Finish your drive in **Himarë**, a Riviera hub with some of Albania's most amazing turquoise beaches.

LOST MONASTERY

One of this region's most important and beautiful monasteries was part of Albania just over a century ago, but now resides just 1km over the border in North Macedonia. Bordering Lake Ohrid, **St Naum Monastery** was initially founded in 905 and rebuilt in the 16th and 17th centuries into a gorgeous Byzantine-style structure with an intricate iconostasis from 1711 and a tranquil garden filled with roses and peacocks.

The monastery was part of Albania when the country declared independence in 1912, but it was handed over to Yugoslavia in 1925 by King Zog I as a peace offering. Head across to North Macedonia for a quick visit if your passport allows for easy entry.

Pogradec (p165)

Lin

TIME FROM KORÇË: 1 HR

Marvellous Byzantine mosaics

In the 6th century, the small fishing village of Lin, at Albania's northern border with Lake Ohrid (p165), was home to a Paleo-Christian basilica with a gorgeous mosaic floor that was destroyed a few centuries later. All that remains is the floor, but it's well worth seeing.

When you arrive, call the janitor, **Roland** *(067 639 9436)*, to open up the gate and see the mosaics. **Lin Mosaics** *(Mozaiku i Linit)* is one of the largest mosaic floors in the Balkans, covering several rooms of the basilica, including its baptistery and curved naves. Featuring intricate designs of birds, grapes, pottery and an interlocking rope-like design, the mosaic is sometimes covered for its protection, but Roland will happily lift the cover to show you. The visit won't take you more than 30 minutes, but the mosaics, combined with the views over the lake, are well worth the trip.

Places We Love to Stay

€ Budget €€ Midrange €€€ Top End

Berat

Berat Backpackers € The best hostel in Berat, and also the oldest, is on the Goricë side. It has dorms, camping, a garden and a fun atmosphere.

Klea Hotel €€ Hilltop hideaway inside the castle, with five compact, wood-panelled rooms, pretty patios and a lovely restaurant terrace.

Bujtina Kodikët €€ Enchanting stone guesthouse within the Mangalem maze, but don't worry about getting lost, as it's just steps from the entrance to the neighbourhood.

Vista €€€ Stylish boutique hotel on the uppermost street of Goricë. A healthy mix of modern comforts while also paying homage to the neighborhood's historic stone decor.

Mangalemi Hotel €€€ Built over Ali Pasha's 1764 palace, this is Berat's first post-communism hotel, and possibly its most charming accommodation, with charming traditional furnishings.

Gjirokastër

Stone City Hostel € Dutch owner Wouter runs Albania's best hostel, with modern-meets-traditional decor and daily activities including fascinating history walks and 4WD tours.

Gjirokastra Hotel €€ Lovely family-run hotel inside a 300-year-old house with huge balconies and gorgeously carved wooden ceilings. The suite (which sleeps four) feels like sleeping inside a museum.

Old Bazaar 1790 €€ Immerse yourself in 18th-century Gjirokastër at this 11-room boutique hotel close to the bazaar. Rooms have ornate, hand-crafted bed frames and cute windows revealing views of the town.

Kalemi 2 €€ A centrally located stone mansion that has some beautiful furnishings in its 16 individually decorated rooms. Modern bathrooms contrast with the elaborate, traditional ceilings. Excellent food, too.

Kerculla Resort €€€ Feel like a sultan in this palatial hotel overlooking Gjirokastër. It features intricate wooden carvings, a relaxing pool area and exquisite views.

Beyond Gjirokastër

Ferma Grand Albanik €€ Escape to this hilltop agrotourism destination between Përmet and Gjirokastër to delve into the region's slow food and enjoy its unparalleled peacefulness. Also does yoga retreats.

Bujtina Mbi Kanion €€ Views don't get any better than from these cabins along the edge of Nivicë Canyon. Get here from Tepelenë or from the coast.

Përmet

Honey House Kastrioti € Small residential house on the Vjosa River with friendly owners. Breakfasts on the picnic table facing the river are especially sweet.

Mosaic House €€ Stay in Përmet's charming old town up on the hill; this stone guesthouse has a garden bursting with flowers and a fascinating mosaic of natural stones. A little oasis.

Villa Përmet €€€ An 1800s villa transformed into a luxurious four-star hotel. The restaurant is one of the best in town for regional dishes.

Leskovik

Farma Sotira €€ Family-friendly wooden cabins surrounded by forest in the very south of Albania, with horse riding and a playground. Trout fished to order from the pond.

Melesin Distillery €€€ Had too much artisanal *raki* (fruit brandy)? The renowned distillery in the tiny village of Leskovik also has comfortable, modern rooms.

Korçë

At Home € Korçë's only hostel consists of two dorm rooms above a friendly local's house. Breakfast isn't included, but guests may use the kitchen.

Vila Eden €€ Artistic boutique hotel that feels straight out of a medieval painting, with a bright turquoise facade and rooms reminiscent of a king's quarters.

Hani i Pazarit €€ Merchants used to trade their horses in the courtyard of this 350-year-old structure close to the central Bazaar; now it's a lavish hotel. Oh, how things change.

Life Gallery €€€ This sleek design hotel would be a surprise anywhere in the Balkans, but in tiny Korçë, it's almost unbelievable. Rooms in the mansion are spacious, with minimalist design and high-thread-count sheets; there's also a pool.

TOOLKIT

Old house in Berat (p138)
NOMAD PIXEL/SHUTTERSTOCK

TOOLKIT

The chapters in this section cover the most important topics you'll need to know about in Albania. They're full of nuts-and-bolts information and valuable insights to help you understand and navigate Albania and get the most out of your trip.

Arriving
p172

Getting Around
p173

Money
p174

Accommodation
p175

Family Travel
p176

Health & Safe Travel
p177

Food, Drink & Nightlife
p178

Responsible Travel
p180

LGBTIQ+ Travellers
p182

Accessible Travel
p183

Driving in Albania
p184

Nuts & Bolts
p185

Language
p186

Arriving

Tirana International Airport Nënë Tereza is Albania's main port of entry, though Vlorë International Airport, opened summer 2025, is a competitor. Another common way to enter the country is via ferry from the Greek island of Corfu. Albania also has land borders with Greece, Montenegro, North Macedonia and Kosovo.

Visas

Citizens of Schengen Zone countries, along with nearly 60 more, including Australia, Canada and China, can enter Albania without a visa for up to 90 days within a 180-day period. US citizens can stay up to one year.

Arriving by Boat

The best way to get to the Albanian Riviera is via a 'Flying Dolphin' boat, which travels between Sarandë and the Greek island of Corfu. There are also ferries to Durrës and Vlorë from Bari and Brindisi in Italy.

Arriving by Car

If entering Albania via a land border, you'll need to present your vehicle registration/ ownership documents and a valid third-party insurance policy, such as a Green Card. Check that your policy covers international border crossings.

SIM Cards

Buy a local SIM from Vodafone or ONE at Tirana International Airport. We recommend Vodafone, which offers 21-day prepaid packages that include 40/100GB of data and 1000/ unlimited minutes of local calling for 2400/7500L.

Travel to Skanderbeg Square, Tirana

Tirana International Airport Nënë Tereza

BUS — From 30 min; **400L**

LUX ELECTRIC TAXI — From 20 min; **1100L**

AIRPORT TAXI — From 20 min; **2300L**

BEACH BUS

RivieraBus *(rivierabus.com; €50)* takes travellers in its seven-person air-conditioned vans from Tirana to Sarandë (or vice versa) along the Albanian Riviera from 31 May to 30 August, stopping at beach towns such as Dhërmi, Himarë and Borsh. The van picks up at accommodation in **Blloku** (p52) at 9am on Tuesdays, Thursdays and Saturdays and charges €50 no matter where you stop. From 2 July to 31 August, RivieraBus does the Vlorë and Sarandë route on Wednesdays, Fridays and Sundays for €30.

Getting Around

There are no easy options when it comes to getting around Albania, with public transport unpredictable and mountain roads dramatic. Decide based on your budget and time available.

TRANSPORT COSTS

Tirana city bus ticket
40L

Tirana to Korçë *furgon*
500L

Shkodër bike hire
500L per hour

Car hire
from 1600L per day

Furgon

The most widespread, and cheapest, way to get around is via *furgon*: a shared minibus (can also be a van or car) that picks up passengers at hubs or at the side of the road. *Furgons* don't leave on predetermined schedules, and they stop along the way. This makes arrival times unpredictable, meaning you'll need a loose schedule. That said, they're a fun way to mix with locals. Bring small lekë to pay in cash.

TRAFFIC STOPS

Traffic stops are common across Albania, as police don't use automated speed meters. Make sure you have your driver's licence and car insurance with you.

Car Hire

Driving in Albania has plenty of issues (erratic drivers, tiny village roads, potholes off highways), but it's the only way to see much of the country, and the drives are gorgeous. Hire a car from a private company (there are very few international brands) in Tirana, Sarandë or Vlorë. Most only accept cash, meaning you won't be able to use the insurance tied to your credit card.

TIP

A beautiful way to experience the Albanian Alps is to embark on the three-hour crossing from Koman to Fierzë via the **Lake Koman Ferry** *(komanilakeferry.com)*. Get on the boat at the **Koman Ferry Terminal** (p120) and head down the Drin River. Reserve ahead, as spots fill up. It's also possible to take smaller private boats from Koman to the hidden beach of **Lumi i Shales** (p126).

Bike

Cycling is a growing mode of transport in Albania, especially in Tirana, Durrës and Shkodër, the latter of which has a strong cycling culture. Many accommodation options in these cities have bikes to use, and rental agencies are around. Bike touring is also becoming popular, especially in northern Albania.

Taxi

Albania doesn't have rideshare taxis such as Uber, Bolt or Lyft. Instead, cities have municipal cabs that use a meter. In Tirana, electric-powered private taxi companies such as **Lux** *(+355 69 844 4487)* are a cheaper alternative to official cabs, and pick-ups can be coordinated via WhatsApp.

Private Transfer

If you don't drive, don't want to hire a car and want to skip the hassle of a *furgon*, **DayTrip** *(daytrip.com)* is an option. It features local, English-speaking drivers who can take you to different sights on a curated schedule. They'll even wait as you do some sightseeing.

DRIVING ESSENTIALS

Drive on the right

Speed limits in towns and cities are 40km/h; highways are 90–110km/h

Blood alcohol limit is 0.01%

Money

CURRENCY: ALBANIAN LEK (L) AND EURO (€)

Cash

Cash is still king nearly everywhere in Albania. Both Albanian lekë and euro are accepted, and most businesses will give you the actual conversion rate. You'll find ATMs dispensing lekë in all major towns and cities, just expect to be slapped with a 500–850L fee and possibly a conversion percentage, in addition to what your home bank charges.

Card Payments

Few businesses in Albania accept debit or credit card payments, though if they do, they'll probably accept contactless. Hotels and restaurants in Tirana and Sarandë are your best shot at paying with card; if they do accept them, expect to be faced with an extra fee.

Tipping

Tipping is not expected in Albania, though it is appreciated. That said, tipping more than 15% runs the risk of influencing the culture.
Restaurant and cafes 5–10%
Tour guides 10%
Taxi drivers round up

HOW MUCH FOR A...

Museum entry ticket
200–1000L

Parking spot
200–500L per day

Beach umbrella and chair
300–1000L

River-rafting tour
from 3500L

HOW TO... Save Money

Albania's recent attention as a tourist destination has led some locals to take advantage of tourists by charging unfair prices, especially for souvenirs, tours and experiences. Ask a trusted local how much something should cost before agreeing to buy. It's also acceptable to kindly push back if you feel the price is too high, and feel free to haggle.

CURRENCY

Both Albanian lekë and euros are accepted everywhere, so there's no need to exchange. Change can often be given in either currency. Hold on to small bills, as €50, €100, 5000L and 10,000L bills aren't always accepted.

CASH = CORRUPTION

How do you avoid the government nosing around in your business? You never leave a paper trail, of course. Being able to hide income is one of the reasons Albania is mainly cash-only. It also has to do with the 1996–97 **pyramid scheme crisis** (p83), which created general distrust in the banks. Another reason? Albania is well behind other countries due to its 45-year communist dictatorship. Nonetheless, card payments are beginning to be accepted – slowly but surely.

Accommodation

Hostels for All

Albania has a strong network of backpackers' hostels, the first of which – **Tirana Backpacker Hostel** (p71) – opened back in 2005. Hostels in the country tend to be social, but with less of a full-on party atmosphere as elsewhere in Europe. They're also frequented by travellers of all ages, though certain age groups tend to flock to certain hostels.

Camping & Boondocking

Albania is one of the few countries where wild or dry camping, aka boondocking, is permitted. If you stay off private property and parkland, you should be good to freely set up your tent or park your van for the night. Alternatively, there are several cool campgrounds along the coast with ready-to-sleep tents and equipment to rent.

Authentic Architecture

More than 500 years of Ottoman rule left plenty of gorgeous homes across Albania, with many being turned into accommodation types. Find authentic stays in 200- or 300-year-old buildings in **Berat** (p138) and **Gjirokastër** (p147). Alternatively, feel Italy and France's impact on Albania by staying in villas on the coast in **Durrës** (p62) or in the colourful, culture-rich city of **Korçë** (p159).

Cosy Cabins

A lack of roads across the Albanian Alps has left the area pleasantly peaceful, with little to do but hike and gaze at the surrounding mountains. Stay in a stone and wood cabin in **Theth** (p128) or **Valbonë** (p121) for a cosy experience any time of year, or book a shepherd's hut in a smaller town for a more isolated experience.

HOW MUCH FOR A NIGHT IN A...

Hostel
from 1000L

B&B
3000–6000L

Beach hotel
from 6000L

Beachfront

Let's face it, many come to Albania to appreciate its wonderful turquoise-tinted water on the Ionian coast. You'll find plenty of modern hotels and resorts steps from the beaches in **Ksamil** (p86), but there are more options throughout the entire coastline. Note that most hotels will require at least some walking to get to the beach.

STAY LOCAL

Albania's rising popularity as a summer destination has undoubtedly been a boost for the country's economy as a whole, but it's worth questioning how many locals benefit from those funds. Many of the hotels and resorts on Albania's beachfront, for instance, are owned and operated by foreigners. The most famous example is the future development coming to **Sazan Island** (p103) and the Vjosë-Nartë Delta Protected Area by a company connected to Jared Kushner and Ivanka Trump. Try to stay at an accommodation owned by locals.

Family Travel

Don't be surprised if your kids are welcomed even more warmly than you are in Albania. The country is still rather traditional, so nuclear families with kids are common, and children are usually welcomed with a smile and a playful tone. And they won't go hungry, with plenty of restaurants serving kid-friendly food options including pizza and *byrek* (flaky pastry filled with spinach, cheese or meat).

Best Areas for Kids

Let their imaginations run wild, along with their legs, inside ancient castles, where there's plenty of space to run around. Or stick to the capital, Tirana, which has the best concentration of kid-friendly activities, including playgrounds, ziplines and a water park. It also has the best hospitals for emergencies. Or make it a beach vacation – there are plenty of long, family-friendly beaches on the coast.

Pro Tips

Don't expect many baby-changing stations, but plenty of restaurants will have high chairs. Essentials such as nappies, wipes and formula aren't always available in rural or beach areas, so bring them with you. Sunscreen isn't always available either, and it's surprisingly expensive. Nursing in public is common. Bringing a baby carrier with you is a good idea, as strollers can be tricky on uneven sidewalks.

Parent Consent Form

With Albanians being most accustomed to two-parent nuclear families, kids travelling with one parent, grandparents or a step-parent could be seen as suspicious. Bring signed permission from one or both parents to show that consent has been given for the trip.

Discounted Entry

Many museums and sites, such as **Butrint** (p88), offer free entry for children under 11 and half-price tickets for adolescents aged 12 to 18.

KID-FRIENDLY PICKS

Borsh Beach (p85)

Ksamil's beaches are hectic. Head to Borsh Beach instead; located north of Sarandë, it has plenty of space to run around.

AquaPark Magic Blue Water (p57)

Cool off with some splish-splashing at this water park north of Tirana.

Berat Castle (p138)

This huge, city-sized castle is perfect for running around in and will spark kids' imaginations.

Lumi i Shales (p126)

Take a day trip on a mini boat to this hidden river beach within the Albanian Alps.

ROAD TRIPPING

With Albania's *furgons* (shared minibuses) being as unpredictable and crammed as they are, having your own wheels is a better bet when travelling with kids. Plus, road trips in Albania are a lot of fun, and distances are never that far in this small country.

Ideally, drive a motorhome into the country and wild or dry camp (permitted across Albania). A car will also do.

A great drive is along the Albanian Riviera, where you can go searching for the best beaches and climb cool castles and fortresses. Or drive north from **Shkodër to Vermosh** (p124), passing up and over the Albanian Alps.

Health & Safe Travel

YES, IT'S SAFE

Many people will warn you about travelling to Albania. These stereotypes date back to the time of Enver Hoxha's dictatorship (1944–92), when the country was mysterious and isolated. It also derives from the movie *Taken* (the kidnappers were Albanian) as well as an admittedly violent Albanian mafia elsewhere in Europe. But travelling here is as safe as anywhere in Europe, if not more so.

Summer Heat

The most common risk to travellers in Albania is sunstroke. Temperatures get surprisingly hot from June to September, often eclipsing 30°C and even reaching 40°C. Cities like Berat and Shkodër offer little shade, and beach towns like Sarandë and Ksamil get steaming hot when you're not in the water. Drink plenty of water (unfortunately, bottled will have to do) and apply sunscreen.

Conflict

Albania is in a prolonged period of peace domestically, which is a feat to be modelled considering the various religious groups the country is home to. Albania also has solid relations with its neighbours (another feat, especially in the Balkans). Serbia, which has an ongoing conflict with Albanians in Kosovo, has no explicit beef with Albania, and many Serbians holiday here.

TAP WATER

Tap water is not drinkable anywhere in Albania, but it's safe enough for brushing your teeth and washing fruit and veggies.

SWIM SAFETY

Green: Safe to swim

Yellow: Swim with caution

Red: Swimming prohibited

The Mafia

Albanians across Europe have become an intimidating force in organised crime, controlling major international drug routes and conducting violent killings. Certainly, many of them visit or live in Albania and use its ports, though the Albanian, Italian and Greek forces keep a close eye. But as travellers, there's no reason to worry about being tangled up with these criminals, unless perhaps you're buying illegal drugs.

INSURANCE

Travel insurance is a smart idea in Albania – you never know what can happen, especially with the potential dangers of driving on narrow mountain roads. Albania's public hospitals aren't the best – go with a private one if your insurance company will cover it. If you plan on trying some adventure sports, make sure your plan covers them.

Food, Drink & Nightlife

When to Eat

Breakfast (Mëngjes) (6am to 9am) Breakfast is just coffee, cigarettes and *raki* (fruit brandy) for most, but it's also prime time for savoury pies like the *lakror* (baked spinach pie).

Lunch (Drekë) (1pm to 3pm) Lunch is the main meal of the day, with plates of salad, bread, and meat or fish, all served individually rather than on one plate.

Dinner (Darkë) (7pm to 10pm) Dinner is typically lighter, though still hearty. A good time for soup.

Where to Eat

Agroturizëm Farm-to-table restaurants and guesthouses with homemade food.

Furre bukë/byrektorë Bakery serving bread, *byrek* and sweets.

Gjellëtore The name translates as 'stew', but it's also come to mean a casual restaurant serving traditional food.

Kafene Cafes that are open all day, with locals sipping espressos and sometimes *raki*, though rarely eating food.

Pasticeri Sells pastries and sweets such as *bakllava* (layered filo dough with honey and nuts).

Piceri Pizzeria.

Restorant Peshku Seafood restaurants, particularly prevalent along the coast.

Zgarë/Tavernë Barbecue restaurants for grilled meats, including cigar-sized meatballs and spicy sausages.

MENU DECODER

Arra Nuts
Birrë Beer
Bukë Bread
Byrek Flaky pastry filled with spinach, cheese or meat
Çaj mali Herbal mountain tea
Dhallë Yoghurt drink
Djathë Cheese
Fërgesë Light summer dip made with pan-fried peppers and ricotta
Japrak/dollma Grape leaves stuffed with meat
Kafe turke Turkish-style coffee
Kripë Salt
Lakror Korçan pie filled with spinach, sometimes also has leeks or cheese
Mish Beef

Moussaka Layered aubergines, meat and potatoes
Perime Vegetables
Petulla Fried dough balls
Peshku Fish
Pulë Chicken
Qofte Spiced beef or lamb meatballs
Raki Fruit brandy
Salatë Salad
Sheqer Sugar
Speca me gjizë/patëllxhan Peppers or aubergines stuffed with rice and sometimes meat
Salcë kosi Yoghurt dip similar to tzatziki
Tavë kosi Baked lamb with yoghurt and rice
Ujë Water
Verë e kuqe/bardhë Red or white wine
Vezë Egg

HOW TO... Drink in Albania

Like elsewhere in the Balkans, *raki* – a fruit brandy made with grapes, plums, mulberries, figs or walnuts – is a national spirit in Albania. Many rural Albanians distil their own *raki* with processing strategies passed down through generations. There's a good chance you'll be offered a small glass of *raki* at any time of the day or night – even for breakfast. But be careful. Don't shoot *raki* as you would tequila in a club. Sip it, as it's stronger than most spirits, often above 45%.

Despite Albania being home to a predominantly Muslim population, beer is common, with most opting for local lagers branded with the cities they're brewed in: Tirana, Korça and Peja. Korça Beer is the best if you ask us. Some craft breweries have been opening up in Tirana, but you'll rarely see craft beers served outside the capital.

CREATUS/SHUTTERSTOCK

HOW MUCH FOR A...

Kafe
60L

Byrek
80L

Korça Beer
150L

Paçe soup
250L

Village salad
300L

Grilled meat
500–700L

Pizza
500–800L

Seafood pasta
800–1000L

HOW TO... Navigate Albanian Food

Traditional Albanian dishes are served one item at a time rather than as a mixed plate. This makes it great for sharing, but costly (and filling) for solo travellers. A typical lunch or dinner will often feature thick country bread, a village/Albanian/Greek salad (tomatoes, cucumber and cheese) and a protein like *qofte* (meatballs) or *tavë kosi* (baked lamb with yoghurt and rice). Vegetarian options include *fasulë* (white bean soup) and *speca me gjizë/patëllxhan* (peppers or aubergines stuffed with rice), though make sure you ask if they've added any meat.

On the coast, expect fresh fish and Italian- or Greek-inspired dishes such as seafood pasta and moussaka (layered aubergine and meat dish). Fish is also common around Lake Shkodër, where baked carp is the speciality, and Lake Ohrid, where *koran* (lake trout) is common.

Dessert in Albania is commonly *bakllava* (layered filo dough with honey and nuts), though keep an eye out for Albanian traditional sweets like *flia* (layered crepes) and *hasude* (cornstarch pudding). You'll also see plenty of gelato on the coast.

If you just want something quick, pop into a *furre bukë* (bakery) for a *byrek* (flaky pastry filled with spinach, cheese or meat). You'll also find plenty of pizzerias, burger joints and, increasingly, falafel and kebab outlets.

Xhiro

Every evening after dinner, Albanians take to their city's loveliest promenade and partake in the age-old tradition called *xhiro*. This is a time for locals to walk off their dinner, chit-chat and get some healthy exercise.

ALBANIAN WINE

Albania has a 3000-year-old winemaking tradition and similar growing conditions to Italy. Despite this, Albanian wine is virtually unknown to most oenophiles. A big reason for this is the country's almost-50-year dictatorship, which was all about producing for quantity rather than quality. But a new generation of winemakers is revitalising Albania's wine tradition and making award-winning bottles with indigenous grape varieties. As of 2022, Albania was producing more than 3 million litres of wine, and from 2000 to 2016, the amount of grapes produced for wine jumped by over 250%.

Shesh grapes are the most widely cultivated in the country's main wine-growing regions – namely, central Albania (around Berat) and in the high-altitude north. Shesh i zi is a dark ruby colour with strong tannins and blackberry notes. Shesh i bardhë is golden with citrus and floral notes. Other grape varieties include the central Albanian pulës, aka the 'gold of Roshnik', that yields citrus and floral flavours; vlosh, a red grape grown near Vlorë, produces an easy-drinking wine with notes of red berries, black olives and dried herbs; kallmet is a grape for red and white wine that's found in the north and is rich in soft tannins and red berry flavours.

Find the best selection of Albanian wines in classy restaurants and hotels, or go directly to the source by tasting at the wineries. Some include **Alpeta Agrotourism** (p143), **Çobo Winery** (p143) near Berat and **Mrizi i Zanave** (p119) near Shkodër.

Responsible Travel

Climate Change & Travel

It's impossible to ignore the impact we have when travelling; Lonely Planet urges all travellers to engage with their travel carbon footprint, which will mainly come from air travel. While there often isn't an alternative, travellers can look to minimise the number of flights they take, opt for newer aircrafts and use cleaner ground transport, such as trains. One proposed solution – purchasing carbon offsets – unfortunately does not cancel out the impact of individual flights. While most destinations will depend on air travel for the foreseeable future, for now, pursuing ground-based travel where possible is the best course of action.

The **UN Carbon Offset Calculator** shows how flying impacts a household's emissions

The **ICAO's carbon emissions calculator** allows visitors to analyse the CO2 generated by point-to-point journeys

Bring a Water Filter

Albania's tap water isn't safe to drink, and you can't trust accommodations to have filtered water to fill up your reusable bottle. Bring a travel water filter (try LifeStraw or Steripen) to cut down on plastic bottles.

Electric Taxis

When landing at Tirana International Airport, WhatsApp an electric taxi to pick you up instead of taking one of the more costly, gas-powered municipal cabs lined up outside the gate.

Albania declared its **Vjosa River** (p156) Europe's first national river park in 2023, but more work needs to be done to convince the government that preservation is good for business. Visit national parks and preserves to show your support.

Përmet in southeastern Albania has styled itself as a hub for slow food, which means leaning towards local ingredients and ancestral recipes. Support restaurants and producers marked with Slow Food stickers.

AVOID OVERTOURISM

Yes, Ksamil has unbelievably turquoise water, but it teems with tourists every summer, taking a heavy toll on the environment. Come during shoulder season or pick a quieter beach north of Sarandë.

COVER UP

While Albania certainly appears secular – you'll rarely see head coverings on the street, for instance – it's still quite religious. Respect locals by not wearing anything too revealing, and cover up when visiting religious sites.

Don't Climb Castles

Albania is lucky to have plenty of ancient castles and fortresses across the country. Keep them intact by avoiding the temptation to climb on them or play on the ramparts.

Pick up Trash

Litter is a serious problem in Albania, with plastic bags and bottles scattered all over what should be gorgeous landscapes. Pick up trash when you see it, and leave no trace. That way, you're not adding to the problem.

Support Agrotourism

An exciting trend in Albania is the number of agrotourism establishments opening up across the country. These farm restaurants and guesthouses stick to seasonal produce and traditional recipes, and they serve some of the tastiest food you'll find in the country.

Stop the Stereotypes

Albania is treated with an ire that is at best misguided, at worst discriminatory. This country is safer than most, and its people are extremely warm. Correct haters when you hear them, and encourage them to find out for themselves.

Buy Artisanal

Albanian *qeleshe* (felt hats) and keyrings are tempting souvenirs, but they're usually made abroad. Support a local artisan instead by buying something from **Margjelo Filigran Jewelry** (p118) in Shkodër or anything from the **Albanian Night** (p52) shop in Tirana.

Staying in a tent has a lower impact on the environment than a hotel.

A simple *faleminderit* (thank you) shows locals you care about their language and culture.

Birds at Risk

Albania is a migration stop for more than 300 bird species, 19 of which are considered globally endangered. Development in the Vjosë-Nartë Delta Protected Area, where the Vlorë International Airport was built, has put them at risk.

RESOURCES

PPNEA.org
Albania's first environmental NGO.

Ecoalbania.org
Supports the preservation of the Vjosa River.

Chwbalbania.org
Restores heritage buildings

CLOCKWISE FROM TOP LEFT: RICHARD L. BOWMAN/SHUTTERSTOCK, ALLA SIMACHEVA/SHUTTERSTOCK, DOROTTYA MATHE/SHUTTERSTOCK

LGBTIQ+ Travellers

Albania is often recognised as one of the worst places in Europe for LGBTIQ+ people. The truth is, it isn't great, but it could be worse. Same-sex relationships are legal in Albania and discrimination is prohibited. However, LGBTIQ+ people can't get married, adopt or change their gender. Overall, LGBTIQ+ travellers are safe in Albania, but it's best to be discreet with PDAs.

Laws

Same-sex sexual intercourse was first decriminalised by the Ottoman Empire in 1858, and Albania enshrined it into law in 1995. Fifteen years later, Albania passed a comprehensive anti-discrimination law that protects LGBTIQ+ people on the grounds of sexual orientation and gender identity. LGBTIQ+ people can serve in the military and donate blood, and conversion therapy was banned in 2020. However, same-sex marriage is still illegal, largely due to pressure from the Christian Orthodox Church and Muslim groups. Unfortunately, there's no reason to believe this will change soon.

LGBTIQ+ TRAVEL

Gay men will generally be safe in Albania, though it's advised to not show displays of affection in public, especially outside of Tirana. Since Albanian women often hold hands, lesbians might not receive unwanted attention for touching, though they are advised to be cautious about more intimate displays of affection. Gay dating or friendship apps such as Grindr and Romeo are popular and perfectly legal.

Tirana Hubs

Tirana is the safest place in Albania for LGBTIQ+ people, with a sizable community. While there are no specific gay bars or clubs, there are frequent events, including drag shows. Some gay-friendly spots include **Hana** (p53) and **Radio** (p52) in Blloku, along with **Hemingway** (p52).

TIRANA PRIDE

Tirana has celebrated Pride since 2012, with every year having a theme. For instance, in 2024, the theme was 'Every Colour, a Family' – a clear response to Albanian laws that don't give same-sex couples the same rights as heterosexual couples.

Tirana Pride is celebrated on 24 May with a march, followed by a big party.

Festival of Diversity

Before and after Pride, LGBTIQ+ organisations bring their communities together for a few weeks in May to host the Festival of Diversity. The 16th edition of the festival in 2025 featured talks, movie nights, poetry, a talent show and a charity gala. See *pinkembassy.al*

LGBTIQ+ RESOURCES

PINK Embassy *(pinkembassy.al)* LGBTIQ+ advocacy group with English-speaking information and events, including the Festival of Diversity.

Streha Centre *(strehacenter.org)* Shelter and resources for LGBTIQ+ youth. Hosts occasional events.

Council of Europe Office in Tirana *(coe.int/en/web/tirana)* Conducting an €850,000 anti-discrimination campaign in the Western Balkans through 2026.

Accessible Travel

Albania has plenty of work to do to develop the necessary infrastructure for accessible travel, though footpaths are improving in major cities and beach hubs. Solo and female travellers will feel safe here.

No Public Transport

Furgons (shared minibuses) can barely run, so it's unsurprising that they don't come equipped with wheelchair lifts. Those with limited mobility will need to arrange private transport if they intend on travelling outside of Tirana.

Airport

Tirana International Airport Nënë Tereza has dedicated parking in front of the terminal for people with reduced mobility. Call airport staff for assistance *(+355 42 381 800)*.

Accommodation

Some modern hotels in Tirana and along the coast in Durrës, Sarandë and Vlorë offer wheelchair-accessible rooms with wide doors and roll-in showers. Getting from the hotel to the beach is, unfortunately, another question. Contact them ahead and check photos online.

SOLO TRAVELLERS

Albania has low crime rates and is in a prolonged era of peace, making it a terrific place for solo travel. Backpacker hostels in Tirana, Shkodër and Himarë are particularly great for meeting fellow travellers.

Parking

Parking in cities is usually a free-for-all on the side of the street or in private lots, with few businesses or hotels having private lots or dedicated parking spaces for those with reduced mobility.

Improving Infrastructure

Freshly paved footpaths and a new, flat **Skanderbeg Square** (p46) in Tirana have made the capital easier for wheelchair users. Paths in Shkodër and Korçë aren't bad. Ottoman-era cities such as Berat and Gjirokastër are mostly hills and cobblestones.

FEMALE TRAVELLERS

Despite warnings from those who've never been, Albania is a terrific place for female travellers, as many can attest – but like anywhere else, it's important to exercise the usual caution.

RESOURCES

Albania Disability Rights Foundation *(adrf.al)* Non-profit founded by Oxfam Great Britain in 1996. Can help connect users with accessibility resources.

Wheelchair Accessible Holiday Taxis *(wheelchairaccessible holidaytaxis.com)* Runs pick-ups from Tirana International Airport and drop-offs across Albania.

Albanian National Association of the Deaf *(anad.al)* Advocacy group that developed Albanian Sign Language. Contact them for interpreters.

North Albania Tours *(northalbaniatours.wordpress. com)* operates wheelchair-friendly tours from Shkodër though the Albanian Alps and neighbouring Balkan countries. It also rents out wheelchairs for €15 to €20 per day.

Driving in Albania

Considering that reliable public transport is virtually non-existent in Albania and the country is filled with stunning drives along the coast and over the mountains, a road trip is a tempting prospect. But if you tell someone you plan to drive here, they'll probably respond with shock and protest. Is driving in Albania really *that* bad? Let's dive in.

Erratic Drivers

Albanian drivers have an awful reputation, but like other negative stereotypes about the country, we're not sure we understand the hate. It's certainly odd and kind of hilarious that drivers stop in the middle of the lane alongside parked cars, put their flickers on and pop into a cafe or bakery – and that nobody seems to mind when they do. There are also your cocky speeders in German sports cars, but they're everywhere. And we're not sure if driving the wrong way on a single-lane road is the driver's fault when the road is only wide enough for one car. In short, drive with caution, and Albanian drivers shouldn't be a problem.

How Are the Roads?

Another criticism about Albanian driving comes from its atrocious road network as a result of the dictatorship, but that's starting to change. Major road construction projects have been completed in the last few years, linking Shkodër to Theth; Vlorë down the Albanian Riviera to Sarandë; and from Tirana east to Kosovo. These highways are well paved and maintained, though be careful and take it slow, as there are some hairpin turns up and around the mountains. The biggest issues arise when you go off the main highway. For instance, this writer tried to drive south from Berat past the Osum Canyon to Gjirokastër on what *appeared* to be a road on Google Maps but ended up being dirt and rocks that trashed the bottom of the car. Other roads that would ordinarily be maintained for tourists, such as one to Bovilla Lake (p59), are riddled with potholes. Be especially careful when driving in the winter, as the roads can be slick with black ice and snow. A 4WD will give you peace of mind any time of year.

Navigation Apps

It quickly becomes clear that Google Maps has no idea what it's doing in Albania. Even in Tirana, you can find yourself being told to turn onto roads that don't exist or are going in the wrong direction. That said, many people seem to use Google's app, as you'll commonly be alerted about an accident or police traffic stop ahead of time (police stops are very common and you'll be asked to show your licence and car registration). Maps.me works a little better than Google Maps and also works with Apple CarPlay.

Hiring a Car

Hiring a car in Albania is a unique and interesting endeavour. Countless private agencies outside Tirana International Airport will rent cars for reasonable day rates, and there are more in the city itself, as well as in Sarandë and Gjirokastër. However, many private agencies don't take card payments, so you won't be able to use the car insurance attached to your card. Thankfully, more international brands are coming to Tirana. Be sure to check online booking sites, which sometimes have better rates than what the agency tells you. If you do happen to get in an accident and don't have insurance (not that this writer has any experience with that...), repairs are very affordable for Volkswagen and Mercedes-Benz cars since there are so many of them.

Parking

Cities in Albania have free public parking on the side of the road, but finding a spot is virtually impossible in high season. Look for blue parking signs for private lots, which charge between 200L and 500L for day use. In Tirana and Vlorë, car parks and garages can be found behind main roads in terrifyingly narrow alleyways. Reach out to your accommodation in Gjirokastër to ask where to park, as there are very few spots near the bazaar. Parking is also a headache in Berat, as there's no parking in Mangalem (p141) or Gorlicë (p141).

WHY SO MANY GERMAN CARS?

For a country with such a high poverty rate, there sure are a lot of Volkswagen and Mercedes-Benz sports cars on the streets. There are many conspiracies about why this could be, but they're hard to prove. Some say that the cars have been stolen from Germany and Switzerland – where there are large Albanian and Kosovar populations – and illegally re-plated here. More straightforwardly, Albanians just love German cars, seeing them as both reliable and as a status symbol – and both King Zog I and Enver Hoxha drove one. And it's not like they're fresh off the assembly line: most models are a decade old or more. One thing's for sure: Albanians love their cars, with the streets always full of traffic when they could just as easily walk.

Nuts & Bolts

OPENING HOURS

Many businesses geared to tourists – tour operators, restaurants and hotels – outside of Tirana, especially on the beach and in the Alps, shut down outside of the June to September period. But generally:

Banks 8am to 4pm Monday to Friday

Cafes 7am to 10pm

Bars noon to midnight

Restaurants 11am to 10pm

Shops 9am to 8pm

Supermarkets 7am to 10pm

Internet

Albania has widespread 4G phone coverage, though reception can be spotty in the mountains. But 5G is growing, especially in Tirana and along the main highways. Hotels, guesthouses and nearly all forms of accommodation have decent wi-fi.

Weights & Measures

Albania uses the metric system (kilometres and grams).

Smoking

Albania has one of the highest smoking rates in Europe. It's prohibited indoors, though rules aren't always enforced outside of Tirana, especially in winter.

GOOD TO KNOW

Time zone
GMT+1 Oct-Mar,
GMT+2 Mar-Oct

Country calling code
+355

Emergency number
112

Population
2.8 million

Electricity
Type F 230V/50Hz

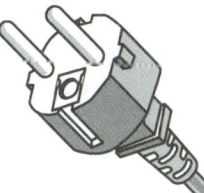

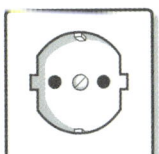

**Type F
230V/50Hz**

PUBLIC HOLIDAYS

New Year's Day 1 January

Dita e Verës (Summer Day) 14 March

Ramadan Bajram/Eid al-Fitr February and March 2026–28

Sultan Nevruz (Bektashi and Persian holiday) 22 March

Easter March or April

Labour Day 1 May

Eid al-Adha May 2026–28

Independence Day 28 November

Liberation Day (From Nazi Germany in 1944) 29 November

Youth Day (Celebrates 1990 student protests in Tirana) 8 December

Christmas Day 25 December

Language

Albanian *(gjuha shqipe dyoo·ha shtyee·pe)* is one of the oldest Indo-European languages, generally considered the only descendant of Illyrian, the language of the ancient inhabitants of the Balkans. With no close relatives and constituting a branch of its own, it's a proud survivor of the Roman, Slavic and Ottoman influxes and a European linguistic oddity on a par with Basque.

Basics

What's your name? Si quheni? see *choo·he·nee*
My name is ... Unë quhem ... *oo·nuh choo·hem ...*
I'm pleased to meet you. Gëzohem që u njohëm. *guh·zo·hem chuh oo nyo·huhm*
Where are you from? Nga jeni? *nga ye·nee*
I'm from ... Jam nga ... *yam nga ...*
 Australia. Australia. *a·oos·tra·lee·a*
 Canada. Kanadaja. *ka·na·da·ya*
 England. Anglia. *an·glee·a*
 New Zealand. Zelanda e Re. *ze·lan·da e re*
 the USA. Shtetet e Bashkuara. *shte·tet e bash·koo·a·ra*

Directions

I'm going to (Tirana). Do të shkoj në (Tiranë). *do tuh shkoy nuh (tee·ra·nuh)*
Where's the ...? Ku është ...? *koo uhsh·tuh ...*
 bank banka *ban·ka*
 city centre qendra e qytetit *chen·dra e chew·te·teet*
 hotel hoteli *ho·te·lee*
 market tregu *tre·goo*
 post office posta *pos·ta*
 tourist office zyra turistike *zew·ra too·rees·tee·ke*
How do I get there? Si mund të shkoj atje? *see moond tuh shkoy at·ye*
Can you show me (on the map)? A mund të ma tregoni (në hartë)? *a moond tuh ma tre·go·nee (nuh har·tuh)*

Is this the road to (Berat)? A është kjo rruga për në (Berat)? *a uhsh·tuh kyo rroo·ga puhr nuh (be·rat)*
Turn left/right. Kthehuni majtas/djathtas. *kthe·hoo·nee mai·tas/diath·tas*
It's ... Është ... *uhsh·tuh ...*
 behind / in front of ... prapa/përpara ... *pra·pa/ puhr·pa·ra ...*
 far away. larg. *larg*
 here. këtu. *kuh·too*
 near (to ...) afër .... *a·fuhr ...*
 next to ... ngjitur me .... *ndyee·toor me ...*
 north/south/east/west. veri/jug/lindje/perëndim. *ve·ree/ yoog/leen·dye/pe·ruhn·deem*
 on the corner. te qoshja. *te chosh·ya*
 opposite ... përballë ... *puhr·ba·lluh ...*
 straight ahead. drejt. *dreyt*
 there. atje. *at·ye*

Time

What time is it? Sa është ora? *sa uhsh·tuh o·ra*
It's (two) o'clock. Ora është (dy). *o·ra uhsh·tuh (dew)*
Quarter to/past (one). (Një) pa/e një çerek. *(nyuh) pa/e nyuh che·rek*
Half past (one). (Një) e gjysmë. *(nyuh) e dyews·muh*
At what time ...? Në çfarë ore ...? *nuh chfa·ruh o·re ...*
since/until (May). që/deri në (maj). *chuh/de·ree nuh (mai)*
next week. javën e ardhshme. *ya·vuhn e ardh·shme*
next month/year. muajin/vitin e ardhshëm. *moo·a·yeen/ vee·teen e ardh·shuhm*

NUMBERS

1
një nyuh

2
dy dew

3
tre/tri (m/f) tre/tree

4
katër *ka·tuhr*

5
pesë *pe·suh*

6
gjashtë *dyash·tuh*

7
shtatë *shta·tuh*

8
tetë *te·tuh*

9
nëntë *nuhn·tuh*

10
dhjetë *dhye·tuh*

EMERGENCIES

It's an emergency!
Është urgjente! uhsh·tuh oor·dyen·te
Help! *Ndihmë! ndeeh·muh*

Five Phrases to Learn Before You Go

Do you speak English?
A flisni anglisht? *a flees·nee ang·leesht*
Do you understand?
A kuptoni? *a koop·to·nee*
I (don't) understand.
Unë (nuk) kuptoj. *oo·nuh (nook) koop·toy*
What does (vrapoj) mean?
Ç'do të thotë fjala (vrapoj)? *chdo tuh tho·tuh fya·la (vra·poy)*
Could you please repeat that?
Përsëriteni, ju lutem. *puhr·suh·ree·te·nee yoo loo·tem*

WORD STRESS

For the vast majority of words in Albanian, the main stress falls on the last syllable of a word (or the last stem of a compound word). In a sentence, the main stress generally falls on the last word of a phrase. In this guide, the stressed syllable is always in italics.

Give It a Go!

Even though many Albanians speak English, you'll find attempts to communicate in Albanian are welcomed. Discovering some of the mysteries of this intriguing language will be rewarding – try learning a few of the 27 words Albanian has for 'moustache' or the other 27 used for 'eyebrows'!

Written Form

Albanian has been written in various alphabets since the earliest written records from the 15th century, including the Roman, Greek, Arabic and Cyrillic scripts. This orthographic confusion was finally settled by the Manastir Congress in 1908, which adopted a modified Roman alphabet as the standard written form of Albanian.

WHO SPEAKS ALBANIAN?

There are two main dialects of Albanian – Tosk (with about 3 million speakers in southern Albania, Greece, Italy and Turkey) and Gheg (spoken by about 2.8 million people in northern Albania, Kosovo and the surrounding areas of Serbia, Montenegro and Macedonia). Tosk is the official language of Albania and is also the variety used in this book.

last night/week/month/year.
mbrëmjen/javën/muajin/vitin e kaluar. *mbruhm·yen/ya·vuhn/moo·a·yeen/vee·teen e ka·loo·ar*
yesterday/tomorrow morning/afternoon/evening. dje/nesër në mëngjes/mbasdite/në mbrëmje. *dee·e/ne·suhr nuh muhn·dyes/mbas·dee·te/nuh mbruhm·ye*

Eating & Drinking

I'd like a table for (four), please.
Dua një tavolinë për (katër veta), ju lutem. *doo·a nyuh ta·vo·lee·nuh puhr (ka·tuhr ve·ta) yoo loo·tem*

Can you recommend a ...? A mund të më rekomandoni një ...? *a moond tuh muh re·ko·man·do·nee nyuh...*
  bar bar *bar*
  café kafene *ka·fe·ne*
  restaurant restorant *res·to·rant*
What would you recommend?
Çfarë më rekomandoni? *chfa·ruh muh ro ko·man·do·nee*
I'd like (the) ...,please. Më sillni ..., ju lutem. *muh seell·nee ... yoo loo·tem*
  bill faturën *fa·too·ruhn*
  drink list listën e pijeve *lees·tuhn e pee·ye·ve*
  menu menunë *me·noo·nuh*
  that dish atë gjellën *a·tuh dye·lluhn*

SIGNS

Entrance/Exit
Hyrje/Dalje
Open/Closed
Hapur/Mbyllur
Rooms (Not) Available
(Nuk) ka vende
Information
Informacion
Police Station
rajoni i policisë
Prohibited
E ndaluar e
Toilets
Banjat
Men/Women
Burra/Gra

STORYBOOK

Our writers delve deep into different aspects of Albanian life

A History of Albania in 15 Places

Albania's history is fit for a Hollywood film, or several.

Joel Balsam

p190

Meet the Albanians

Fiercely proud and endlessly hospitable, Albanians live by a mixture of old codes and grit. Family, food and honour define us.

Linda Alia

p194

World Heritage

Despite thousands of years of occupation, Albanians have managed to preserve their cultural traditions.

Joel Balsam

p196

Skanderbeg's Sword

The Albanian hero who fended off the Ottomans in the 15th century remains a powerful symbol of national identity.

Joel Balsam

p198

Tourism Boom or Burden?

Everyone's going here these days, but is it too much, too soon?

Joel Balsam

p200

House museum (p150), Gjirokastër

A HISTORY OF ALBANIA IN
15 PLACES

Albania's history is fit for a Hollywood film, or rather, several. Sandwiched between Rome, Greece, Türkiye and the Slavic countries, Albania was conquered by various empires and brutal dictators over an action-packed 2800 years, leading to countless bloody wars and rebellions. Buckle up – it's a wild ride. By Joel Balsam

THINK OF ALBANIA as that little flag in the middle of the rope in a tug of war, constantly being pulled back and forth between powerful empires. Ethnically and linguistically linked to the ancient Illyrian tribes that controlled the southwestern Balkans before our common era, Albania has been conquered by the Greeks, the Byzantines and the Ottomans from the east, and the Germans, the French, and various Italian empires (Rome, Venice and Mussolini) from the west at different points over the past few thousand years.

On the brink of being taken over by neighbouring Balkan nations in 1912, Albania was granted statehood by the Great Powers, only for it to suffer one of the most tumultuous 20th centuries of any country in the world – a self-declared king and a brutal 45-year dictatorship, capped off by a near civil war that bankrupted the country. No wonder neighbouring Kosovars, who share an ethnic history, joke that Albanians have more PTSD than they do, despite Kosovo's more recent war with Serbia.

Somehow, Albania is still standing, and in fact, it's thriving as a tourist destination. Learning about its intense, fascinating history is crucial before any visit.

1. Butrint
CITY OF CIVILISATIONS

For 2800 years, virtually every empire that set foot in this territory decided to set up shop in a strategic patch of land on the Ionian coast known as Butrint (Buthrotum). Greek Hellenistic tribes kicked things off in the 8th century BCE with the first *polis* (city) walls before adding a theatre at a later date. Then the Romans conquered it and added an aqueduct, bathhouses and a forum. Further additions were made by the Byzantines, Angevins and Venetians, but Butrint was neglected by the Ottomans and abandoned in the 18th century. As a way to justify its occupation, Fascist Italy excavated the area in the 1930s and uncovered Albania's finest archaeological ruins.

For more on Butrint, see page 88

2. Apollonia
ILLYRIAN ROOTS

Albanians link themselves ancestrally with the ancient Illyrians, an Indo-European people who ruled swathes of the western Balkans from the 6th century BCE to 168 BCE, though some sources say they lasted much longer. The name Albania, first given by the Romans, derives from the Illyrian Albanoi tribe who lived here in the 2nd century BCE. Throughout Illyrian rule, tribes established kingdoms and city-states, and defied Greek and Roman control, with Queen Teuta, aka the Pirate Queen, leading the way in this regard. Walk where the Illyrians did in the ruined city of Apollonia. Other Illyrian stomping grounds include Byllis and the Rozafa Fortress.

For more on Apollonia, see page 105

3. Durrës Amphitheatre
IN THE FOOTSTEPS OF GLADIATORS

Albania's second-largest city is filled with white, Italian-style buildings that face the Adriatic coast. But in between its 20th-century architecture are ruins much, much older. After Rome defeated Queen Teuta and the Illyrians, it took control of the territory and built Epidamnus and Dyrrachium (modern-day Durrës), one of its major cities in the Balkans. Rome began the construction of the Durrës Amphitheatre in the early 2nd century CE, during the reign of Emperor Trajan (98–117 CE). In its day, the stadium hosted gladiator battles and could seat as many as 18,000 people. The amphitheatre was active for another 200 years until it was destroyed by an earthquake.

For more on the Durrës Amphitheatre, see page 62

Durrës Amphitheatre (p62)

JOEL BALSAM/LONELY PLANET

4. Reconciliation Tower
BLOOD FEUDS IN THE NORTH

Since at least the 15th century, northern Albania was governed by a moral and legal code known as the Kanun. Rules for living ranged from the mundane – like what to do if bees escaped your farm – to the arcane – including controversial practices such as *gjakmarrja* (blood feuds) and sworn virgins (women who pledged celibacy to gain social privileges). Influences of the Kanun can still be felt in remote villages across the Albanian Alps, including in Theth, where you may visit the 400-year-old Reconciliation Tower, which was used for negotiation and protection during blood feuds.

For more on the Reconciliation Tower, see page 129

5. Berat
OTTOMAN EMPIRE AT ITS PEAK

While the history of the city of Berat dates back to the time of the Illyrians in the 4th century BCE – when the hilltop Berat Castle was first built – the city is most known for the period when Albania was controlled by the Ottoman Empire, between 1385 and 1912. After taking Berat in 1417, the Ottomans built beautiful neighbourhoods, residences and stone mosques, while the repressed Christians built pretty churches. Protected as a 'museum city' in 1961 during the Enver Hoxha dictatorship and given special status by UNESCO in 2008, Berat is the perfect place to get a feel for what city life under the Ottomans might have looked like.

For more on Berat, see page 138

6. Krujë Castle
STRONGHOLD OF A NATIONAL HERO

There was a blip in the Ottomans' 527-year control of Albania, and his name was Gjergj Kastrioti (1405–68), later known as Skanderbeg, Albania's national hero. Born in Krujë, Skanderbeg was taken hostage as a child and trained to be a soldier in Türkiye. He deserted the military in 1443 and returned to his homeland, where he renounced Islam and united Albanian tribes against the Ottomans. Based out of Krujë Castle, Skanderbeg led a guerrilla campaign that fended off the Ottomans for 25 years, until he died of malaria (or

7. Porto Palermo Castle
ALI PASHA'S AUDACITY

Born in Tepelenë, Ali Pasha of Ioannina (1740–1822) took charge of managing Albania for the Ottomans and became one of the strongest leaders in the empire. Ali Pasha is credited for his religious tolerance, and for building and renovating bridges and fortresses across the country, including the triangular Porto Palermo Castle, a gift for one of his wives. At the same time, Ali Pasha ruled with an iron fist, imprisoning dissidents and irking the sultan, who declared him a rebel in 1821. After a short standoff, Ali Pasha was shot and killed, with his head taken to Istanbul as a warning to others.

For more on Porto Palermo Castle, see page 95

8. Marubi National Photography Museum
CAPTURING ALBANIAN CULTURE

As parts of Albania were modernising in the 19th century, many were still living a traditional life, with elaborate clothing and remarkable traditions. We know this partly due to the amazing photographs taken by Pietro Marubi (1832–1903) and his heirs, whose work is on display in Shkodër at the Marubi National Photography Museum. Born in Italy (he was forced to leave after being accused of being involved in the murder of a duke), Marubi moved to Albania, where he captured some of Albania's first photographs of people and political events. Marubi's heir, Kel, carried on the family tradition, as did Kel's son, Gegë.

For more on the Marubi National Photography Museum, see page 112

9. Independence Monument
CRADLE OF ALBANIAN INDEPENDENCE

With the Ottoman Empire crumbling and WWI on the horizon, the Balkan League (consisting of Serbia, Montenegro, Greece and Bulgaria) led a successful rebellion that pushed the Ottomans out of the region, including Albania. Meanwhile, Ismail Qemali, an Albanian statesman who'd been campaigning for independence for decades, travelled to Vlorë and led a congress on 28 November 1912 to declare Albania a state, with the Independence Monument marking this occasion. Despite not having backing from the Balkan League (who wanted Albania for themselves), the Great Powers met at the London Conference of Ambassadors on 17 December and granted Albania statehood with its first borders.

For more on the Independence Monument, see page 101

10. King Zog Villa
ALBANIA'S 20TH-CENTURY MONARCH

Albania was plunged into chaos with WWI, creating a power vacuum that a 27-year-old Ahmed Muhtar Zogolli (1895–1961), aka King Zog I, was happy to fill. Zog was first elected prime minister of Albania in 1922, then served as president before declaring himself king in 1928. With no royal bloodline, Zog was ridiculed by other European monarchs, but his rule was propped up by a close relationship with Benito Mussolini's Italy. In 1939, allies became enemies when Italy invaded Albania and deposed King Zog. Visit the abandoned King Zog Villa in Durrës for a taste of how the 20th-century monarch used to live.

For more on the King Zog Villa, see page 65

11. House of Leaves
COMMUNIST SPY HEADQUARTERS

Fascist Italy controlled Albania for just four years (1939–43) before it was ceded to Germany during WWII. Nazi rule didn't last long either, with Albanian rebels and Allied forces liberating the country in 1944. Later that year, Gjirokastër-born Enver Hoxha (1908–85), as leader of Albania's Communist Party, was elected prime minister. Hoxha quickly imprisoned or killed any opposition, leading to a brutal, isolated dictatorship that lasted 45 years. The lengthy repression of Albanians was in part due to the vast network of spies, whose headquarters was a former obstetrics clinic and Gestapo base in Tirana, ominously called the House of Leaves.

For more on the House of Leaves, see page 51

King Zog Villa (p65)

12. Cold War Tunnel
PARANOID LEADER'S BUNKER

Hoxha began his rule as an ally and admirer of Josef Stalin, imitating the Soviet dictator's gulags with brutal internment camps of his own and hosting Russian submarines. But when Stalin died, Hoxha broke ties with Russia, turning instead to Communist China, but that didn't last long either – this time, because Mao Zedong shook hands with President Richard Nixon. Alone and paranoid, Hoxha ordered Albanians to build roughly 175,000 concrete bunkers in case the country was attacked. Most of these bunkers remain today. Tour the Cold War Tunnel in Gjirokastër to get a glimpse into what they were like.

For more on the Cold War Tunnel, see page 152

13. Blloku
PRIVATE COMMUNIST NEIGHBOURHOOD

Despite mass poverty and the desperate attempts of thousands of Albanians to escape the country, the dictatorship was still kicking by the time Enver Hoxha took his last breath in 1985. Three years later, the government erected the Pyramid in honour of its pharaoh near the Former Residence of Enver Hoxha in the Blloku neighbourhood of Tirana. At the time, Blloku was restricted to party elites, but when communism finally fell in 1991, the gates to the neighbourhood swung open, turning it into a bright symbol of a (very) capitalist Albania, with plenty of snazzy shops, cocktail bars and clubs.

For more on Blloku, see page 52

14. Sarandë
FROM REBELLION TO RESORT

After the fall of communism, Albanians could start buying foreign goods (Coca-Cola and bananas weren't allowed in the country during the dictatorship), accumulate money and spend it at will. In the 1990s, an estimated 66% of the population were convinced to invest in financial products that turned out to be pyramid schemes. Thousands lost their life savings, prompting widespread violence in 1997 that killed around 2000 people. Now remarkably a beach resort, the city of Sarandë was the site of major violence during the crisis, with rebels from Vlorë arriving by boat to burn down government buildings and seize weapons.

For more on Sarandë, see page 80

15. Vjosa River
PROTECTED WILD RIVER

The last two decades have seen major economic growth in Albania, particularly in its tourism sector as the country is repeatedly listed as one of the top places to visit. This attention has prompted rapid and unfettered development, especially on the Albanian Riviera, causing environmental organisations to sound the alarm. After a star-studded international campaign, a major conservation victory was declared in 2023, when the Vjosa River was protected as a national river park – Europe's first. There's still plenty of work to do, as evidenced by the trash on the river seen when rafting, but it's a start.

For more on the Vjosa River, see page 156

MEET THE ALBANIANS

Fiercely proud and endlessly hospitable, Albanians live by a mixture of old codes and grit. Family, food and honour define us. LINDA ALIA introduces her people.

WE ARE A small country with deep roots. In Albania, you are never just yourself, you are someone's daughter, son, cousin, neighbour. This is how we map the world, through kinship, not road names (which are often missing anyway).

Hospitality here isn't a nice extra, it's an unshakeable law. Literally. The Kanun, a centuries-old set of customary laws still deeply woven into northern culture, commands: 'Before the house belongs to the owner, it first belongs to God and the guest'. That philosophy remains alive in every corner of the country. If you visit my mother's house, you'll find a table overflowing with *byrek,* pickles, feta and homemade *raki,* followed by a humble apology of 'I'm sorry, this is all we had'. Then, you'll leave with reused supermarket bags filled with cucumbers or whatever was picked that morning from her garden.

We express love through action, not language. We insist you eat, pack leftovers into containers for your trip, and slip fig *gliko* or Turkish coffee into your coat pockets. Affection is practical: never declared, always present. Every region has its own dialect, dishes and stubborn pride, but we share the same core: protect your people, respect your elders, feed your guests.

When I think of Albanian gatherings, I think of movement, people coming and going, voices rising, laughter echoing. There's a rhythm to it all: someone is always brewing coffee, someone else is slicing fruit. A guest doesn't stay a guest for long; you're quickly handed a spoon, a seat and advice, whether you want it or not.

Despite decades of communism and years of forced atheism, Albanians today live in rare religious harmony. It's common for neighbours to attend each other's celebrations, Bajram lunches, Christmas dinners and Orthodox name days. And we especially love how this harmony means more public holidays.

Politics are passionate, history still hurts and many of us carry the scars of transition. Our parents survived isolation and dictatorship, and many left to seek better lives abroad. The diaspora is immense. But even abroad, ties remain strong. We send money home, visit in the summers and gather in backyards to eat and argue like we never left.

We are shaped not just by history, but also by legends. Ask any Albanian child, and they'll tell you of Rozafa, the woman who sacrificed herself to be walled up alive into a castle so it would stand strong, her milk still flowing to feed her son. Or of Muji and Halili, warrior brothers and protectors of the poor and brave. Or of Queen Teuta, who ruled the seas and defied empires. These stories are not fairy tales to us, they're blueprints for endurance, sacrifice and defiance.

To meet Albanians is to be swept into a whirlwind. You won't just shake hands here. You'll be welcomed, interrogated, fed, teased, hugged and possibly renamed. And when you leave, you'll do so with full hands and an even fuller heart.

A Small Nation, a Global People

Albania has a population of around 2.7 million, but nearly twice that number live abroad. Our diaspora spans continents, yet the pull of home remains strong in language, family ties and the summer return to the homeland.

Pictured clockwise from top left: Grandmother teaching traditional Albanian cooking (p152); Independence Day celebrations; man near Gjirokastër (p147); woman in traditional dress, Tirana (p46)

THE HOUSE MY GRANDFATHER BUILT

I was born in Kryezi, a village nestled in the mountains of Pukë. That's where my grandfather built the stone house that became the beating heart of our family. It was where we hosted weddings, mourned losses, celebrated births and always shared food. When I was young, each celebration meant dozens of cousins arriving with pans and platoo from their own kitchens. Everything had initials scratched into the metal to make sure it found its way back. We'd eat and laugh under the sun, then fall asleep side by side on floors layered with thin mattresses and wool blankets. Those nights, filled with giggles and whispers, remain my favourite memories. I now live in Tirana and work across Europe, but that northern village taught me everything: how to share, how to welcome, how to belong. It's the blueprint I carry with me, in every room I walk into, every story I tell and every guest I host.

WORLD HERITAGE

Despite thousands of years of occupation, the people of Albania have managed to preserve their cultural traditions. By Joel Balsam

ALBANIAN CULTURAL TRADITIONS date back hundreds, if not thousands, of years to the time of the Illyrians (Albania's ethnic and linguistic ancestors). Against all odds, dancing, music, clothing and transhumance all remain in Albania today and are pivotal expressions of national identity.

Dancing

Albanian weddings are something else. Along with traditional vows, feasting and, let's face it, plenty of gossip, locals get up to link pinkies or arms and twirl and stomp to traditional Albanian folk dances. If you're lucky enough to get invited to one, you'll be treated to a unique event. If not, you can see see a staged one at Albanian Night (p52).

According to some experts, Albanian dancing dates back to Illyrian fertility or sun rituals, but it was also likely influenced by Slavic, Greek and Ottoman traditions. During the Enver Hoxha dictatorship (1944–92), Albanian dancing was preserved and promoted as part of the country's national identity, though only if the dance adhered to socialist ideals – the working class – and was in no way related to religious ceremonies or the legal and moral code of Kanun law.

Pictured clockwise from top left: Albanian Night (p52), Tirana; women in traditional dress, Tirana (p46); shepherd leading his flock to pasture, Butrint (p88); homemade cheese

Albanian folk dances feature various moves and music, and they differ across the north, south and centre of the country, though if you go to a traditional wedding, you'll likely see several styles. In northeastern Albania, you could see *K'cimi tropojës,* a folk dance that gained international notoriety when it was listed as a UNESCO Intangible Cultural Heritage in 2024. It's performed by men, women and children – both young and old – with dancers moving to a bouncy beat without touching each other, arms raised above them like the heads of the eagles on Albania's flag. You'll know it's *K'cimi tropojës* if you see the female dancers waving a red handkerchief over their heads.

Valle Pogonishte originates in southern Albania and is slower and more melancholic, with participants gently gliding in a line or semi-circle. *Shotë* is the most typical Albanian folk dance; it's named after a female freedom fighter and is a lively, syncopated line dance performed in unison.

You can see traditional Albanian dancing, along with music and clothing, at the National Folk Festival (p150).

Music

Albania likes DJs and international pop hits as much as anywhere else, but it also has a long tradition of music that dates back to Illyrian times, with chilling ballads of love and loss, legends and migrations that are performed at weddings, funerals and seasonal rituals. Albanian music is often accompanied by instruments such as the *lahutë* (single-stringed fiddle), the *çifteli* (two-stringed instrument similar to the Turkish saz) and the *fyell* (shepherd's flute made from wood or bone). It's also sometimes accompanied by iso-polyphony singing, which managed to survive the secular dictatorship, despite being related to Byzantine Christian church singing. In 2005, it was proclaimed a Masterpiece of the Oral and Intangible Heritage of Humanity by UNESCO. Heard especially in southern Albania, iso-polyphony involves one or two *marrësi* (lead singers) carrying the melody while one *kthyesi* (returner) sings a countermelody with a sustained choral drone. The result is a haunting, quivering tune, sure to lead to tingles and shivers in all those who hear it.

Enjoy traditional Albanian music with dinner and drinks at restaurants such as Oda (p51) in Tirana, Vila Cofiel (p162) in Korçë and Black Rose (p150) in Gjirokastër.

Clothing

While young Albanians clearly have an affinity for greyscale wardrobes, Albanian culture has an amazing tradition of vibrant clothing that dates back 4000 years. There are over 200 documented types of traditional Albanian clothes, with vivid colours and intricate motifs that harken back to Illyrian pagan beliefs. Historically, traditional clothing depended on the region, religion and class, but men generally wore a *fustanella* (pleated skirt) or pantaloons, a *xhamadan* (embroidered wool vest) and a *qeleshe* (felt cap). Women's clothing was more varied, with ladies in the south wearing embroidered silk dresses and layered skirts with magnificent filigree jewellery, an artisanal tradition dating back 5000 years and still made in Shkodër and Prizren (Kosovo). In the north, women could be seen wearing *xhubleta* (long woollen dresses often adorned with metals that chime with movement). In 2022, the *xhubleta* was added to UNESCO's List of Intangible Cultural Heritage in Need of Urgent Safeguarding.

See vibrant Albanian clothing at museums in Krujë (p60), Gjirokastër (p151) and Shkodër (p115).

Migration

Drive around Albania in spring or autumn and you're bound to hit a traffic jam – not of cars, but of large herds of sheep or goats. Shepherd culture is alive and well, and the biannual transhumance – the migration of animals between the uplands and the lowlands – is another UNESCO-protected element of Albanian culture.

Also practised across Europe, in countries such as Austria, Croatia, Spain, France, Greece, Italy and Romania, transhumance preserves grazing areas and is good for the animals. It's also pivotal to the practice of making traditional Albanian cheeses such as *mishavinë* and *djathë i zier*. Transhumance is often accompanied by rituals, celebrations and, of course, food.

Ask locals, especially in the Albanian Alps, if they know of a transhumance celebration going on, or if they know of a shepherd you can accompany on their transhumance route.

SKANDERBEG'S SWORD

The Albanian hero who fended off the Ottomans in the 15th century remains a powerful symbol of national identity. By Joel Balsam

GJERGJ KASTRIOTI (1405–68), aka Skanderbeg, did what no other rebel leader could in more than five centuries of Ottoman occupation – he resisted, going undefeated in 13 battles. But despite Ottoman reoccupation of Albania for four more centuries following Skanderbeg's death, his legend lives on and is pivotal for understanding Albania today.

Ottoman Captive

The power of the Ottoman Empire shouldn't be understated: for half a millennium, from the 14th century onwards, it controlled much of West Asia, North Africa and southern Europe, including the Balkans and Albania. Along with its infamous taxation system for minorities, one way the empire asserted control over its territories was with a *devshirme* (blood tax or child levy), which took the children of noble families captive and trained them as warriors in its army. One such captive was Kastrioti, born to a noble family in northern Albania and taken to be trained at a school in Edirne, now western Türkiye. Converted to Islam, he became a skilled soldier, earning the name Skanderbeg, a combination of the Turkish word *bey* (lord) and 'Iskander', after Alexander the Great.

Pictured clockwise from top left: Skanderbeg bust, Krujë Castle (p60); Skanderbeg Square (p46), Tirana; mosaic, Krujë Castle (p60); Krujë Castle (p60)

Christian Rebel

In 1443, following defeat by the Serbs at the Battle of Niš, Skanderbeg deserted Sultan Murad II's army along with 300 men and led them to his homeland. Arriving in Krujë, Skanderbeg cleverly used a forged letter from the sultan to become the city governor and began to take over Albanian castles, including Petrelë (p57) and Prezë (p57) near Tirana.

After converting to Christianity, Skanderbeg gathered Albanian tribal leaders in Lezhë and declared his intention to liberate Shqipëria from Ottoman occupation. The League of Lezhë, as the rebels were called, united under Skanderbeg. Their red flag featured a double-headed black eagle standing boldly in the centre, a symbol of Albanians at the time, along with the pre-Ottoman Christian Byzantines.

Despite partnerships with Naples, Venice, several popes and King Alfonso V of Spain, Skanderbeg's rebellion was undermanned. He led between 10,000 and 15,000 men against Ottoman forces that numbered as many as 25,000. But with hit-and-run guerrilla tactics, a fruitful defense of Krujë Castle (p60) under four sieges and a magic sword (according to some), Skanderbeg went undefeated in 13 battles, fending off the Ottomans for 25 years, from 1443 to 1468. At the age of 62, Skanderbeg died (of malaria or poison, depending on the source) in Lezhë and was buried beneath a church (today's Skanderbeg Memorial; p123). The rebels managed to last another 12 years before the Ottomans regained control of Albania in 1480.

National Icon

It didn't take long for Skanderbeg to be immortalised as a hero, starting with an official biography published in Rome by Shkodër priest Marin Barleti. Centuries of books and art followed, including an opera, *Scanderbeg,* by Antonio Vivaldi, first performed in Florence in 1722. Skanderbeg's legend picked up steam again in the 1800s as a symbol of the Rilindja (Albanian National Awakening), marked by the first Albanian language school (today's Museum of Education; p162) in Korçë and a nationalist political movement that campaigned for independence from the Ottomans.

After the First Balkan War, Albanian nationalists would get their wish. On 28 November 1912, exiled statesman Ismaïl Qemali gathered Albanian leaders in Vlorë, and under Skanderbeg's double-headed eagle flag, they declared a state. Skanderbeg's dream of an Ottoman-free Albania was then guaranteed by the Great Powers at the Conference of London, and the first national borders were drawn in 1913.

In 1914, the Great Powers anointed Prince Wilhelm of Germany as Albania's head of state. He hoped to earn respect among Albanians by styling himself as Skanderbeg II, but Wilhelm didn't last more than a year, as WWI broke out soon after. After the war, yet another leader deployed the name of Skanderbeg as a way to win over Albanians. This time, it was Ahmed Muhtar Zogolli, who called himself Skanderbeg's heir, and with the help of Benito Mussolini Fascist Party in Italy, declared himself King Zog I in 1928.

WWII saw Albania taken over by Italy and Germany from 1939 to 1943, when Albania's infamous Communist Party filled the void. Elected and led by Enver Hoxha, who – surprise, surprise – also said he descended from Skanderbeg, the brutal dictatorship lasted 45 years. As the country became poor and isolated, Hoxha frequently deployed the legend of Skanderbeg as justification for Albania's resistance, not just against its neighbours, but the entire world.

After communism fell in 1992, Skanderbeg's symbol and flag were adopted by Albanians in Kosovo, whose resistance against Serbia, with the help of NATO bombs, led to the formation of their own country in 2008.

Today, Skanderbeg's legend is as strong as ever. He remains a symbol of national identity among Albanians in Albania, Kosovo, North Macedonia, Montenegro, Greece, Italy and elsewhere in the large diaspora. There are statues of him in Tirana, Skopjë (North Macedonia), Pristina (Kosovo) and Brussels (Belgium). For some, Skanderbeg is a historic hero to be proud of. For others, his legend is a reminder that Albanians are not yet free until Albanian-populated territories in Albania, Kosovo and Greece are united as one country under a red and black flag. But with persisting conflict between Serbia and Kosovo, and both Albania and Kosovo hoping to join the European Union, a Greater Albania won't happen. Then again, Skanderbeg wasn't supposed to defeat the Ottomans, either.

TOURISM BOOM OR BURDEN?

Everyone's going to Albania these days, but is it too much tourism, too soon? By Joel Balsam

IN 1992, ALBANIA emerged from a near half-century of communism, where locals weren't allowed out, and almost no one was allowed in. The Hoxha dictatorship (1944–92) earned Albania a reputation as a mysterious, dangerous country, amplified by ethnic tensions and the rise of Albanian organised crime in western Europe. Locals fled in one of the largest emigrations in recent history, and the economy was left in shambles after a 1997 pyramid scheme bankrupted nearly everyone who stayed.

Then, sometime in the 2000s, backpackers and US Peace Corps volunteers started coming to Albania for its wild landscapes and warm people.

Nowadays, Albania is a hotter-than-hot destination, frequently at the top of must-travel lists from your favourite travel publications, including Lonely Planet, who just published their first Albania title (this very one) in English. In 2024, Albania received 11.7 million foreign visitors, up 15.2% from 2023. That's a heck of a lot of people for a country of fewer than three million residents, and it has undoubtedly benefited the economy. Tourism accounted for a staggering 20% of Albania's €20.7

Pictured clockwise from top left: Houses under construction on the Albanian Riviera (p72), sign in Gjirokastër (p147); Bazaar (p149), Gjirokastër; farm stand, Përmet p156)

billion GDP in 2024, twice that of the UK and 12% more than France, the world's most-visited country. Tourism in Albania is now estimated to support 274,000 jobs, representing 21% of employment.

Yet critics are concerned that it could be too many visitors, too fast for little Albania. Development is quickly taking over the coast, with huge resorts – many of them foreign-owned – ripping out chunks of mountains and paving over once-pristine landscapes. Sarandë went from a small beach town to a full-on tourist hub in a matter of years. Just think what'll happen to other popular stops along the Albanian Riviera.

The country is also (in)famous for having limited regulations when it comes to opening businesses – one of the reasons so many open up shop here. But without limits, especially when it comes to environmental regulations, Albanian ecosystems are at risk. It already has trouble managing trash at popular local sites like the Cape of Rodon – how is the country going to keep things clean with millions more tourists arriving every year?

Vjosa River & Delta

Responding to an international environmentalist campaign from NGOs, the Patagonia clothing company and actor Leonardo DiCaprio, Albania declared the Vjosa River a national park in 2023 – the first in Europe to centre around a river. This was undoubtedly an environmental win, but it's not a knockout. When rafting down the Vjosa River in 2025, this writer saw hundreds of plastic bags and other forms of rubbish along the riverbanks. The situation is even more troublesome on the river delta. Despite being labelled the Vjosë-Nartë Delta Protected Area, this is where Albania decided to build the new Vjosë International Airport. The delta, which is rich in biodiversity, with 250 bird species, as well as loggerhead turtles and monk seals, is also expected to be the site of a 6000-room luxury resort. One of the proposed investors in said resort is Donald Trump's son-in-law Jared Kushner, who also made a deal with the Albanian government to build a resort on Sazan Island, Albania's largest island, located off the coast of Vlorë.

Lessons from Abroad

This all comes at a time when other countries are limiting overtourism. Venice proposed a tax on visitors, while Spain banned tens of thousands of Airbnbs. Nearby Dubrovnik in Croatia has launched regulations on cruise ships and the number of souvenir stands the UNESCO city can have. At the same time, as outlined above, Albania needs the tourism dollars. This is a developing country that's pushing to join the European Union as soon as possible. It's also still losing a high number of its young people to emigration. In 2022, the number of people leaving Albania for the UK tripled from the previous year – a phenomenon that's been blamed on Kanun blood feuds and TikTok videos advertising smuggling services. Albania doesn't want to scare tourists and their money away. Besides, tourism in Albania is really only for a few months of the year. The rest of the time, most accommodations and hotels are shut, giving the environment some time to recover before the next round of visitors arrive.

What You Can Do

We're not going to sit here and tell you not to visit Albania – this is a travel guidebook, and tourism can have a positive impact on developing economies. So go, enjoy yourself and spend your hard-earned cash – but you can also try to limit your impact.

The Albanian Riviera, especially Sarandë, Ksamil, Himarë and Dhërmi, teems with tourists from June through August. Go in May or September instead to avoid overtouristed areas and times and get the best of the warm weather with fewer crowds. At the very least, avoid Sarandë and Ksamil.

Support local businesses and stay with a locally owned guesthouse or B&B rather than a foreign-owned hotel or resort. There are plenty, and they tend to offer a much more authentic experience.

Albanians are passionate about their locally grown veggies and fruits, especially grapes, which are used for wine and raki (fruit brandy). Eat local and seasonal products where possible, including by picking up produce from markets or stands on the side of the highway. Also celebrate Albanian cuisine by enjoying traditional food at agrotourism or slow-food restaurants.

Leave no trace is always an important travel principle, but worth re-emphasising, as there's clearly work to be done in Albania, with many natural areas filled with rubbish.

INDEX

A

accessible travel 183
accommodation 71, 107, 131, 169, 175
activities 8-9, 16-17, 36-7, 38-9, **38-9**, *see also individual activities*
agrotourism 34, 143-4, 181
Albanian Alps 109-31, *see also Northern Albania*
amusement parks 57
ancient sites 12-13, 15
  Antigona 153
  Apollonia 105, 190-1
  Berat 138, 191
  Butrint 88-91, 190
  Byllis 146
  Durrës
    Amphitheatre 62, 191
  Krujë Castle 60, 191-2
  Lin Mosaics 168
  Porto Palermo Castle 95, 192
  Reconciliation Tower 129, 191
  Synagogue (Sarandë) 83
  Via Egnatia 65
archaeological sites 12-13
  Antigona 153
  Apollonia 105, 190-1
  Butrint 88-91, 190
  Byllis 146
  Durrës
    Amphitheatre 62, 191
  Lin Mosaics 168
  Synagogue (Sarandë) 83
architecture 15
art 14
art galleries, *see museums & galleries*
Asim Zeneli 153

Map Pages **000**

B

bazaars
  Gjirokastër 149
  Korçë 159
  Krujë 61
beaches 78-9, 80
  Borsh 85
  Cape of Rodon 70
  Dhërmi 97-9
  Durrës 65
  Himarë 92-3
  Ksamil 86-7
  Lukovë 85
  Lumi i Shales 126-7
  Porto Palermo 95-6
  Sarandë 82
  Seman 106
  Shëngjin 123
  Spille 67
  Vlorë 104
beer 34, 161-2
Berat 138-42, **21**, **139**, **142**
  food 140, 141
  itineraries 21
  travel within 138
birds 37, 69, 103, 181
boat travel 172, 173
  Dhërmi 99
  Durrës 63
  Himarë 92
  Ksamil 87
  Lake Koman 126
  Sarandë 80, 82
  Shkodër 120-1
  Vlorë 103
Boks 119
books 31, 150
boondocking 94, 175
Borsh 85
Bovilla Lake 59
budget 174, 175, 179
bus travel 172, 173
business hours 185
Butrint 88-91, **90**
Byllis 146

C

cabins 175
cable cars 56, 57

Caesar, Julius 100
camping 94, 175
canoeing, *see rafting*
Cape of Rodon 70
car travel, *see driving*
castles & fortresses 146
  Bashtovë Fortress 67, 70
  Berat Castle 138, 140-1
  Borsh Castle 85
  Gjirokastër Castle 149-50
  Himarë Castle 94
  Kaninë Castle 104
  Krujë Castle 60
  Lekursi Castle 82-3
  Lezhë Castle 123
  Libohovë Castle 155
  Petrelë Castle 57-8
  Porto Palermo Castle 95, 192
  Prezë Fortress 57
  Rodon Castle 70
  Rozafa Fortress 115
  Tepelenë Castle 155
  Tirana Castle 53
caves
  Dhërmi 99
  Haxhi Ali Cave 103
  Pëllumbas 58
  Sari Salltik 61
cell phones 172
Central Albania 20-1, 43-71, **21**, **44**
  accommodation 71
  activities 45
  Bovilla Lake 59
  Cape of Rodon 70
  climate 45
  Durrës 62-6, **63**, **64**
  festivals & events 45, 54
  food 57, 67, 69
  itineraries 20-1, 45
  Krujë 60-1, **61**
  Mt Dajti 55-9
  navigation 44
  Pëllumbas 58-9
  Petrelë 57-8
  Spille 67-70
  Tirana 46-56, **48-9**, **50**
  Tirana Airport Area 57
  tours 56
  travel seasons 45
  travel within 44, 55, 67
  weather 45

churches & cathedrals, *see also monasteries*
  Holy Trinity Church 140
  Prophet Elijah Church 164
  Resurrection of Christ Orthodox Cathedral 160
  St Anthony Church 70
  St Athanasius Church 164
  St Mary Church (Labovë e Kryqitë) 155
  St Mary Church (Leus) 156
  St Mary Church (Voskopojë) 163-4
  St Nicholas Church 164
  St Stephen Cathedral 117
  Theth Church 129
climate 28-9, 180-1
clothes 30, 197
communist history & sites 46-7, 51-2, 53, 57, 65-6, 87, 115, 151-2, 155, 161, 192-3
costs 174, 175, 179
credit cards 174
crime 82, 83, 174, 177
culture 117, 128, 194-5, 196-7
currency 174
cycling 37, 112, 173

D

dance 196-7
Dardhë 164-5
Dhërmi 97-100, **98**
  food 99
  itineraries 23
  travel within 97
disabilities, travellers with 183
diving & snorkelling 36, 37, 83
Divjakë-Karavastë National Park 68-9
drinking 142-3, *see also individual locations*
driving 172, 173, 176, 184
  itineraries 99, 124-5, 154, 166-7
Durrës 62-6, **63**
  drinking 66
  food 65

itineraries 20
tours 64
travel within 62
walking tour 64, **64**

earthquakes 70
electricity 185
emergencies 185
etiquette 30, 181
events, *see* festivals & events

family travel 176
ferries 172, 173, *see also* boat travel
 Butrint 90
 Durrës 63
 Ksamil 86, 87
 Lake Koman 126
 Sarandë 80, 82
 Shkodër 112, 120-1, 126
 Vlorë 103
festivals & events 29, 33, *see also individual locations*
Fier 105-6
films 31
Fishtë 119-22
food 11, 32-5, 152, 178-9, *see also individual foods, locations*
fortresses, *see* castles & fortresses
furgon 173

galleries, *see* museums & galleries
gay travellers 182
Gjirokastër 147-52, **148**
 drinking 150
 festivals & events 150
 food 149
 itineraries 27
 shopping 149, 151
 travel within 147
grapes 144

health 177
highlights 8-17
hiking 36-7, 56, 120-1, 130
 Divjakë-Karavastë National Park 69
 Langarica Canyon 158

Mt Çika 100
Mt Taraboshi 118
Mt Tomorr 144-5
Northeastern Albania 122
Peaks of the Balkans Trail 123
Pëllumbas 59
Theth 128-9
Himarë 92-4, **93**
 drinking 93
 food 93
 itineraries 22
 travel within 92
historical sites 10, 15
 Adriatik Hotel 65
 Ali Pasha Bridge 149
 Ali Pasha Tower 96
 Clock Tower 47
 Cold War Tunnel 151-2
 Englishman's Clocktower 117
 Enver Hoxha's Former Residence 52
 Goricë 141
 Kadiu Bridge 158
 King Zog Villa 65-6
 Mangalem 141
 Mesi Bridge 119
 Palace of Culture 47
 Reconciliation Tower 129, 191
 Skanderbeg Square 46
 Tepelenë Internment Camp 155
 Venetian Tower 62-3
 Via Egnatia 65
history 190-3
 ancient 58, 65, 100, 106, 190-1
 communist 47, 51-2, 53, 57, 66, 87, 115, 152, 155, 161, 192-3
 modern 70, 83, 193
 Ottoman Empire 96, 103, 191-2, 198-9
holidays 185
horse riding 153, 163
hostels 175
hotels 175
hot springs, *see* springs & pools
Hoxha, Enver 52, 53, 151, 155

insurance 177
internet 185
itineraries 20-7, 45, 76-7, 111, 136-7, *see also individual locations*

jet-skiing 36, 65

Kadare, Ismail 54, 150-1
kayaking, *see* rafting
kitesurfing 37, 106
Koman 127
 itineraries 24
Korçë 159-62, **160**
 drinking 162
 food 161
 itineraries 26
 travel within 159
Kosovo 117, 122
Krongj 84
Krujë 60-1, **61**
 food 61
 itineraries 20
 shopping 61
 travel within 60
Ksamil 86-7, **86**
 drinking 86
 food 86, 89
 itineraries 22
 travel within 86

Labovë e Kryqitë 155
Lake Koman 126
language 31, 186-7
lesbian travellers 182
Lezhë 122-3
LGBTIQ+ travellers 182
Libohovë 155
Lin 168
Lipa, Dua 59
Lukovë 85
Lumi i Shales 126-7

markets, *see* bazaars
measures 185
migration 197
mobile phones 172
monasteries, *see also* churches & cathedrals
 Ardenicë Monastery 106
 Monastery of the 40 Saints 83
 St John the Baptist Monastery 164
 St Mary Monastery 99, 103-4
 St Naum Monastery 168
 St Nicholas Monastery 84

St Theodor Monastery 99
money 46, 174
monuments & statues
 Independence Monument 101
 Skanderbeg Memorial 123
 Skanderbeg Statue 46
mosques
 Bazaar Mosque 149
 Ebu Bekr Mosque 117
 Et'hem Bey Mosque 47
 Lead Mosque 115, 117
 Muradie Mosque 101
 Xhamia e Iljaz Mirahorit 159
Mother Teresa 164
motorcycling 37
Mt Dajti 55-7, **56**
Mt Tujani 56
museums & galleries
 Apollonia Archaeological Museum 105
 Archaeological Museum (Durrës) 63, 65
 Archaeological Museum (Korçë) 160-1
 Army Museum 150
 Bunk'Art 1 55
 Bunk'Art 2 51-2
 Diocese Museum 115
 Ethnographic Museum (Berat) 141
 Ethnographic Museum (Gjirokastër) 151
 Ethnographic Museum (Krujë) 60
 GADK 161
 Gjirokastër Museum 150
 Gjon Mili Museum 161
 House of Leaves 51
 House of Sali Shijaku 54
 Kadare House 150-1
 Marubi National Photography Museum 112-14
 Medieval Art Museum 159-60
 MiG 53
 Museum of Archaeology 83
 Museum of Education 162
 Muza Ime Musine Kokalari 151
 National Gallery of Arts 54
 National History Museum 46
 Onufri Museum 140
 Saranda Art Gallery 82
 Shkodër History Museum 115
 Site of Witness & Memory Museum 115

museums & galleries, continued
  Skanderbeg Museum 60
  Skenduli House 151
  Solomoni Jewish Museum 141
  Studio Kadare & Agolli House 54
  Zekate House 151
music 31, 59, 99, 149, 197
mussels 87

N

national parks, *see also* wildlife reserves
  Butrint 91
  Divjakë-Karavastë National Park 68-9
  Drilon National Park 165
  Llogorë Pass National Park 99-100
  Mt Dajti National Park 57
  Mt Tomorr 144-5
  Theth National Park 128
  Vjosa River 156-7
Northeastern Albania 122
Northern Albania 24-5, 109-31, **25**, **110**
  accommodation 131
  activities 111
  Boks 119
  climate 111
  festivals & events 111, 129
  Fishtë 119-22
  itineraries 24-5, 111
  Lezhë 122-3
  Lumi i Shales 126-7
  navigation 110
  Shëngjin 123-6
  Chkodër 112-10, **113**, **114**
  Theth 128-30, **129**
  tours 116, 120-1, 121, 124-5, 130, **116**, **121**, **125**, **130**
  travel seasons 111
  travel within 110, 119
  weather 111

O

opening hours 185
Osum Canyon 145-6

Map Pages **000**

Ottoman Empire 96, 103, 191-2, 198-9
overtourism 180, 200-1

P

paragliding 36, 57, 104
parasailing 65
parking 184
parks & gardens 54
Pasha, Ali 96, 155
Pëllumbas 58-9
people 194-5
Përmet 156-8, **157**
  food 157, 158
  itineraries 27
  travel within 156
Petrelë 57-8
planning 30-1
  clothes 30
  etiquette 30, 181
podcasts 31
Pogradec 165
  itineraries 26
pools, *see* springs & pools
population 185, 194
Porto Palermo 95-6
public holidays 185

Q

Qemali, Ismail 101, 103
Qeparo 96

R

rafting 16, 37
  Lukovë 85
  Osum Canyon 145-6
  Vjosa River 157
raki 11, 34, 166, 178
religion 141
religious sites, *see also* churches & cathedrals, monasteries, mosques
  Bektashi World Headquarters 54
  Sari Salltik 61
resorts 175
responsible travel 180-1, 200-1
Riviera, the 22-3, 72-107, **22**, **74-5**
  accommodation 107
  activities 76-7
  Borsh 85
  Butrint 88-91, **90**
  climate 76-7
  Dhërmi 97-100, **98**
  festivals & events 76-7, 99, 101

Fier 105-6
Himarë 92-4, **93**
itineraries 22-3, 76-7
Krongj 84
Ksamil 86-7, **87**
Lukovë 85
navigation 74-5
Porto Palermo 95-6
Qeparo 96
Sarandë 80-3, **81**
travel seasons 76-7
travel within 74, 84, 95, 105
Vlorë 101-4, **102**
weather 76-7
Roshnik 143-5
ruins 12-13

S

safe travel 47, 177
Sarandë 80-3, **81**
  food 82
  itineraries 22
  nightlife 80-1
  travel within 80
Shëngjin 123-6
Shijaku, Sali 54
Shkodër 112-18, **113**, **114**, **116**
  drinking 117
  festivals & events 118
  food 114, 119, 122, 123
  itineraries 24
  shopping 117-18
  travel within 112
SIM cards 172
Skanderbeg 61, 198-9
skiing 37, 164-5
smoking 185
snorkelling, *see* diving & snorkelling
solo travellers 183
Southeastern Albania 26-7, 132-69, **27**, **134-5**
  accommodation 169
  activities 136-7
  Asim Zeneli 153
  Berat 138-42, **139**
  Byllis 146
  climate 136-7
  Dardhë 164-5
  festivals & events 136-7, 162
  Gjirokastër 147-52, **148**
  itineraries 26-7, 136-7
  Korçë 159-62, **160**
  Labovë e Kryqitë 155
  Libohovë 155
  Lin 168
  navigation 134-5
  Osum Canyon 145-6
  Përmët 156-8, **157**
  Pogradec 165
  Roshnik 143-5

Tepelenë 155
tours 142, 154, 166-7, **142**, **154**, **167**
travel seasons 136-7
travel within 135, 143, 153, 163
Turan 163
Ura Vajgurore 143
Voskopojë 163-4
weather 136-7
Spille 67-70
springs & pools
  Benjë Hot Springs 158
  Blue Eye 84
  Blue Eye Kaprre 128
  Syri i Sheganit 124-5
stand-up paddleboarding 37, 85, 118
sustainability 85, 180-1, 200-1

T

taxis 173
Tepelenë 155
Teuta 106
theatres 54, 117
theme parks, *see* amusement parks
Theth 128-30, **129**, **130**
  itineraries 25
  travel within 129
time zone 185
tipping 174
Tirana 43-71, 46-56, **48-9**, **50**
  accommodation 71
  activities 45
  climate 45
  drinking 52, 53
  entertainment 52-3
  festivals & events 45
  food 47, 51, 52
  itineraries 20, 45
  navigation 44
  nightlife 52
  shopping 53
  tours 50, 51
  travel seasons 45
  travel within 44, 46
  walking tour 50, **50**
  weather 45
Tirana Airport Area 57
tourism 200-1
tours 50, 51, 56, 64, 120-1, 124-5, 130, 142, 154, 166-7
transhumance 197
travelling with kids 176
travel seasons 28-9, 35
travel to/from Albania 172
travel within Albania 173, 184
Turan 163

Ura Vajgurore 143

vacations 185
Valbonë 121
  itineraries 24
vegetarian travellers 34
Via Egnatia 65
villages
  Northern Albania 118
  Pogradec 165
  Tushemisht 165
  Voskopojë 163-4
  Vuno 99
visas 172
Vjosa River 85, 156-7, 180, 201
Vlorë 101-4, **102**
  drinking 104
  food 104
  itineraries 23
  travel within 101
Voskopojë 163-4
  itineraries 26

W

walking 36-7, 50, 56, 64, 120-1, 130, 142
  Divjakë-Karavastë National Park 69
Langarica Canyon 158
Mt Çika 100
Mt Tarabosh 118
Mt Tomorr 144-5
Northeastern Albania 122
Peaks of the Balkans Trail 123
Pëllumbas 59
Theth 128-9
war 177
water 177
waterfalls 128
weather 28-9, 177
weights 185
white-water rafting, *see* rafting
wildlife 69, *see also* birds
wildlife reserves 126, *see also* national parks
wine 11, 34, 143, 144, 179
women travellers 183

xhiro 138, 179

ziplining 58, 129
Zog I 66

NOTES

NOTES

"I busted rental cars not once but twice. Worth it!"

JOEL BALSAM

"I visited Nivicë Canyon (p167) in spring and it was like a Garden of Eden of wildflowers and waterfalls."

JOEL BALSAM

All rights reserved. No part of this publication may be copied, stored in a retrieval system, or transmitted in any form by any means, electronic, mechanical, recording or otherwise, except brief extracts for the purpose of review, and no part of this publication may be sold or hired, without the written permission of the publisher. Lonely Planet and the Lonely Planet logo are trademarks of Lonely Planet and are registered in the US Patent and Trademark Office and in other countries. Lonely Planet does not allow its name or logo to be appropriated by commercial establishments, such as retailers, restaurants or hotels. Please let us know of any misuses: lonelyplanet.com/legal/intellectual-property.

Mapping data sources:
© Lonely Planet
© OpenStreetMap http://openstreetmap.org/copyright

THIS BOOK

Destination Editor
Daniel Bolger

Production Editor
Will Allen

Book Designer
Norma Brewer

Cartographer
Dorothy Davidson

Coordinating Editor
Shauna Daly

Assisting Editors
Imogen Bannister,
Melanie Dankel,
Helen Koehne

Cover Researcher
Kat Marsh

Thanks Kellie Langdon,
Chris Lee-Ack,
Darren O'Connell,
Saralinda Turner

MIX
Paper | Supporting responsible forestry
FSC™ C021741

Paper in this book is certified against the Forest Stewardship Council™ standards. FSC™ promotes environmentally responsible, socially beneficial and economically viable management of the world's forests.

Published by Lonely Planet Global Limited
CRN 554153
1st edition – March 2026
ISBN 978 1 83758 726 1
© Lonely Planet 2026
10 9 8 7 6 5 4 3 2 1
Printed in Malaysia